DOOMSDAY DECEPTION

DOOMSDAY DECEPTION

THE RISE AND FALL
OF
THE WATCHTOWER SOCIETY

GEOFF UNWIN

Argyle Books

ISBN-9798675603626

To my wife
JUDY

ACKNOWLEDGEMENTS

Top of the bill in my show of appreciation of those who have helped spur me on in the writing of this book, is my wife for without her dedicated assistance and encouragement in all my endeavours over the years, I think I would not have achieved very much at all. So, Judy my love, my wise and patient amanuensis of many long-suffering years, take a bow. Take another, this book is just as much yours as it is mine.

We met at the old Argyle Theatre, Birkenhead, Merseyside, in the winter of 1957/58 when I joined the cast of a touring production of Alice in Wonderland during a brief tenure as an actor. Judy played Alice and I was cast as the White Rabbit (I think I only got the part because they wanted a piano-playing rabbit to top and tail the production with a song from the cast). We have had many adventures together since then, not least of which was a somewhat eccentric, yet eye-opening, period in our lives during which we were baptised as Jehovah's Witnesses.

I had been drawn into the Watchtower Society as a young idealistic and impressionable session musician much influenced by the trendy recording artists, (the famous and the not so famous from both side of the Atlantic) with whom I worked throughout the 'swinging sixties' who were Jehovah's Witnesses. For some reason I also remember two footballers on the team sheet at a popular London club at that time who were said to be JW's as well as the trademark strongman banging a huge gong in the J Arthur Rank movies. I saw all this as a community, of which I was part, rejecting the politically sponsored money-making crowd-controlling racket of the world's religions. Believing Jehovah's Witnesses inhabited an alternative world of their own – 'the Truth' – I jumped in at the deep end and was soon followed by my wife.

For us, the rot began to set in when we attended an international Watchtower convention at the Wembley Stadium in 1969 where we found ourselves surrounded by a thronging mass of fixed smiling plastic faces, dressed-down sensibly shod women accompanied by earnest-looking briefcase-carrying collar and polyester tie-wearing men all spouting Watchtower-talk as they shepherded their restless young ones into listless submission for hours on end. It was a depressing and alienating shock. We felt like a couple of film extras on the set of a remake of The Body Snatchers – (a 1950's horror film about a small-town community whose minds were controlled by brainwashing invaders from outer space). Consequently, in the early 1970's, I wrote an open letter of disassociation to Watchtower president N H Knorr, (no, he never replied), copies of which were sent to the British press. It was the first of my sporadic forays into the world of investigative journalism. Perhaps it was also the time when I started writing this book.

***

My thanks to Prime Minister Boris Johnson – former Commissioning Editor of *The Spectator* – for a previous opportunity to address his well informed and influential readership on the dubious tax-free charitable status of the Watchtower Society in both the UK and the USA (although nothing has changed on that score – yet). Likewise, in that regard, I thank Stephen Bates of *The Guardian* and Ruth Gledhill, religion correspondent of *The Times*.

From the old school of the numerous Watchtower Society breakaway persuasions, I am enormously grateful to Jonathan A. Ross of the Adventist Heritage Library, Richard Doidge of the Layman's Home Missionary Movement along with James Parkinson, Jerry Leslie, and Robert Wagoner for sharing their unique recollections with me. My thanks also to Dr Jerry Bergman, Carl Olof Jonnson, James Penton, Barbara Anderson, former resident researcher at the Brooklyn Bethel, and to the late Ray Franz, a previous member of Watchtower Society's Governing Body, who was unstinting with his help and encouragement in answering all my nosey questions. Special thanks also to Anthony Bowyer, my eagle-eyed research assistant, for digging out the most obscure tale-telling Watchtower books and documents; not forgetting affable Irishman Eddie Cooney. My thanks also to the late Albert Hudson and William (Bill) Simmons – former contemporary associates of Pastor Russell's close friend and British representative, Jessie Hemery – for their generous co-operation and first-hand memories of what really took place in New York and London back in those early formative days of the Watchtower Society. Finally, my thanks to so many others around the world who have shared their – sometimes sad and unbelievably tragic – Watchtower experiences with me over the years.

During an early gestation period of this biography of a belief quite some years ago I concluded that although the Watchtower story had a fascinating beginning and an absorbing main theme, it lacked a satisfactory conclusion at that time. However, in recent years explosive internet exposure and 21st century enlightenment has fired the organisation into an irreversible trajectory of ever-decreasing circles as it spins itself into an all-consuming black hole of obscurity and irrelevance.

Contents

PREFACE

TRACING THE ROOTS OF CHRISTIAN END-TIME BELIEF

The development of radical politics in Britain between 1790 and 1900 reflected the social changes which transformed a predominantly rural country into an urban and industrial society. Small towns grew into cities as industry spread throughout the land and the population increased accordingly. It was during this period that the established church in Britain, a powerful supporter of the aristocratic conservative state, began to lose its grip.

While they sympathised with the 'lower orders', who were at the mercy of their political and aristocratic masters, most of the Anglican clergy at that time chose to equate the social injustice of the day with biblical interpretations that justified this human condition as self-inflicted and temporary. It was a stranglehold that was notably challenged by Thomas Paine (1737-1809), the son of a Quaker and a former confirmed member of the Church of England. Paine, like Voltaire and Newton before him, was a religiously minded man, but one who controversially denounced the partnership between church and state as an unholy alliance: 'The systems of one are as false as those of the other and are calculated for mutual support.'[1]

However, there were other voices to be heard. Pioneering evangelists who preached the imminence of social change often attracted the attention of many who had lost faith in the established church. They pointed out that the early Christians believed that one day, Christ would return to earth in much the same way as his disciples are said to have witnessed him ascending to heaven from the Mount of Olives when 'he was taken up; and a cloud received him out of their sight'.[2] That he would descend in a similar manner – 'and they shall see the Son of man coming in the

[1] The Rights of Man – Thomas Paine, 1791.
[2] Acts 1:9 KJV.

clouds of heaven with power and great glory'[3] – seemed to be a perfectly reasonable assumption for the faithful to make.

Such considerations were nurtured by the early Christians for more than five hundred years before St. Augustine imposed his own controversial biblical interpretations on the Church of Rome thereby introducing a fearful and threatening element of heavenly reward or hellish punishment for the submissive Catholics. Consequently, the controversial doctrine of Christ's return and the restoration of the earth to its former biblical glory as an everlasting paradise was all but forgotten for a thousand years, only to surface again after the Reformation.

In 19th century Britain Christ's 'second coming' was once the subject of much intellectually focused analysis and debate. Most notable of these was the Albury Second Advent Conference which took place at the Surrey home of politician and religious leader, Henry Drummond, in 1826. This meeting of religious minds was convened annually for five years and attended by such luminaries as Jewish evangelist Joseph Wolff and Scottish clergyman and mystic Edward Irving, an accomplished speaker and successful preacher at the Caledonian Church, Hatton Garden in London.

The general view adopted at Albury Park was that the 'second coming' would commence with the unseen spiritual arrival of Jesus Christ to prepare his collective 'bride' of chosen ones for celestial life with him in the heavens. When all those selected had passed on from the earth the marriage feast, mentioned in Revelation,[4] would then take place. Seven years later Christ would return to earth once more and visibly appear to the world at large. A restoration of Israel to the Holy Land would then signal the commencement of the Millennium. At least that was the agenda conference delegates set for God at the time, a period when many worshippers assumed the Church of England, with its Authorised King James Version of the Bible, to be the very epicentre of Christianity.

The annual Albury Conference was superseded by the fortnightly Powerscourt Conference which ran continuously between 1830 and 1833 and focused on developing what had now become known as the 'secret rapture'. This theory was designed to accommodate the beliefs of those who considered themselves worthy of being counted as part of the bride class, those who believed themselves destined to live forever

---

[3] Matthew 24:30 KJV

[4] Revelation 19: 7-8 KJV

with Christ Jesus in heaven. Such ones would never experience death and, in the words of St. Paul,[5] would be rapturously transformed from physicality to spirituality 'in the twinkling of an eye'. The fate of the rest of mankind – both the living and the dead – lay in whatever took place during and after what Jesus Christ referred to as the 'great tribulation'.

Chronological speculation came about during the 1st century when Jewish rabbis attempted to predict when the Messiah would appear utilising the day-year principle, first mentioned in the Bible when the Israelites learned they were to wander in the desert for forty years as a punishment for the number of days (40) they had impatiently spied out the promised land against God's will. A further example is recorded by the prophet, Ezekiel, who applied the day-year principle retrospectively when he revealed how he was instructed by God to lie on his left side for 390 days and then on his right side for 40 days in atonement for the sins committed by Israel and Judah during periods of just as many years.

This allegedly God-given mathematical equation was initially applied to numerous time-based interpretations of the 'seventy weeks' prophecy of Daniel as rabbi scholars counted forward in day-years from numerous significant dates in Jewish history to the hoped-for year of fulfilment, but without success. By the 9th century the day-year formula was being arbitrarily applied to endless interpretations of other timescales to be found in Daniel's prophecies as one uneventful messianic date after another passed into history. For many Jews, the future remained as unpredictable as ever and the much anticipated and hoped-for appearance of the Messiah on earth remained just that; in effect the same hope that Christians have been nurturing since the time of Christ.

Joachim of Floris, a 12th century Roman Catholic abbot of the Cistercian monastery in Corace, Italy, appears to have been the first Christian who attempted to put a date on Christ's return to earth when he looked beyond the prophecies of Daniel and Ezekiel. Turning to the Christian Greek scriptures he applied the original rabbinic day-year calculating method to the 1,260 days period mentioned in the Bible.[6] Counting from the time of Christ he believed the day-years of St. John's prophecy would end in 'an age of spirit' sometime in the year 1260 C.E.

Following the non-event of Joachim's prediction succeeding end-time expositors began to link the 1,260 years period with the Gentile

---

[5] 1 Corinthians 15: 53 KJV

[6] Revelation 11; 12:6 KJV

Times, a belief commonly held by the Reformers, branded as heretics by the Church of Rome, who soon identified the 'trampling Gentiles' of Luke's apocalyptic visions with the papacy. Such believers (Martin Luther among them) saw themselves as the true church of Christ's followers, depicted in the Bible as a pregnant woman 'clothed with the sun, and the moon under her feet, and upon her head a crown of twelve stars' who sought sanctuary in the [spiritual] wilderness for 'a thousand two hundred *and* threescore days.'[7]

Writing in the London Evangelical Magazine of 1796, one George Bell predicted the downfall of the Antichrist (in his estimation, the Pope) in either 1797 or 1813, according to his interpretation of the 1,260 days of Luke's gospel. It was the time of the French Revolution during which the Pope was taken captive by French troops and forced into exile. This turn of events was interpreted as a remarkable fulfilment of Bible prophecy and gave rise to the belief that 1798 marked the end of the prophetic 1,260 days and that the following year must therefore mark the beginning of the 'last days'. On the August 12th, 1799, Napoleon paid a visit to Egypt's Great Pyramid. Afterwards it was said that after spending some time inside the Kings Chamber, alone at his request, the conqueror of Europe emerged pale-faced and shaken. The illustrious Freemason, so the story went, had foreseen the future.

In 1823 Londoner John Aquila Brown published Even-Tide, a book in which he interpreted the 'seven times' of Daniel's prophecy as a grand week of seven prophetic years. He based his understanding on a 17th century Protestant interpretation of the Bible book of Revelation when the phrase, 'a time, times, and half a time'[8] was believed to signify the period of 1,260 days leading to the Day of Judgement while the indefinite time itself was thought to be the length of a prophetic year.

Applying the day-year theory to Daniel's prophecy Brown multiplied 360 days by seven to give himself 2,520 prophetic years beginning in the first year of Nebuchadnezzar's reign in 604 B.C. and ending, according to his calculations, 'at the close of the Last Judgement in 1917, when the full glory of the kingdom of Israel shall be perfected'. Utilising the same calculating method, he also predicted the 'destruction of Papal Power in the year 1843, or 1844'.

By the year 1834 six journals devoted to Second Advent Truth were regularly appearing in Britain and some sixty books on the subject had

---

[7] Revelation 12: 1, 6 KJV

[8] Revelation 12:6, 14 KJV

been published. That the Bible contained a mathematically coded key to identifying the year of Christ's return to earth was now simply taken as read. Then in 1844 the Reverend E.B. Elliot A.M. (1793-1875) an incumbent of St. Marks Church, Kemptown, Brighton and late Fellow of Trinity College, Cambridge, published Horæ Apocalypticæ in which he identified the Gentile Times as the period between the accession of Nebuchadnezzar, which he mistakenly believed at that time, dated from 606 B.C.E to 1914 C.E., one of the 'extreme dates' he set for the 'second coming' of Jesus Christ.

Elliot's book – sub-titled The Scripture Chronology of the World – became a best-seller throughout an eighteen-year period of continuous publication. The book also featured an illustrated table depicting world events past, present and future in tandem with Bible prophecy, which had been drawn up by his friend and fellow preacher the Reverend Christopher Bowen B.A., M.A. of St. Mary Magdalene Church, Southwark. Now, for the first time ever, it was claimed, Christians could see for themselves and understand what was taking place on earth as a physical reflection of a cosmic drama being played out in the heavenly realm and glean just where they were in the stream of time by studying Bowen's chart of eschatological expectations, his road map to paradise.

Meanwhile increasing numbers of Church of England ministers consistently preached about the imminence of the 'second coming' from their pulpits, but to diminishing congregations. Many of those confined to the lower orders of society were increasingly less inclined to accept their lot in life with humility and grace at the behest of a well-fed clergy. In 1846 the Leicester Unitarian Domestic Missionary reported: 'there is an almost universal neglect of public worship in those parts of the town that are occupied by the working class.' The historian of adult education, J.W. Hudson, wrote in 1851: 'In one manufactory in Lambeth, where upwards of one thousand men were constantly employed, it was ascertained that no more than thirty-three attended public worship.'

A Religious Census, which was taken on Sunday, March 30th, 1851, noted: 'A sadly formidable portion of the English people are habitual neglecters of the public ordinances of religion. Nor is it difficult to indicate to what particular class of the community this portion in the main belongs . . . the classes which are most in need of the restraints and consolations of religion are the classes which are most without them.'

Christianity was dealt a further blow in 1859 when English naturalist Charles Darwin published his Origin of Species, a revolutionary biological theory which effectively dismissed the Bible account of creation as religious allegory. Further intellectual criticism of organised religious worship came from other thinkers of the day such as Karl Marx, Sigmund Freud, Friedrich Nietzsche, and Ludwig Feuerbach whose philosophical, psychological, and sociological opinions boldly articulated the nagging doubts and suspicions long harboured by many. The clergy survived this storm of criticism, but the boat had been rocked and from then onwards it would not all be plain sailing for the established church in Britain.

The last of the 'second coming' talks took place in 1878 when millennium fervour was at its height in Britain. Among the many earnest speakers who attended the Mildmay Conference was Anthony Ashley Cooper (1801-1885), the seventh Earl of Shaftesbury. Educated at Harrow and Christ Church College, Oxford, he entered parliament when he was twenty-five years old where he undertook leadership of the Factory Reform movement. His Coal Mines Act of 1842 prohibited underground employment of women and children under the age of 13. He actively assisted Florence Nightingale with her schemes for army welfare and took an interest in missionary work. A committed evangelist he was absolutely convinced of the imminence of Christ's return to earth in the flesh.

During the 1880's such debates were dismissed by many as an intellectual pooling of religious fantasy and fable. However, that was not to be the end of the matter for Anglican seeds of millennial hope and expectation had already crossed the Atlantic Ocean and taken root in the burgeoning 'new world' of America. The Christian Observer (founded 1802), a London periodical that frequently dealt with Bible prophecy, also had an American edition which was published in Boston. The November 1810 issue featured an article by John Aquila Brown in which he first drew attention to the 'prophetic significance' of the year 1844. Thus, his chronological speculations and those of numerous other British millenarians of the day were spread abroad thereby fuelling similar beliefs in America, notably those of William Miller (1781-1849), a New York farmer who came to believe that the return to earth of Jesus Christ would first take place in 1843 then, in 1844.

The inevitable failure of both prophecies led to what became known as the 'great disappointment' for many thousands of Miller's followers, some of whom went on to establish the Seventh Day Adventist Church in 1863, a movement to which the founder of the Watchtower Bible and Tract Society, Charles Taze Russell, was drawn.

INTRODUCTION

The saga of the Watchtower Society is essentially the story of self-styled 'Pastor Russell' (b.1852) and self-appointed 'Judge Rutherford' (b.1869) and of the two distinctly different religious movements that were founded by these two charismatic men.

Both persuasions are inextricably linked by their legal connections with the Watchtower Bible & Tract Society (founded 1884), the organisation that originally represented the interests of Russell's followers, who came to be known as International Bible Students, and latterly of Rutherford's followers who are known today as Jehovah's Witnesses, a name that rings a bell with millions all over the world.

Yet, despite their fame, little is known about these earnest doorstep preachers. Even more surprising is the fact that most of the dedicated rank and file members of this controversial religious cult know little of their own hidden history and even less of the Watchtower Bible & Tract Society, the vast multi-billion-dollar commercial publishing organisation to which they and their children devote, and sometimes tragically sacrifice, their lives.

For decades, the spectre of religiously motivated suicidal behaviour has haunted the public image of Jehovah's Witnesses who also stand accused of callously breaking up families through their practice of shunning and employing brainwashing methods of indoctrination. But are these things true? How do the Witnesses themselves respond to such allegations?

'The brains of millions need a washing, but not with the political or religious propagandas of this system of things under Satan. Rather everyone needs regular cleansings with the bath of water by means of the word of Jehovah God. Jehovah's Witnesses have been targets of false accusations, barefaced lies, and twisted presentations of their beliefs. As a result, they have been the object of unjustified attack in some lands. They have wrongly been labelled 'child murderers' and 'a suicide cult'. The accusation that numerous children of Jehovah's Witnesses die each year [by] refusing blood transfusions is totally unfounded. In addition, because Bible truth does not have the same effect on all family members, Witnesses have also been accused of breaking up families. Yet, those acquainted with Jehovah's Witnesses know that they highly regard family life.'[9]

In a Foreword to Jehovah's Witnesses – Proclaimers of God's Kingdom (a 750 page somewhat cryptic history of the movement published by the Watchtower Society in 1993), we read: 'Who really are Jehovah's Witnesses? Certainly, no one knows their modern-day history better than they themselves do. The editors of this volume have endeavoured to be objective and to present a candid history.'

However, after reading through this much detailed and lavishly illustrated Watchtower tome, Ray Franz, a prominent critic of the movement, noted: 'Most of Jehovah's Witnesses have no access to the records of the past and no personal knowledge of the events relating to the organisation's development. The operations of the central authority structure or of the men forming that inner authority structure are likewise unknown to them. They are thus essentially at the mercy of the editors of this supposedly impartial 'candid history'. I have seldom read a more sanitised, less objective presentation. Its depiction of organisational history and policy paints a picture that differs measurably from reality.'[10]

Franz should know because for many years he was one of the principal writers for the Watchtower Society and a former member of the hallowed Governing Body of Jehovah's Witnesses no less. Indeed, the events surrounding his defection from the movement in 1980 and his subsequently published disclosures have since been covered up by the Watchtower Society and consigned to its officially forgotten past.

***

Undoubtedly sincere and utterly devoted to their cause, Jehovah's Witnesses are, often, looked upon as quite harmless and usually dismissed as religious eccentrics. Their activities are largely ignored throughout the world as of no consequence to mankind – certainly, no threat – while the Witnesses themselves are generally derided and good-naturedly lampooned by all and sundry. When they call to tell us that the world is about to end, the attitude they are met with is often one of patronising toleration. They tend to be essentially good hearted and well-meaning folk (and so they surely are) but misguided and something of a tragic joke.

---

[9] Watchtower – June 15, 1956; Dec. 1998.

[10] Crisis of Conscience – Raymond Franz, Commentary Press, 1992.

There is however a darker potential to the homespun doorstep philosophy advocated by the secretive leadership of the sect, an elite group of men who distinguish themselves with extravagant claims of divine authority as they dream of theocratic world domination and the downfall of democracy. They maintain that in the not-too-distant future 'Jehovah's day will arrive with shocking suddenness' when almost the entire population of the earth will be wiped out within just a few short days of apocalyptic terror, with much of the dirty work – according to their reading of the Bible – being carried out by man himself: 'For God hath put it into their hearts to fulfil his will.'[11]

Jehovah's Witnesses in the 21st century see themselves as champions of spiritual freedom and ironclad truth in a bourgeois world which is dominated by corrupt capitalist values, a world that God has allowed to become temporarily enslaved and bitterly divided by a confusing and distracting array of false religious beliefs. For them there can be only one true religion which of course is theirs. There are more than 1·5 billion professing Christians in the world today divided into as many as 20,800 differing sects and denominations.

In a world of lip-serving religious obfuscation and politically motivated religious patronage we might applaud the Witnesses (perhaps reservedly) for their candour; the Watchtower Society, like the Roman Catholic Church, regarding itself as a separate divine authority along with the Bible. Indeed, the organisation arbitrarily dismisses all the preaching of the gospel which has taken place since the death of the Apostles and claims to be the only Christian denomination that promotes the true gospel throughout the world today: 'Let the honest-hearted person compare the kind of preaching of the gospel of the Kingdom done by the religious systems of Christendom during all the centuries with that done by Jehovah's Witnesses since the end of World War One in 1918. They are not one and the same kind. That of Jehovah's Witnesses is really 'gospel' or 'good news,' as of God's heavenly kingdom that was established by the enthronement of his Son Jesus Christ at the end of the Gentile Times in 1914'.[12]

This 'enthronement of Jesus Christ in 1914' – the most distinctive feature of their gospel and one which is pivotal to their countdown to Armageddon – is, as history clearly shows, a theological delusion. Furthermore, the deceptively accommodating religious pragmatism of the

---

[11] Revelation 17:17 KJV.

[12] Watchtower May 1, 1981.

Watchtower Society, which has so effectively camouflaged and nourished its constantly withering credibility, is now hopelessly outdated.

According to their unique eschatology the world entered its 'last days' when Satan and his demons were hurled out of heaven and down to earth during 'the difficult conditions foretold for the last days [that] would prevail . . . those events have been clearly in evidence since 1914. Before the last members of the generation that was alive in 1914 will have passed off the scene, all the things foretold will occur, including the 'great tribulation' in which the present wicked world will end.'[13]

During these 'last days' humanity has been dividing itself into two groups – the 'sheep' (Jehovah's Witnesses) and the 'goats' (all the rest of mankind) – in readiness for the final showdown between God and his arch enemy Satan the Devil. This satanic clash of spiritual personalities will be reflected on earth with a cataclysmic global disaster which will be sparked off when the United Nations – long identified and vilified by Jehovah's Witnesses as the biblical 'scarlet coloured beast'[14] – initiates an attack upon the world headquarters of the sect in New York which, in turn, signals the onset of Armageddon.

The Watchtower Society explains: 'The outworking of history identifies this image as the organisation proposed, promoted, and supported by Britain and the United States and known initially as the League of Nations . . . the United Nations is a 'beastly image' and represents an international conspiracy against God's kingdom . . . [it] represents all the political power of Satan the Devil's visible earthly organisation. The Greek Har Ma-ge-don, taken from Hebrew and rendered Armageddon by many translators, means Mountain of Megiddo or Mountain of Assembly of Troops. The Bible associates the name, not with a nuclear holocaust, but with the coming universal 'war of the great day of God the Almighty'[15] This name is applied specifically to the place (Greek, to'pon; that is, condition or situation) to which earth's political rulers are being gathered in opposition to Jehovah and his Kingdom by Jesus Christ. Such opposition will be shown by global action against Jehovah's servants on earth, the visible representatives of God's Kingdom.'

At that time, the Witnesses believe, Jehovah God will authorise Jesus Christ and his heavenly armies to sweep across timeless infinity into the present terrestrial world to protect 'his people' during a world-wide

---

[13] Reasoning from the Scriptures – WTBTS, 1985.

[14] Revelation 17:3 KJV

[15] Revelation 16; 16, 14. NWT

breakdown of society. Billions of men women and children all over the world will then be 'destroyed' – apart from those individuals who have identified themselves before their God and the world at large as 'Jehovah's Witnesses'. In mentally preparing believers for such an ordeal the Watchtower Society's New World Translation of the Bible cautions the faithful: 'Seek Jehovah, all you [sic] meek ones of the earth, who have practised His own judicial decision. Seek righteousness, seek meekness. Probably you may be concealed in the day of Jehovah's anger.'[16]

The Witnesses are further admonished to find comfort in the words of the Apostle Paul who, in his letter to the Romans, implored: 'Everyone who calls on the name of Jehovah will be saved.'[17] Believers are periodically reminded: 'Only Jehovah's Witnesses, those of the anointed remnant and the 'great crowd', as a united organisation under the Supreme Organiser, have any Scriptural hope of surviving the impending end of this doomed system dominated by Satan, the Devil.'

As for the dead, they will neither be mourned nor buried for, according to the Old Testament prophet Jeremiah, 'In that day those whom the Lord has slain shall lie like dung on the ground from one end of the earth to the other; no one shall wail for them, they shall not be taken up and buried.'[18] However, the malevolence does not end there. The apostle John continues: 'I saw also an angel standing in the sun, and he cried out with a loud voice and said to all the birds that fly in mid-heaven: "Come here, be gathered together to the great evening meal of God, that you may eat the fleshy parts of kings and the fleshy parts of military commanders and the fleshy parts of strong men and the fleshy parts of all, of freemen as well as slaves and of small ones and great."[19]

In the ensuing pandemonium every democratically elected government on the face of the earth will collapse leaving the way clear for the Witnesses to institute a global theocratic government of their own before embarking upon a thousand year-long restoration programme during which the entire planet will be manually transformed into a garden paradise. The Watchtower Society offers us an intriguing glimpse into how this will be done:

'All the material goods that the war survivors will gather after the destruction of their international enemies will be [used] in the service of

---

[16] Zephaniah 2:3. NWT

[17] Romans 10: 13, NWT

[18] Jeremiah 25:33. NEB

[19] Revelation 19:17,18. NWT

the God-King Jehovah. No wrecked war equipment will be preserved as relics. It will be a time for construction, not destruction. The literal earth will doubtless have suffered from the 'military service' of the enemies of Jehovah's Messianic kingdom. The selfish ruiners [sic] of the earth will themselves have been brought to ruin, but many effects that their ruinous course will have produced down to the end of the final war will still be on hand.'[20]

As earth's transformation takes place the survivors of the apocalypse will then prepare to welcome back from the dead every single man, woman and child who had ever lived and died on earth prior to the end of the world. In stark contrast billions of others – those who had actually lived and consequently perished for not embracing the Watchtower creed during the 'last days' – would never ever be resurrected. Sensitive believers are comforted by the widely accepted notion that sentimental memories of such ones – former relatives or 'worldly acquaintances' – will eventually pass and be forgotten altogether.

The resurrected ones will then be 'educated in the ways of the Lord during a millennium of peace and security' in preparation for a global re-enactment of Eve's temptation in the Garden of Eden when Satan the Devil will once again be 'let loose in the cleansed earth' to challenge Jehovah's sovereignty in the minds of now perfected mankind. Nobody knows exactly just how this test of loyalty to Jehovah will manifest itself at that time, but one thing is certain; those who succumb to temptation, (and there could be some, the Bible hints), will be promptly despatched into oblivion along with the Devil himself.

Watchtower Society founder, Charles Russell explains: 'Now, if they are not able to stand the test after all the experiences of the fall and redemption and restitution processes, and with all that knowledge of God and the principles of justice and good and evil . . . then they are not fit for eternal life . . . with Satan they will be destroyed.'[21] Following this 'second death' – the final extinction of potential heavenly and earthly opposition to his sovereignty – God will then pronounce the world and everyone in it to be 'very good' and worthy of a physical permanency as originally intended.[22] Immortality will cease to be a dream and a global race of indestructible, permanently happy and ever youthful people will populate the 'new world' for ever and ever. An unofficial

[20] Paradise Restored to Mankind – WTBTS, 1972.
[21] What Pastor Russell Said – Dr L W Jones, 1917.
[22] Genesis 1: 31 KJV.

consensus within the movement favours the 'middle thirties' – believed to be the time in Christ's life when he was in his prime shortly before he was crucified then resurrected – as the ideal age to be in perpetuity.

Eventually human procreation will cease, and sexual desire will be a thing of the past as the last children on earth mature into permanently young adults. The violence of survival in the animal kingdom will gradually disappear as the food chain magically unlinks itself amid scenes of unprecedented tolerance and harmony among the species. As foretold by the prophet Isaiah, carnivores will become herbivorous as wildlife evolves into tame life and the earth becomes 'subdued' as biblically intended. At least that is the dream or, as the Witnesses themselves call it, 'the Truth'. Styling itself 'an organisation to direct the minds of God's people', today's movement, which is irrevocably linked to the debatable ministries of both Pastor Russell and Judge Rutherford, remains a motivating influence in the lives of millions.

***

The Watchtower Bible & Tract Society is the official title of the legal arm of the sect. Its world headquarters were previously situated in numerous purpose-built factory buildings and former hotels in New York which had been adapted into offices and living accommodation for the large volunteer residential work force. Indeed, the organisation's considerable real estate holdings in Brooklyn occupying some thirty blocks – 42 buildings in all – were once a massive and imposing presence in the city throughout the 20th century, but not anymore.

Now, somewhat condensed and relocated 40 miles northwest of New York City, the new world headquarters of Jehovah's Witnesses occupies a 253-acre site in Sterling Forest alongside Blue Lake in Warwick, NY, having four residential buildings providing accommodation for the 800 volunteers who live and work there. The newly built campus, which was completed in 2017, also boasts green roofing, bio-retention tanks, recycled wood, and geothermal wells. Seven-hundred volunteer Witnesses helped in its construction.

In addition to its dedicated Warwick conglomerate, the Watchtower Society also operates a 670-acre training centre in rural New York State. Patterson Farm, a 27-building campus, boasts 6 apartment houses 2 to 5 stories high with 624 apartments, a 450-car garage, a 144-room hotel, a huge kitchen, and dining room to serve 1,600 people at one sitting, an office building, a classroom building and several service units. This religious complex sits on a hill overlooking Route 22 in Putnam County and, like much of the Watchtower Society's real-estate holdings, it too was built by unpaid volunteers, all of them Jehovah's Witnesses.

During its construction, which was completed in 1996, volunteer, Matt Higgs, a former golf course landscaper who came from Kansas City to lay carpets, told a newspaper reporter, 'I am working to serve God'. Another volunteer, carpenter John Roth, Jr., a contractor from Albany, added, 'We feel it is part of our service to God'.[23] The entire workforce – engineers, architects, draftsmen, carpenters, concrete workers, electricians, plumbers and labourers – who volunteered their services for periods of weeks, months and, in some cases, years at a time, were housed and fed by the Watchtower Society but received no pay, excepting for a small monthly stipend toward 'incidental expenses'. In total 400 men and women toiled willingly on the five-year project.

Elsewhere in New York State, the Wallkill Farm complex – about 95 miles northwest of Brooklyn – is home to the organisation's computing technology and subsidiary printing plant. Both the Wallkill and Patterson properties are active livestock and arable farms where volunteers work on the land or in the bakeries and canned food facilities producing meat, poultry, dairy products and fruit and vegetables for the entire Bethel family – the term used to describe those Witnesses who live and work in the Watchtower Society's principal locations to be found in and around New York State. Across the globe other similar, but somewhat smaller, Bethel families produce Bible literature and provide support services for more than one hundred thousand congregations of Jehovah's Witnesses throughout the world.

For these industrious believers, the production and distribution of the Watchtower Society's religious literature takes precedence over all other considerations. Believing they are striving toward their own immortality 'in the short time remaining' they happily work voluntarily for 'Jehovah's organisation' before Armageddon strikes. 'The successful printing of books and Bibles by persons of little or no previous experience is evidence of Jehovah's oversight and the direction of his spirit,' the faithful were told throughout the 20th century. However, printing and bookbinding activity has, in recent years, diminished considerably as corporate attention re-focussed on audio/video production.

The physical labour involved in the smooth running of the organisation is undertaken by the youth of the movement who are encouraged and conditioned from childhood to eschew higher education and the

---

[23] The New York Times – April 7, 1991.

realisation of personal ambition and enlightenment in favour of entering the 'full-time service', either as part of the voluntary workforce in Watchtower branches around the world, or as travelling pioneering ministers. The avoidance of higher education in favour of 'labouring in the vineyard of the Lord' was instituted by Pastor Russell: 'I advise all Christians not to send their children to colleges or universities; for if they do, they will risk a great deal through infidelity and unbelief . . . most children would be better off if they would not go beyond, or much beyond, a common school education. I do not know of a college anywhere that would do them any good.'

The principal organ of the sect is the Watchtower, originally a 32-page magazine 'Announcing Jehovah's Kingdom' with Bible-based articles designed to inspire loyalty and faith in the organisational structure and functioning of the Watchtower Society. At its peak, toward the end of the 20th century, it had a print run of more than 58 million copies in 254 languages and was published 24 times a year. Once hailed as 'the most widely-circulated magazine in the world' it was also among the least read. Likewise, its companion publication *Awake!* was previously an illustrated 32-page magazine written in Readers Digest style with articles of general interest and significantly reflective of the apocalyptic beliefs of the sect. Having a total print run of more than 50 million copies in 103 languages, it was also initially published 24 times a year. However, in 2016 both magazines were unexpectedly much reduced in size and content to just three copies a year. A further reduction to a single copy of both is tentatively scheduled for 2022.

In addition to these magazines, a constant stream of auxiliary publications is circulated world-wide with a dogged and determined regularity by those who measure not only their own faith but that of others with an unquestioning loyalty to 'God's visible organisation on earth'. Such devotional allegiance to the organisation can only be acceptably demonstrated by those who publicly take part in the familiar doorstep preaching activities for which they are known throughout the world.

It was principally this non-stop production and distribution of apocalyptic literature that gave life and meaning to the movement. Without that fervent activity the organisational infra-structure of the Watchtower Society – which, since its inception in the late 19th century, has attracted millions of predominantly nominal Christians and their families – could well collapse. Indeed, in recent years the organisation found itself in retreat, closing branch offices, laying off many live-in workers and struggling to justify its presence and purpose in the internet-savvy world of the 21st century as various aspects of its global printing and preaching work were officially 'delayed, reduced in scope or, in some cases, cancelled'.[24] Consequently, many of the 83,790 full-time special pioneers and residential staff (in receipt of a small monthly stipend) across the globe were 'invited' to return to the regular (self-supporting) pioneering work in the outside world as part of an ongoing cost-cutting programme first introduced in 2015.

Nonetheless, preaching targets continue to be set before the Witnesses as directives from God and the amount of time each believer spends persuading others to accept a magazine displayed on street carts is carefully noted and documented by the elders at local level in 239 lands across the globe. This information is then collated at the New York State Headquarters into a grand total of 'hours spent in the field' by the global community of Jehovah's Witnesses.

Previously, details of meeting attendance – which on special occasions would peek at upwards of 20,000,000 – were published in the Yearbook of Jehovah's Witnesses along with interesting accounts of preaching activities throughout the world as an encouraging indication of the spiritual well-being of a thriving and expanding organisation. However, publication of this once popular and encouraging source of information ominously ceased in 2017.

Householders who accept the offer of a 'free home Bible study' conducted by one of Jehovah's Witnesses are sooner or later invited to attend one of several meetings which are held each week. On these occasions prospective subjects of the New World Society are warmly welcomed – love-bombed – by their new 'brothers and sisters'. Once a regular pattern of meeting attendance has been established, baptism – in which the newcomer is totally immersed in water – follows in symbolic recognition of dedication to Jehovah and unquestioning loyalty to his organisation on earth. The new subject of Jehovah's Kingdom is now on the way to becoming a mere object within the Watchtower Society, in effect an unpaid part-time representative – and potential full-time volunteer worker – for one of the largest corporations in the world.

For many years all baptized members of the sect were obliged to spend at least two hours a week going from door to door 'on the work' spreading the 'good news' but in recent years this requirement has been relaxed. Today, those who report spending just 15 minutes per month

[24] Public announcement broadcast on Wednesday, September 23, 2015 (www JW.org).

preaching are counted as active members of the New World Society in the annual service report. Jehovah's Witnesses are required to regularly attend several meetings each week. Here powerfully persuasive organisational propaganda is featured in repetitive programmes of indoctrination designed to keep everyone in a constant state of alert and expectation.

Forever on the watch for the signs of the impending doom they so look forward to, the apocalyptic hopes of believers are reinvigorated by any human tragedy or natural disaster in the news which underscores mankind's eternal struggle to survive. Consequently, news reports of war, civil disruption, and natural disasters such as earthquakes and flooding as well as news items on famine and the spread of disease are eagerly assessed during meetings as taking place in fulfilment of Bible prophecy. Whenever any of these things occur, they are meticulously tabulated, chronicled, listed, and endlessly and methodically studied in detail. Such grim facts are regularly portrayed in gory words and graphic pictures in Watchtower literature as evidence of the nearness of Armageddon. Climate change, terrorism and the recent pandemic Covid-19 outbreak are relatively new additions to the list of apocalyptic precursors.

Jehovah's Witnesses are chiefly motivated by a consuming fascination with immortality, a morbid interest which encourages and promotes a suicidal loyalty to their 'mother organisation' and a readiness to die for their intangible beliefs. Believing that Armageddon is 'imminent' they place small value on their present lives and focus all their longing on a never-ending future life in paradise. As we shall see, the opportunity to put such beliefs first in a life-or-death situation is often seized upon to publicly demonstrate one's depth of feeling and intensity of faith, thereby encouraging and strengthening the beliefs of others.

For decades, the Witnesses have dutifully obeyed numerous life-threatening directives from their spiritual leaders and denied themselves and their children crucial medical treatment such as blood transfusions, vaccinations, and organ transplants, including sight-giving corneal grafts. Some have lost their sight. Many have lost their lives. Former Jehovah's Witness elder and presiding overseer, David Reed, comments: 'Between the years 1931 and 1952 vaccinations were prohibited, and during the years 1967 to 1980 organ transplants were banned. Those medical procedures are now permitted again, but who knows how many Witnesses, or their children got sick or died during the interim for lack of a vaccination or for want of a kidney or cornea transplant? (A former

Jehovah's Witness elder in England told reporters that he resigned after a woman in his congregation turned down a cornea transplant in obedience to the Watchtower and went blind.) How high will the death toll climb – already estimated by some to be in the thousands – as loyal followers continue to refuse blood transfusions, adhering to an interpretation introduced in the 1940's but not yet rescinded?'[25]

Both Russell and Rutherford were roundly dismissed by their critics as cranks, Bible-freaks, power-hungry tricksters on the make. Nonetheless, they were enthusiastically patronised by their followers who, in turn, were led to believe that they too were intended by God to dispense the Watchtower Society's 'lifesaving literature' to the masses prior to the outbreak of Armageddon and the 'imminent' end of the world's 'system of things'. For example, in 1987, long serving Jehovah's Witness, Melvin Sargent, then 91 years of age and hoping to live through Armageddon – at that time expected to break sometime 'soon' toward the end of the 20th century – proffered: 'Those of us inside the Lord's organisation have tried, in every way possible, to turn attention to the message of life. We have used slogans, full-page advertisements, radio, sound cars, portable phonographs, gigantic conventions, parades of information-walkers carrying signs, and a growing army of house-to-house ministers. This activity has served to divide people – those in favour of God's established Kingdom on the one side, those against it on the other. This was the work foretold by Jesus for my generation.'[26]

Likewise, today's Jehovah's Witnesses continue in that tradition – seeking out and separating the 'sheep' from the 'goats' of this doomed world in 'the short time remaining' – singing the praises of Jehovah as they go, convinced that their activities are of paramount importance to the everlasting survival of humanity:

We're Jehovah's Witnesses,
We speak out in fearlessness.
Ours is the God of true prophecy,
What, he foretells comes to be!

***

For some 140 years, the non-stop production and circulation of its flagship magazine has been the only constant factor in the kaleidoscopic history of the Watchtower Society. Founder Charles Russell initially published Zion's Watch Tower and Herald of Christ's Presence for

---

[25] Watchtower Errors – David A Reed, Baker Books 1990.

[26] Jehovah's Witnesses – Proclaimers of God's Kingdom. WTBTS 1993.

thirty years before removing the word Zion from the main title in 1909 to clarify and redefine its eventual Christian focus. Under Rutherford's control Watchtower became one word in 1931 and in January 1939 Christ's Presence in the subtitle was quietly altered, first to Christ's Kingdom and then to Jehovah's Kingdom a couple of months later, in effect, reducing the established deity of Jesus to something of a lesser god than his father Jehovah God.

This Arian interpretation of the Scriptures, which lies at the heart of Watchtower theology, reveals, in part, how nominal Christians and others, usually disadvantaged by a generalised and vague conception of a 'three-in-one God', are sometimes persuaded to reject confusing 4th century Trinitarian beliefs in favour of the comparatively reasonable logic of the Watchtower Society, and it is easy to see why. Jehovah's Witnesses readily, and quite rightly, point out that neither the word Trinity, nor any allusion to such a contradictory interpretation of its biblical monotheistic root source – the Shema [27] – appears anywhere in the Scriptures.

After being trained in Antioch the Libyan theologian Arius became a presbyter in Alexandria and soon found himself at odds with his bishop when, in the year 319, he began promoting the belief that Jesus was not co-equal or co-eternal with his heavenly father but rather the first of creatures both heavenly and earthly that existed by the grace of God. At that time, the Holy Spirit was understood to be the active force or power of God which was utilised by Christ (a lesser god) to demonstrate his supernatural powers during his sojourn on earth in the guise of a man. This official clarification had been largely adopted in Egypt, Syria, and Asia Minor and inevitably, in the year 321, Arius, for his pains, was deposed and excommunicated by a synod of bishops at Alexandria, prior to Christianity becoming a state religion in 324.

In the year 325 Emperor Constantine 1 convoked the Church Council of Nicaea (Nice) in Blithynia when a court of some three hundred and eighteen, mainly Greek speaking, bishops as well as priests, deacons, and acolytes, formalised the majority view on the vexing questions previously posed by Arius. From then on, the God of the Bible was to be understood as a composite triune entity of Father, Son and Spirit. It was a controversial interpretation which introduced a potentially divisive

---

[27] 'Hear, O Israel: the Lord our God *is* one Lord.' (Deuteronomy 6:4 KJV).

fault line in the shifting layers of Christian thinking down through the centuries.

The Watchtower Society points out: 'Neither the word Trinity, nor the explicit doctrine as such, appears in the New Testament. It developed gradually over several centuries and through many controversies.' And for good measure, they point out that even the New Catholic Encyclopaedia supports their argument: 'The formulation "one God in three Persons" was not solidly established, certainly not fully assimilated into Christian life and its profession of faith, prior to the end of the 4th century. Among the Apostolic fathers, there had been nothing even remotely approaching such a mentality or perspective.'

To nominal Christians, and others who profess a vague but nonetheless sincere belief in God, such authoritative reasoning sounds impressive and appears to undermine many of the teachings and traditions of Christendom. Consequently, some householders find themselves attracted to the chatty informality of the Witnesses when they call. They are intrigued by the fact that there appears, at first, to be no clergy/laity distinction and no pecking-order of status or privilege in the organization. Indeed, as the Witnesses tell those who may feel put off by such things, the elaborate trappings of piety and pomp, along with the distinctive garb usually associated with traditional acts of Christian worship, are significantly absent in the Kingdom Halls of Jehovah's Witnesses.

Most notable is the fact that the Witnesses seem to be so knowledgeable about the Bible, utilising any translation – not, as is widely believed, just their own. Above all, they appear so ready to openly discuss their beliefs with anyone. And for some Christian 'believers' this candid down-to-earth approach can be disarming, irresistible almost. It is at this point that inquiring minds, sometimes unwittingly, open the door to the tenacious end-time philosophy of the Watchtower Society as mind-controlling indoctrination gains a tentative foothold. Inevitably, those who go on to embrace the implausible agenda of the Watchtower Society, in the hope of living on earth forever in the New World Society of Jehovah's Witnesses, sooner or later find themselves indulging in the collective denial and self-deception upon which the entire movement depends. Thus, the doomsday-mentality cycle continues.

Since its inception, the promising exegesis of the Watchtower Bible & Tract Society – a strange, yet fascinating, piety – has captivated millions of devotees all over the world. Although tens of thousands of dissenters are ceremoniously expelled from the organisation each year – in addition to the countless others who independently manage to break free from its manipulative organisational control – substantial numbers of 'newly interested persons' inexplicably continue to join the ranks of Jehovah's Witnesses marking time on their never-ending road to paradise.

For example, following a determined recruitment campaign in third world and east European countries early in the 21st century the Watchtower Society announced: 'During the 2003 service year, 2,340 Kingdom Halls [places of worship] were completed around the world. This represents an average of 195 halls per month, or just over 6 per day! Since November 1999 when the construction programme in lands with limited resources began, 7,730 Kingdom halls have been built. In many areas, once a hall is finished, meeting attendance soars and halls are soon filled.'[28]

In glaring contrast to this alleged bustling preaching activity, the future of the Church of England was said to be in the balance at the end of the 20th century. Attendance figures had fallen to less than 2% of the U.K. population, with only half of those taking communion. Christian Research, an independent agency, also revealed that more than half of the country's churches had no teenagers or young people attending services. Professor David Martin, a sociologist of religion at the London School of Economics, said that the Church's established social status would have to be questioned.

'Churchgoing in Britain has declined by 50 per cent in 25 years. The latest English Church census shows that the overall decline is centred in the traditional, liberal, and middle-of-the-road churches of mainstream traditions. Since the last census, in 1998, the Methodists have closed down some 300 churches while the Anglicans have lost more than 100.'[29]

Today, in the USA, the fastest growing religious affiliation is 'no affiliation', according to a Pew Research poll which indicated 36% of younger millennials identify as either atheist or agnostic or 'nothing in particular'. The report found the vast amount of information available via the www is leading many away from the churches. In Britain, a more telling sign of religious apathy is the Church of England's ongoing catalogue of redundant properties for sale. During the past thirty-odd years more than 1,650 churches have been commercially disposed of in this way only to be born-again as homes, offices, art galleries or warehouses.

---

[28] 2004 Yearbook of Jehovah's Witnesses.

[29] The Times – September 18, 2006.

In some happy instances deserted and abandoned places of Christian worship have been converted into theatres, thriving temples of entertainment where, it is sometimes said, the deepest truths are to be found in the wondrous world of music, make-believe, and drama.

***

Honed to a toweringly disproportionate presence in the 21st century by generations of disillusioned defectors from tired-out traditional faiths and fragmenting orthodoxies of all persuasions, the Watchtower Bible & Tract Society owes its existence primarily to the collective efforts of a host of – predominantly 19th century – Christian intellectuals, Protestant philanthropists, and diverse millenarians from all walks of life and from both sides of the Atlantic. Indeed, we can more readily understand – perhaps, in some ways, sympathise with – Jehovah's Witnesses when we view their outdated creed dispassionately as a naive distillation of the religiously inspired delusions (apocalyptic hopes, fears and fantasies) of others who lived in less informed times; a Bible-based prescience which is now hopelessly discredited by time itself.

For example, a whole string of previously 'significant' years of expectancy that once fuelled the date-driven movement along its road to paradise is today no longer referred to. Having served their purpose at the time, those misleading signpost dates (1799, 1874, 1878, 1881, 1910, 1914, 1915, 1918, 1919, 1922, 1925, 1935, 1942, 1975 and latterly the year 2000) are now redundant and preferably forgotten. However, there is just one tenacious exception, the year 1914 – the ubiquitous pivotal date upon which the credibility of the Watchtower Society's doomsday agenda now hangs by an ever-weakening thread.

Notwithstanding the implausibility of the predictions of Pastor Russell and Judge Rutherford, both men are customarily revered by today's Witnesses as the principal architects of the movement, respected pillars of the Watchtower Society. To the outsider (not to mention millions of faith-blinkered Jehovah's Witnesses), these two 'God-fearing' men would appear to have been genuinely sincere and well-meaning in their biblical deliberations and Christian preaching activities. However, when we consider their private lives quite different images emerge – deeply flawed hypocritical personalities living on the edge of reality but able nonetheless to galvanise support for an exuberantly fatuous eschatology with a succession of money-making schemes that barely conceal their rapacity.

In the beginning of course, Charles Russell was innocent enough; after all, he was a respectable businessman and a well-intentioned Bible-reading Christian to boot. However, he was also one of a growing number of disillusioned Christian traditionalists who came to reject the faulty logic and reasoning of Christendom but were loath to abandon the cherished source of that demonstrably flawed rationale – the Bible itself, unquestioningly considered by many to be the very 'word' of God.

His relentless disaffection from mainstream Christianity may have been unintentionally initiated in his infancy, more than likely by his mother. His rejection – and subsequent rediscovery – of religion in his youth, along with repressed teenage angst, probably accelerated the process. The Adventist movement beckoned, and subsequently young Charles acquired a passion for divining the future when he found himself charmed and fascinated by the 'secrets' of Freemasonry and the 'mysteries' of ancient Egypt.

It was during this period in his life that he began to formulate his Plan of the Ages – an apocalyptic interpretation of the Bible which incorporated a pseudo-scientific study of one of the ancient Seven Wonders of the World. Convinced he had been chosen by God to disseminate an allegedly new and enlightened interpretation of Bible prophecy regarding the ultimate destiny of the Jews and the Gentile nations of the world the young millionaire launched his own controversial religious campaign as a Christian Zionist. He claimed that his remarkable understanding of the Bible was due to 'the simple fact that God's due time had come'. His growing flock eventually conferred on him the unofficial title Pastor and came to look upon him as God's lone spokesman and guiding light because the young preacher so convincingly led them to believe they were living in the 'last days' of a doomed planet earth.

Of those early beginnings the Watchtower Society comments: 'As Jehovah's Witnesses today review the work that he did, the things he taught, his reason for teaching them, and the outcome, they have no doubt that Charles Taze Russell was, indeed, used by God in a special way and at a significant time.' Indeed, he attracted much favourable attention on both sides of the Atlantic by rejecting the doctrine of the Trinity, the teaching that human souls are inherently immortal, and the reverently accepted Christian image of the death-dealing God of the Old Testament he was introduced to as a child during his strict Presbyterian upbringing. Having been whipped by his mother into believing that the God of the Bible would burn all doubters in hell, who could blame him? The determined young preacher focused instead on an altogether different God of love, a merciful one who cared for all the human family.

He maintained that only those who embraced his promising interpretation of the much loved and respected Holy Bible would win God's favour and gain everlasting life. In forcefully negating the depressing hellfire beliefs which had been taught by the established church for centuries he came to be revered among his followers as 'the man who turned the hose on hell'. In his own eyes he was special – 'If I did not speak, and no other agent could be found, the very stones would cry out,' he once said. His adoring followers in turn persuaded themselves that such conceit was unassailable Godly devotion. His books sold by the million.

As the circulation of Russell's writings steadily grew, both Catholic and Protestant clergy angrily denounced his works from their pulpits and instructed their flocks not to accept any literature from the Bible Students. In some places in the United States clergymen encouraged and supervised the public burning of books written by the infamous Pastor. Because of such attacks the beleaguered preacher was in a permanent state of self-righteous readiness for imaginary spiritual conflict, an entirely unnecessary attitude which led to a string of costly lawsuits and non-productive confrontational debates with theologians and others who did not share his views. However, when gossipy rumours about his alleged sexual dalliances were published in the New York press he remained uncharacteristically silent.

Like many individuals of exceptional achievement Russell tended toward over-activity and denying himself proper rest and relaxation. Thus, as God's only channel of communication on earth, he tried to be everywhere at the same time, hence his constant world tours. An unlikely pioneer of 'motion pictures' he produced the world's first million-dollar block-buster. His epic Photo Drama of Creation premiered off Broadway (where it ran for two years) and in London's West-End in the spring of 1914, the long-awaited year of doom. Expectations among the Bible Students at that time heightened. What on earth would happen? Characteristically, Russell prevaricated: 'If we have the correct date and chronology, Gentile Times will end this year – 1914. What of it? We do not surely know. Our expectation, true or false, is that there will be wonderful manifestations of Divine judgements against all unrighteousness, and that this will mean the breaking up of many institutions of the present time, if not all.'

Fortuitously for the disappointed prophet, the outbreak of World War One in 1914 coincided with his predicted date for Armageddon and lent a measure of credence to his doomsday warnings to the world. With hindsight the global conflict was now interpreted as a curtain raiser to the 'great tribulation', God's final two-part execution of judgement of the world in which all other religious organisations, and civilisation itself, would be drawn into confusion and conflict prior to the battle of Armageddon. Sick and disillusioned, Russell lived on for a further two disappointing years. Unsurprisingly, he died earthbound and was buried in mawkish and meandering splendour surrounded by crowds of broken-hearted mourners who felt they had been abandoned by 'God's messenger'.

In the confusion that followed, one of Russell's followers, Joseph Franklin Rutherford, a former Missouri small-town lawyer resorted to forgery and physical intimidation to seize power at the Watchtower Society's New York headquarters, eventually duping board members into accepting him as their new spiritual leader. The organisation's second president was now obliged to kick-start Russell's stalled countdown to doomsday. He did this by pointing out that 1914 was not the date for Armageddon, as had previously been thought, but rather 'the beginning of sorrows' as detailed in the 24th chapter of the Bible book of Matthew. With war raging around the world at that time, it all seemed to make apocalyptic sense to Russell's confused and disappointed followers.

Rutherford, an unfulfilled lawyer, was a restless, stentorian man. Irrationally impulsive and driven by religiously motivated personal ambition he frequently experienced alcohol-induced flights of fancy during which he dreamed up his own doomsday predictions. However, many of Russell's original die-hard followers gradually ceased to associate with Rutherford's increasingly totalitarian administration but confusingly continued to identify themselves as Russell's original International Bible Students as opposed to Rutherford's International Bible Students.

To distinguish between the two factions Rutherford sought to discredit his predecessor and proceeded to formulate a creed of his own in which he incorporated Russell's failed but necessary pivotal 1914 date for the Apocalypse. It was a shrewd move on Rutherford's part and one which not only signalled the inevitable decline and demise of Russell's International Bible Students Association, but one which also heralded the birth of its mutant offspring. He eventually formalised its inception in 1931 with the emergence of his very own Jehovah's Witnesses movement laying down the 'solid Scriptural foundations' upon which the creed of today's Watchtower Society is based:

'In the secret place of the Highest there have been revealed, to those who love Jehovah, certain great truths which they are commanded to proclaim to the nations (Matthew 10:27). Among such truths revealed are these: That Jehovah is the true God; that Jesus Christ is his anointed King, who is earth's rightful ruler; that in 1914 he took office, and his first work was to cast Satan out of heaven; that in 1918 he began to gather the faithful into a compact company and make known to them that Satan has built a mighty organisation in the earth consisting of religion, politics and commerce; that within a short time the battle of Armageddon will be fought; that knowing there is but a short time for him, Satan now brings greater burdens upon the people; that in order to vindicate His holy name and save the people the battle of Armageddon will result in the complete destruction of Satan's organisation, including all the nations of the earth; that the people must now be notified, and that such notice or testimony will be given amidst great opposition, but will be given just the same; and that such notice is not a threat, but a solemn warning, and those who hear it may receive it or reject it; take it or leave it. Those who take Satan's side and oppose Jehovah's truth shall die; those who serve Jehovah shall live forever.'[30]

The power Rutherford came to exercise within his Jehovah's Witnesses movement was concentrated to such an extent that there was little room for others to act in any other way than in a subordinate role to the man himself. He died early in 1942, soon after America entered World War Two, leaving his followers with apocalyptic expectations for that year. Rutherford was succeeded by Nathan Homer Knorr who then became the third president of the Watchtower Society. He, in turn, was succeeded in 1977 by Vice president Frederick William Franz, who remained in power until his death at the age of ninety-nine in 1992.

Under the combined stewardship of these two men the Watchtower Society expanded impressively encircling the globe throughout the second half of the 20th century. In post war America its persuasive influence penetrated the very heart of government reaching into the White House and the president himself – a fact that so intrigued Prime Minister Winston Churchill that when the opportunity unexpectedly presented itself the British Bulldog requested a home visit from one of Jehovah's Witnesses and subsequently bought some Watchtower Society literature. It was during this period that the one-time 'fastest growing religion in the world' gradually acquired a stifling bureaucratic complexity of Talmudic proportions.

---

[30] Dividing the People – J F Rutherford. WTBTS 1933.

Yet, having survived some 140 years of failed prophecies and predictions, doctrinal U-turns and accusations of corruption and scandal involving those at its heart, the movement inexplicably continues to attract expectant worshippers today. Indeed, today's Watchtower Bible & Tract Society – now bereft of idiosyncratic leadership – appears to have gained an inscrutable theocratic life and personality of its own, having a compliant administration that wields unbridled hierarchal executive power over the personal lives of millions of its followers.

Jehovah's Witnesses are forbidden to attend any birthday or Christmas celebrations. They do not stand to sing any national anthems, school songs, or even figuratively join in any chorus of appreciation or congratulation which may have been accorded to a work colleague or school friend. Witnesses cannot do jury service, stand for civic election, or hold office in any political capacity. They do not take up arms, salute any flag or pay respects at any remembrance service or commemorative event. Unavoidable national holidays such as those marked by Easter or Christmas are taken but never acknowledged. Among a silent but rebellious minority surprise gifts may spontaneously appear a few days prior to a birthday and many a Christmas pudding and other unmentionable seasonal goodies are known to be secretly consumed by guilt-ridden Witnesses in the privacy of their own homes.

Without exception Jehovah's Witnesses are required to dress and behave 'modestly'. Teenagers and youthful male Witnesses in general are regularly warned not to draw attention to themselves with extreme styles or outlandish fashions. Tight trousers and underwear 'displaying the buttocks and genitals'[31] are to be avoided at all costs. The organisational pressures to be sensible, rather than sensuous, are enormous. Young men are admonished to get a 'theocratic haircut' – a modest and unremarkable 'short back and sides'. School dances and outings are looked upon as inappropriate for the youth of the Watchtower Society. Dating is forbidden along with participation in school plays and any activity connected with Christmas. Additionally, Jehovah's Witnesses may not become members of the YMCA.

For adults and children alike, every sphere of life is affected, in one way or another, by the baleful influence of the corporate paranoia of the

---

[31] From a leaked, graphically detailed, Watchtower instructional video on the evils of masturbation. Governing Body member Anthony Morris has adopted a questionable interest in tight-fitting menswear in recent years, even to the extent of flying (business class) to Trinidad and Rome, Italy, to prioritize his obsessive homo-phobic take on the subject.

Watchtower Society: 'The ideal situation is for parents to have such a fine programme outlined for their children that little or no time remains for outside associations.'[32] Almost all sporting activities and most forms of entertainment are frowned upon, if not roundly condemned, by the movement: 'Participation in organised sports . . . would expose Witness youths to unwholesome associations . . . the competitive spirit in modern sports . . . has harmful effects.'[33]

While theatregoing and visits to the cinema are not banned outright, they are not encouraged. The evils of listening to almost every genre of music are regularly analysed and featured in Watchtower literature along with pep-talks at local Kingdom Halls and Witness conventions. Those with any musical aptitude are encouraged to stifle such worldly aspirations and wait until they find themselves in the 'new order of things' when they will have 'all the time in the world' to pursue music making in a 'God-honouring frame of mind'.

Wives are held in subjection to their husbands and are expected not only to take care of their husbands' needs and looking after the children, but to take part in the door-to-door preaching work. Women are permitted to answer questions at meetings but forbidden to teach directly as individuals. When required to give a short talk at the Kingdom Hall women must never address the audience directly. They get around this by addressing themselves to another female who appears with them on the platform. In this way, the men in the audience feel they are not being taught by a woman – they are merely eavesdropping on two women in a domestic situation. Women cannot be appointed as ministerial servants or elders. In short, they can never take the lead or be in a teaching position in the presence of a man; in effect they are subordinate.

A Witness cannot buy a lottery ticket or a raffle ticket or play card games for money. A game of chess cannot be played with a clear conscience for it is a war game. Conjuring and magical illusions are considered as pagan practices, derivative of the works of Satan, 'the greatest deceiver of all'. There are no tears at the funerals of Jehovah's Witnesses for to cry would signal a weakness of faith. Such occasions are routinely exploited as an opportunity to deliver a public talk on the Watchtower Society's 'glorious hope ahead' along with a brief passing reference to the deceased. Indeed, those conducting funerals are specifically told not to eulogize the individual who has died.

---

[32] Watchtower – February 1, 1974.

[33] School and Jehovah's Witnesses – WTBTS 1983.

A Witness may not be hypnotised, not even under medical supervision, and so on. Clearly, the lifestyle of the average believer is severely curtailed and self-censored by an almost irresistible conditioned loyalty to the 'mother organisation' which rigorously promotes an unhealthy dependency on itself. Adopting and insidiously adapting individuals to its extraordinarily suppressive demands in this way, the Watchtower hierarchy constantly reminds its adherents that they are 'in the world but are no part of it'. With St. Paul's second letter to the early Christians of the ancient Greek city of Corinth in mind, today's Watchtower Society explains:

'Jehovah's Witnesses have good times with their families and friends. But they do not participate in holidays and celebrations that are linked with pagan gods (as is true of such holidays as Easter, New Year Day, May Day, Mother's Day, and Father's Day). Like the early Christians, they do not even celebrate birthdays. They also respectfully refrain from sharing in national holidays that memorialise political or military events and refrain from giving worshipful honour to national heroes.'

Consequently, the faithful cultivate a deplorably circumscribed view of the world and everyone in it; indeed, Jehovah's Witnesses can hardly wait to see the back of it. Mentally constrained, socially isolated, and spiritually marooned, each on his or her own little island of private dreams, typical believers can see nothing wrong in any of this for their eyes of understanding are continually focused on the pronouncements and requirements of Jehovah's organisation, God's mouthpiece on earth.

Mindful of the sentiments penned by the Apostle Mark – 'If thou canst believe, all things *are* possible to him that believeth.'[34] – Jehovah's Witnesses tell us it is a simple matter of faith. However, such blind faith is common to all believers in any god and given the disagreeable history (to say the very least) of organised religion in general, intellectual honesty and simple common sense tell us that such unquestioning conviction can only be a matter of opinion, not fact.

The 'end of this system of things' is still yet to come for the worldwide community of Jehovah's Witnesses while the future of their Watchtower Society remains as unpredictable as ever. Exposed as never before by a constellation of informative websites and whistle-blowing social media, history tells us that the seeds of the organisation's present

---

[34] Mark 9:23. KJV

decline and much speculated demise were sown by Charles Russell from the start.

Many commentators view the recent sale and disposal of its New York City headquarters and closures of branch offices and Kingdom Halls across the globe as the beginning of the end for the time-locked Watchtower Society itself, and they may well be right – who knows? The only thing we can be sure about in this instance is the story so far, a story that begins neither with the troublesome birth of Christianity, nor with the genesis of Judaism, but rather with the building of a pyramid in ancient Egypt.

GENESIS

Chapter One

IN THE BEGINNING

To the medieval Arabs the pyramids of Egypt were known as 'Pharaoh's mountains'. 'Man, fears time,' they said, 'but time itself fears the pyramids.' The largest, most imposing, and majestic of them all is the Great Pyramid of Giza which stands proudly on a rocky plateau ten miles west of Cairo. More than 450 feet high and covering an area of 13 acres the 5,000-year-old mysterious edifice sits on a base which is a perfect square with its four sides aligned to the four points of the compass. Such ancient mathematical accuracy attracted the attention of Oxford scholar John Greaves who explored the pyramid in 1638. The perfect pyramid form in such colossal proportions exuded an ethereal quality which seemed to hint at a hidden theological significance. Could God have had anything to do with its construction?

Upon his return to Britain Greaves shared his Egyptian experiences with his fellows, among them Isaac Newton who was fascinated by the prospect of solving the riddle of the silent monument. Consequently, throughout the rest of the 17th century numerous other British and French scientists and mathematicians took an interest in deciphering the allegedly built-in secrets of the pyramid. Even the aged Galileo was said to be involved in correspondence with some of the pyramid researchers on the subject.

This intellectually fashionable trend continued throughout the 18th and 19th centuries as a whole range of scholars, religionists, mystics, and eccentrics joined in the debate. One school of thought defined the pyramid as having been built for astronomical purposes; it was a gigantic ancient observatory from which maps of the starry sky were drawn, while another ventured that it had been constructed as the mystical headquarters of an ancient secretive movement; embryonic Rosicrucian or Masonic, perhaps. Other observers took the comfortable majority view that, although awe-inspiring in its colossal proportions, the Great Pyramid of Giza was simply an unused, though remarkable, tomb which had been built for King Khufu, otherwise identified today by Herodotus' Grecianized appellation of Cheops.

However, the persistent legend that it had been exquisitely constructed by the ancient Egyptians under God's direction to convey a divine revelation, believed to be encoded in the pyramid's extraordinary structure, at a future 'appointed time' continued to fascinate numerous theorists who were determined to solve the alleged cabbalistic mystery of the mighty edifice. Besides, it was entertaining and stimulating for those driven by the mathematical challenge rather than the alleged esoteric belief.

Among the earliest of the 19th century investigators of the Great Pyramid were English astronomer Sir John Herschel who pioneered celestial photography and carried out research on photo-active chemicals. Another was General Howard Vyse who, in 1837 after taking measurements both inside and outside the structure, came to believe that the pyramid had been built for astronomic purposes. During this period of archaeological exploration in Egypt some Christian believers busied themselves with an altogether different kind of dig seeking to make a connection between early Hebrew history and Britain.

Convinced the Reformation of the16th century that established Protestantism was now ready for further clarification and refinement one Richard Brothers subsequently claimed the British were the actual descendants of the lost tribes of Israel. Although this self-styled 'Nephew of the Almighty' was eventually confined to a lunatic asylum for prophesying the death of the king, the notion of British Israelites took a firm hold on certain probing religionists, archaeologists among them. As for the pyramid theory, it first came into prominence in 1859 when 69-year-old John Taylor, the somewhat eccentric son of the editor of London's Observer newspaper, published The Great Pyramid: Why was it built? And who built it? It was a short work which embraced Brothers' strange British Israelite hypothesis in which he proposed 'to recover a lost leaf in the world's history'.

Although he had never visited the Great Pyramid, he claimed to have discovered the length of the ancient biblical cubit. He wrote of 'sacred cubits' and 'pyramidal inches' (said to equal the 500 millionth part of the polar diameter of the earth). He also observed that the length of two sides of the pyramid divided by its height equalled a number remarkably close to the transcendental number π (3·41 . . .) It was an astonishing and imaginative claim and one that attracted the attention of numerous religionists at the time.

Taylor pointed out that as there is no evidence that the ancient Egyptians had anything other than the most rudimentary command of mathematics they could never have known about such geometric and geodetic accuracy. Therefore, he claimed, the Egyptian stone masons of long ago must surely have laboured under divine guidance. He also suggested that the architect concerned was none other than Old Testament boat-builder himself, Noah. However, when Taylor presented a thesis on the subject to the Royal Society of Edinburgh it was rejected – but all was not lost.

After reading John Taylor's curious little book on the subject Professor Charles Piazzi Smyth (1819-1900), a British Israelite and Astronomer Royal for Scotland, remarked that it had 'opened for archaeology a purer, nobler, more intellectual pathway to light than that study had ever enjoyed before. But academic archaeology would not accept it; indeed, the whole reading world stood askance; and I can hardly now explain how it came about that something induced me, in February 1864, to commence an independent examination of Mr. Taylor's theory'.

However, while he was quite taken with 'the principal thread of Mr. Taylor's chief and most startling discovery', he concluded that that Taylor had demonstrated 'a lamentable deficiency in the accurateness [sic] of almost all the numerical data required; and which necessary exactitude, nothing but practical examination and instrumental measure at the place could hope to supply'. Consequently, Piazzi Smyth journeyed to Egypt with his wife where, during a four-month period of investigation, he attempted to validate the existence of Taylor's 'pyramid inch' sometimes called the 'polar diameter inch'. To do this he photographed the interior passages, using for the first time a magnesium light, and employing 'a variety of surveying and astronomical instruments, in obtaining many measures of the mighty monument; some of them to far more exactness [sic] than had ever been attempted before, and others descending to numerous details unnoticed by former observers'.

After calculating the number of stones used in the construction of the inner chambers of the pyramid, the measurements and shape of the stone coffer found in the King's Chamber and the number of courses of masonry which divided various chambers within the empty tomb, he derived a complex system of interrelated numbers to produce the result he was searching for. In addition to scrutinising the pyramid's linear measurements, Smyth investigated the temperature and barometric pressure of all the inner chambers of the pyramid in his search for the perfect unit of measurement – the revelatory standard that he believed was used by God in the creation of the ancient Egyptian time-capsule.

Heaping scorn on the metric system as 'atheistic and unnatural' his 'pyramid inch' was then put forward as the five-hundred-millionth part of the earth's polar axis. He measured the circumference of the building and dividing it by 365·242 (the number of days in a year) and again by 100 which gave him his pyramid inch. Smyth also claimed to have discovered the base length of the Great Pyramid divided by the width of a casing stone equalled the number of days in a year. If the number π defined the shape of the pyramid, a mathematical equation just too incredible to be ignored, then its size must be of equal importance, he reasoned.

His arithmetical contortions were as infinite as the grains of sand in the desert upon which this enigmatic ruin stands, so much so that he filled 616 pages with his wondrous computations fusing mathematics with a perceived religious significance as he advanced his theory in his book, Our Inheritance in the Great Pyramid (1864). Smyth derived his prophecies primarily from the lengths of passages which he measured in 'pyramid inches'. From these the intrepid Egyptologist expected something to happen in 1881, something quite drastic.

His pyramid theory was weakened considerably among sceptics by the existence of other pyramids, all of which had been constructed within the same one hundred or so year (Fourth Dynasty) period. This did not seem to worry the explorer too much and he dismissed those as 'imitation pyramids'. He went on to publish Life and Work at the Great Pyramid (1867) and On the Antiquity of Intellectual Man (1868). He became known as the Father of modern Egyptology and for his efforts he was awarded a gold medal by the Royal Society of Edinburgh.

However, not everyone saw things from his angle and his paper on the religious significance built into the design of the Great Pyramid was rejected by the Royal Society. This came as an unexpected blow to the Astronomer Royal and led to his resignation in 1874. Two years later he published an article in The Bible Examiner, a journal owned by one George Storrs of Brooklyn, New York, thus introducing the American Second Advent community to 'the Glory of the Great Pyramid' which was read with great interest by 24-year-old Charles Taze Russell.

William Flinders Petrie (1853-1942), whose father was a friend of the celebrated archaeologist and Egyptologist, was a frequent guest at Smyth's home and it was here that he met and courted the woman he eventually married. Many years later Petrie, now Sir William, wrote: 'A new stir arose when one day I brought back from Smiths bookstall, in 1866, a volume by Piazzi Smyth, Our Inheritance in the Great Pyramid. The views, in conjunction with his old friendship for the author, strongly attracted my father, and for some years I was urged on in what seemed so enticing a field of coincidence. It was this interest which led my father to encourage me to go out and do the survey of the Great Pyramid.' Petrie did just that and saw the famous pyramid for what it was. In 1932 he subsequently published Seventy Years in Archaeology in which he termed those who insisted there was more to Khufu's empty tomb than met the eye as 'pyramidiots'.

Some thirteen years after Smyth had published his findings on the Great Pyramid, one Joseph A, Seiss reasoned: 'If the primeval man were nothing but a gorilla or troglodyte, how, in those prehistoric times, could the builders of this mighty structure know how to even make and handle the tools, machines and expedients, indispensable to the construction of an edifice so enormous in dimensions, so massive in its materials, so exalted in its height and so perfect in its workmanship that to this day it is without a rival on earth? How could they solve the problem of the squaring of the circle, calculate the proportions or determine the four cardinal points?'

His book[35] proved popular but like Smyth's earlier work it was far from original. A significant portion of his 'findings' had simply been lifted from Smyth's material and embellished with his own religious hopes and prejudices. Charles Russell ventured beyond Taylor, Smyth, Seiss and others when he published Volume III of Studies in the Scriptures (1890) in which he championed his own bespoke version of Pyramidology, as the pseudo-science came to be known. Prior to publication the manuscript was amended and impressively endorsed by 'Professor C. Piazzi Smyth, F. R. C. E., F. R. A. S' who also agreed to the inclusion of his original diagrams in the book.

According to Charles Russell the prophet Isaiah refers to the pyramid as 'a witness in . . . the land of Egypt'[36] and describes Christ as its 'precious corner-stone'. He saw this 'stone Witness of Egypt' as the 'silent but eloquent symbolism of the plan of God – the 'Plan of the Ages' and suggested that its top cornerstone represented Christ because of the

---

[35] A Miracle in Stone: or The Great Pyramid – W. F. Petrie. Porter & Coates, 1877.
[36] Isaiah 19: 19-20; 28:16. KJV.

numerous references to the symbol by the prophets and apostles and by Jesus Christ himself.

Here, Russell takes us on a tour of the ins and outs and the ups and downs of selected interior measurements of the pyramid as he guides us through time and space according to his reading of the Bible: 'It has an entrance passage downward to a pit representing the broad road to destruction. From this a passage starts upward [which] in due time enlarges and becomes a grand gallery, representing the Gospel Age. Thirty-three inches from the beginning of the grand gallery is a well, representing the death and resurrection of Jesus. The grand gallery measures 1,874 inches long at the top, 1,878 inches at the bottom. Now notice how ably they [Russell's 'significant' dates, 1874 and 1878] support the teachings of the Bible.'

During the summer of 1891 Pastor Russell and his wife Maria made a pilgrimage to Palestine where they saw the Great Pyramid for themselves. For Mrs Russell, who never shared her husband's interest in Pyramidology, it would be her first and her last visit to the ancient wonder. Twenty years later, in the spring of 1910, the intrepid Pastor, now divorced, journeyed back to Egypt, but this time with an entourage of his closest followers.

Anticipation among these devotees was especially heightened on this occasion for some twenty years earlier Russell had predicted: 'we may well accept as correct the testimony of the Great Pyramid, that the last members of the body or bride of Christ will have been tested and accepted and will have passed beyond the veil before the close of A.D. 1910 . . . though not furnished in the Scriptures, date 1910 seems more than a reasonable one for some important event in the Church's experience and final testing, while A.D. 1914 is apparently well-defined as its close.'[37]

Among those who travelled with Pastor Russell in an official capacity on that occasion were his close associate and personal attorney Judge Rutherford and one Dr Leslie W. Jones, a wealthy and enthusiastic follower who independently chronicled and published Russell's activities throughout his ministry: 'Tuesday, April 4th, was our day for sailing. That morning we were at Bethel for our last breakfast before sailing. Brother Russell gave quite a talk at the table to the friends, urging them to faithfulness, even more so, if possible, during his absence than when he was there, realising that the Adversary would do all in his power to

---

[37] Studies in the Scriptures, Volume III, WTBTS.

hinder the work. He also said it was not beyond the bounds of possibility that some would not return alive, but as far as he was concerned personally, he had endeavoured to leave matters in such shape that the [preaching] work could go on nicely anyway.'[38]

Later that day Russell, accompanied by a contingency of twenty-one hopefuls, embarked on the Kaiser Wilhelm II. As the ship was being tugged out into the Hudson River an anxious crowd of 150 or so Bible Students, who had gathered on the quayside to see them off, watched and waved and sang hymns. Many of them wondered if they would ever see their Pastor on this side of the veil again.

On board ship that evening, after supper had been taken in a specially reserved corner of the dining saloon, Russell announced that he had obtained special permission 'to invade a portion of the Pyramid seldom visited – the King's Chamber'. He then gave a foretaste of what they were about to experience during their explorations: 'The very stones of this Great Pyramid of Testimony are crying out in no uncertain tones. Every inch of this massive structure is eloquently proclaiming the wisdom and power of our God. Firmly encased in this solid rocky structure, beyond the power of nature's storms, the outline drawings of God's great plan have stood for four thousand years, prepared to give their testimony at the time appointed.'

'The Great pyramid, the Scriptures declare, is a "pillar and altar unto the Lord of Hosts, in the midst of the border of Egypt," a witness to the divine plan of the ages. We will go through its various passages, which symbolize the downward course of humanity and the upward leadings of divine grace, and the glorious outcome of the divine purposes, the giving of the Jewish Law Covenant blessings, and secondarily the blessings of the Gospel Age, and finally the blessings to both the Church and the world – the former to be accomplished at the beginning of the Millennial Age, and the latter before its close.'

Russell then pointed out how the Kings Chamber, by its ventilating tubes, indicated that it symbolised a permanent residence, an everlasting condition: 'The Scriptures say of those who attain the condition represented by the Kings Chamber, that they partake of the divine nature, and are immortal . . . they cannot die there-after.' Everyone listened in expectant silence and wonder. Might they too slip 'beyond the veil' and attain immortality when they present themselves at that very spot within

---

[38] Souvenir Notes – Bible Students' Conventions 1910 – Dr L W Jones, Peoples Pulpit Association.

the mysterious interior of the ancient tomb? There were no questions and soon afterwards they all retired to their cabins.

Eventually, having journeyed though France, Switzerland and Italy, the Pastor and his entourage found themselves in Cairo. His travelling diarist describes what happened next: 'After breakfast twenty of our party prepared to visit the Wonderful Pyramid of Giza. We took the electric line for the pyramid. All the party went by trolley, except brother Russell and brother Rutherford who came out later in carriages. On the way they stopped to purchase some long white robes.'

When the hopeful explorers gathered at the main entrance to the pyramid, the sheik, who was caretaker, arranged for guides to assist the party as they made their way into the darkness. When they arrived at the descending passage it was found to be locked; whereupon the sheik produced a key, explaining that few people were permitted to go into the downward passage. His native assistants hesitated at first, but at his command they reluctantly agreed to accompany the determined tourists during their descent. The passage itself proved to be quite long, 'very narrow and difficult to navigate in some parts without crawling backwards'. Once at the bottom they found themselves in a small room 'measuring about 20 x 20 feet, but not exactly square' cut out of the solid rock.

Brother Jones continues: 'The floor is uneven and contains large piles of debris. The ceiling is also uneven. Many bats infested this place. With our long white robes, which all our party wore, and by the dim light which each one of us carried in his hand, the rough and rugged appearance of the room, together with the numerous bats which flew about our heads, gave a weird and hideous appearance. It reminded us of Dante's 'inferno'. We found the return trip more difficult than the descent. We then entered the Queen's Chamber . . . and then the King's Chamber.'

As Russell and Rutherford made their way toward the centre of the tomb, they held their lanterns aloft beckoning the rest of the party to join them. Anticipation peaked when lanterns were lowered to the floor as the faithful linked hands and formed a circle. Our eyewitness describes the scene: 'We were glad to get in here and spoke some words to each other of the Lord's blessings, and then joined in singing If I in Thy Likeness, O Lord, May Awake. This was very appropriate, being in the symbolic King's Chamber. As our voices resounded through this great stone structure of the Lord, our hearts were filled with love and praise to the heavenly Father, and we longed for the day when we may indeed by his grace enter the King's Chamber of eternal glory.'

In the shadowy silence that followed the impassioned singing, an expectant peace fell upon the waiting assembly. Eventually, in the flickering gloom of the King's Chamber, unmentionable disappointment self-consciously dawned. It was not the first time Charles Russell had draped himself in white in anticipation of the secret rapture – that 'twinkling of an eye' moment when the faithful are physically 'taken up' to heaven – and, as we shall see, it would not be the last.

***

Without doubt 'Pyramidology' was the inspirational driving force behind the esoteric biblical interpretations of Charles Russell. Indeed, it remained fundamental to the Watchtower Society's doomsday agenda for more than a decade after his death – up until 1928 in fact, when the second president of the Watchtower Society, Joseph F. Rutherford, denounced his predecessor's pyramid-based theology as unscriptural and of the Devil: 'If the pyramid is not mentioned in the Bible, then following its teachings is being led by vain philosophy and false science.'[39]

The present-day Watchtower Society has ensured the shifting sands of time have effectively covered over this pi-eyed, but once fundamental, aspect of their faith. Today at his lonely graveside a scaled down replica of the Great Pyramid of Giza stands as an embarrassing reminder of Russell's obsession with ancient Egypt and Freemasonry as being corroborative to his eschatology. Hewn from pink-tinted granite (the Pastor's favourite colour), from Marble Falls, Texas, the weighty monument, seven feet high and nine feet across at the base, was designed and paid for by Freemason J.A. Bohnet, a wealthy bachelor and one of Russell's principal benefactors and staunchest supporters. The graves of several of Russell's followers, including that of brother Bohnet, also lie within a few yards of the pyramid. Today the area is home to the Greater Pittsburgh Masonic Centre.

A wreathed cross and crown (a Knights Templar logo) above an open Bible are etched on each of the four triangular slabs which, together with a solid capstone, form a hollow pyramid. Watchtower legend has it that encased within lies a wooden chest containing a complete set of Russell's Studies in the Scriptures along with a Bible and a photograph of the man himself – an eerie simulation of ancient Egyptian burial rites

[39] Watchtower – November 1, 1928.

and rituals and a silent witness to the glory days of the Watchtower Society's International Bible Students, latterly Jehovah's Witnesses.

However, before we eliminate Charles Russell's 'pyramidology' from the unravelling enigma of his Christian eschatology there remains just one irrefutable fact – the uncanny mathematical certainty of Khufu's pyramid with its angle (51°52′) built at a ratio of $1/2\pi$. This geometric riddle was first proven more than a century ago and over the years numerous triangulations of the Giza plateau have been carried out all of which verify the mysterious dimensional accuracy of the early pyramid builders.

Contrastingly, the relatively primitive two-dimensional artwork of the ancient Egyptians suggests they had yet to form the concept of isotropic three-dimensional space whereby measures of vertical height and horizontal distance are calculated using the same unit. To measure heights, they used the royal cubit, based on the upward distance from elbow to fingertips, which in the Old Kingdom had already been standardized to a length of 52 centimetres. The royal cubit suggests itself as the standard diameter of a drum which provided 'rolled cubits' as an accurate method of calculating the horizontal base measurements of a large pyramid, for example, as the revolutions of the drum were counted. This technique was considered much more precise than utilising ropes of palm fibre which tended to stretch.

Egyptologist Kurt Mendelssohn tells us that, using this system of measurement, the Egyptian architects never did anything more sophisticated than to build pyramids according to the simple gradients of 4:1 and 3:1. 'Taking the former first, the height of the pyramid will be 4 x n cubits, where n is the number chosen to determine its size. The horizontal distance from the centre of the building to its side will then have to be 1 x n rolled cubits or in our mathematical terms, $n\pi$ cubits. Since this distance is half the side length of the pyramid, the latter's circumference comes to 8 x $n\pi$ cubits. Therefore, the ratio of height to circumference is 4 x n/8 x $n\pi$ cubits or, by dividing this fraction by 4 x n cubits, simply $1/2\pi$. This is the mysterious ratio used in pyramid construction and which, at the same time, leads inevitably to an angle of elevation of 51°52.'[40]

In other words, Dr Mendelssohn concludes, 'the pyramid builders of long ago discovered the transcendental number π (3·41 . . .) without trying and without knowing. This hypothesis is made even more likely

---

[40] The Riddle of the Pyramids – Kurt Mendelsohn, Thames & Hudson, 1974.

by the fact that using in this way the lower gradient 3:1 instead of 4:1 the angle of elevation comes out correctly as 43½°.' Apart from its enduring mathematical fascination there is no built-in messianic symbolism to be found in the constructional dimensions of the Great Pyramid of Giza.

Decades after Russell's death historian George Swetnam observed: 'It is an amazing thing that no Pittsburgh history has ever even so much as contained the name of Charles Taze Russell, since his influence has easily been the widest of any man who ever lived in the city, not even excepting Andrew Carnegie. He founded the one major religious movement to have appeared in the Pittsburgh district, a movement which has reached world-wide scope.'

From the beginning of his ministry Pastor Russell 'privately admitted that he was chosen [by God] for his great work from before his birth'. However, a consideration of the politically driven religious divide that shaped 19th century Ireland, and of the sectarian piety he inherited from his Irish/American parents, might well provide us with a rather more down-to-earth assessment of his ministry.

Chapter Two

THE PROMISED LAND

The 17th century Irish had been the first Europeans to accept the potato as their main crop and, for many of the poverty-trapped labourers who worked on the land it soon became their only food. The water loving vegetable proved well suited to the damp Irish soil and turned out to be a life saver for a hungry peasantry that grew strong and fertile on the vitamin-rich fibrous potatoes, but it was a precarious dependency that would lead to disaster.

Most of the land was owned by English landlords and while a smallholder in Britain enjoyed certain rights of tenancy and security his counterpart in Ireland had no security at all, living in serf-like bondage to a distant 'foreigner' he would never know or meet. The enslaved Irish farmer was usually required to pay his rent in grain, a food he was unaccustomed to eating. Surplus land he utilised to produce food for his large and numerous family that survived entirely on year-round crops of potatoes, perhaps supplemented with a pig or two.

Ireland, as the nearest overseas Crown possession, had been subject to British influence and rule since Henry II first staked his claim some 700 years earlier, but the emerald isle was never really subdued. The Irish remained determinedly Catholic and stubbornly refused to become anglicised. Under laws passed by Oliver Cromwell, which were rigorously maintained for 150 years, Catholic Irishmen were forbidden to buy or bequeath land or even own a horse. Some were too poor to own cattle or a plough. Catholics could not hold office of any kind or even vote. They were forbidden to practice law or enlist in the army and possession of a gun, or a sword was a punishable offence. Moreover, religious devotion was outlawed, and Catholic priests were reduced to officiating in pious and determined secrecy.

At the end of the 18th century there was a notable attempt to bring an end to the British occupation of Ireland when Irish nationalist Wolfe Tone (1763-98) and a small squadron of French Republicans led the Irish rebellion of 1798. Tone was captured during fierce fighting in Lough Swilley then taken to Dublin where he was tried and condemned to be hanged as a traitor. Waiting for the hangman's visit, he committed suicide by cutting his throat. The British government then decided to institute administrative changes to pre-empt any further uprising with a legislative act of parliament – the Act of Union – which was imposed by Westminster upon an already humiliated but nonetheless still fiercely proud nation.

The idea was to bind the two countries into one, with the Protestant voters of Ireland dispatching 100 representatives of their own to speak on behalf of the entire Irish population at Westminster. This led to the collapse of the fragile Irish economy and further alienated an already poverty-stricken Catholic peasantry. Although a significant proportion of the Anglo-Irish were powerful, having great estates and property holdings, there were other British sponsored settlers somewhat lower down the social pecking order to be found mostly in the Protestant communities in the north. Having enjoyed religious freedom in the preceding two centuries and a certain degree of financial independence, rural life continued to be a struggle in the shadow of those in bondage to the crown.

It was against such background that Thomas and Fanny Russell, a young Protestant farming couple in Donegal, decided to sell up and get out of the troubled countryside. In 1805 they travelled north with their three children and settled in Londonderry, an industrial town which provided at least some employment for increasing numbers of rural Irish families struggling on the land. They went on to have four more children, but it was Charles Tays Russell, the second eldest of four sons, who set a precedent for the whole family. In 1822, when the young adventurer was sixteen years old, he joined the crew of a ship bound for the 'new world' of America. He was never to see Ireland again for Charles jumped ship in New York and eventually made his home and his fortune there.

Proud Protestants by birth and Presbyterians by choice, the men folk in the Russell family also attended the local Masonic Lodge, a connection which to a certain degree enabled them to transcend the religious strife and social division which rent apart entire communities. As Freemasons they were required to maintain themselves 'in reputable circumstances' and to conform to Rule 135 on the initiation application form for the Irish Grand Lodge: 'No Lodge shall initiate any person who shall not be able to read and write.'

Working-class Protestants invariably fulfilled their Christian obligations by mentally directing their inbred hatred of Catholicism to Rome and the Pope himself. However, hunger was no respecter of any shade of piety and for many on both sides of the religious divide one hopeless day followed another. In 1845 there was a partial failure of the potato crop when potato blight (phytophthora infestans) struck again. Overnight, entire plots of thriving potato plants were reduced to blackened dying vegetation and within days the crunchy firm tubers that lay beneath the soil cruelly self-destructed into a stinking mess of rotting vegetation. Potato crops had often failed before, leaving destitute Irish folk scrimping through life at starvation level, but this time it was different; within weeks of the outbreak the first casualties of hunger drifted into Londonderry.

It was a curtain-raiser to years of famine when beggars would roam the streets like stray dogs. Hospitals, prisons, and workhouses were overcrowded with desperate men, women and children all reduced to hungry despair. Typhus, dysentery, and consumption would add to their misery as the ruling classes remained in wealthy isolation, aloof but certainly not unaware of the sufferings of their fellow countrymen. There were, however, some notable exceptions and the more decent and sensitive of the Anglo-Irish set up soup kitchens and took to visiting their sick and dying tenants, often forgoing rents and consoling the bereaved. Such acts of spontaneous compassion publicly demonstrated contempt, at least on the part of some, for Westminster's official policy of none-involvement.

Alarmed at the immediacy of the depressing effects of this latest crop failure the Russell family began to feel that there was no future for them in Ireland. One day, quite unexpectedly, there was word from Charles. Having settled in New York some twenty years earlier, the former runaway cabin boy was now a naturalised American and proud owner of a thriving Dry-Goods Store (established 1831). It was one of the largest in New York at that time, he boasted in his letter. Consequently, throughout an uneasy summer and a darkening autumn, the Russell family realised modest assets and pooled their resources to finance their emigration to America the 'land of the free'.

The first leg of the journey would be to the British mainland, birthplace of Protestantism and the spiritual heartland of the British Empire. Loathed by Irish Catholics, and a substantial segment of the Scots Irish working-class Protestant population alike, Britain was spurned and cursed as an impostor of a mother nation who had, effectively, elected to abandon her own. Londonderry was the most northerly port in Ireland and the bustling quayside witnessed tearful partings and brave farewells on the day the Russell family boarded a ship bound for the port of Liverpool on the British mainland.

The fare for the relatively short trip of two days, sometimes three, was just a few shillings (less than a dollar). Once on British soil the now displaced but determined family set about finding lodgings for the few days it would take for them to arrange their emigration and secure berths for the long sea voyage ahead. Nineteenth century Liverpool, which had long been associated with the infamous slave trade, was one of the biggest and busiest ports in the world with more than 36 miles of quays lining both sides of the deep river Mersey.

Ships which had previously borne sad clutches of brutalised humanity across the Atlantic were once more deployed in transporting hordes of desperate people overseas. Hapless emigrants travelled in conditions little better than those of the slaves who had made the same journey before them. Commercially driven skippers, along with their invariably incompetent and sometimes brutal crews, often failed to measure up to their official responsibilities toward those in their charge as ragged and rootless people filled the holds of ships (and the pockets) of those who had formerly profited from the slave trade.

The fare for the Atlantic crossing in 1845 was usually three pounds ten shillings (US $17.50) for a cramped cot space in a communal steerage berth or five pounds (US $25) for a cabin berth. The ship's rations, which were included in the fare, usually amounted to 6 pints of water daily, for drinking, cooking, and washing, plus a total of 7lbs of flour, bread, biscuit, oatmeal, or potatoes each week for every passenger, a mere one pound of food a day. Those who could afford it supplemented this subsistence level of survival as best they could with their own extra provisions which were stowed away in the ten cubic feet of luggage space allotted to each passenger. Firing and hearths – usually metal boxes lined with bricks – were also made available up on deck where the most basic of culinary skills were tested to the limit.

Passengers were medically screened for infectious diseases by Government appointed surgeons who were charged with identifying those who might pose a threat to the health of others. But few, if any, were declared unfit to travel following a fleeting and rudimentary consultation. The medical officers who were specially appointed to undertake this task were paid one pound (US$5) per hundred such medical examinations. Tickets were then stamped as proof of favourable medical assessment and official British endorsement of the proposed long and arduous sea voyage about to be undertaken by ticket holders. Pamphlets, warning passengers of the tricksters and robbers who would be waiting for them on the other side of the Atlantic Ocean, were handed out to those who could read.

Embarkation was little more than a scrum of an affair. Once they were on board, all emigrants came under the captain's rule and were subject to the same harsh discipline as were the crew. Under the auspices of the Board of Trade the captain was licensed to exercise absolute authority at sea as 'Master under God'. His rule was law and passengers were soon made aware of that fact; they could be charged with mutiny if they showed signs of rebellious and disorderly conduct. The penalty for mutiny was death by hanging.

Steerage passengers were corralled below decks for most of the time; forced to subsist on their meagre survival rations during those hazardous Atlantic crossings. The inevitable sickness and suffering added to the misery of starving emigrants at a time when Britain once more exported human cargo and desperation ruled the waves. The sad plight of Irish emigrants was considered even worse than those endured by criminals who were sentenced to Transportation from the shores of Britain to far away Australia. When the annual Irish emigration figures had passed 100,000 by the end of 1846 politicians in Dublin half-heartedly appealed to the British government: 'We would recommend that free emigrants should be treated at least as well as convicts in transport ships.'

Most of the passengers in those desperate times were Catholics who outnumbered Protestants such as the Russell family by about eight to one. Passengers were only allowed up on deck in small groups to wash themselves and to cook their meagre rations. During bad weather, when they were confined to their bunks, sometimes in bewildering darkness, the vessel would roll and sway, and rise and fall, with a sickening regularity that brought on wave after wave of vomiting misery. Nonetheless, during those claustrophobic trips, some of which could last for anything up to eight weeks at a time in putrid and airless communal quarters, a friendly air of shipmate co-operation often ensued as opposing Christian believers journeyed into the unknown.

Over the six-year period of Irish famine more than a million desperate souls left the shores of their homeland and embarked on the tortuous 3,000-mile voyage across the mountainous and moody Atlantic Ocean in their quest for freedom and refuge from a politically inspired nightmare existence in occupied Ireland. Many of them did not complete the journey. Passengers who died during the voyage were buried at sea following a rudimentary huddle of a ceremony, usually presided over by a grim-faced and indifferent skipper.

A century and a half later the Famine years were officially recognized by the Irish Government as 'the darkest moment in Irish history'. In 1995, following an official visit from Dr Mary Robinson, the President of Ireland, the British government issued an official 'Statement of Regret' regarding its callous indifference during a shameful episode in the swaggering history of Imperial Britain when Protestant-inspired political expediency took precedence over the human rights of millions of, largely Catholic, Irish peasants.

When eventually the coastline of America came into view it was usually some days, depending on the coastal weather conditions, before soddening, creaking barques, brigs, and packet-ships of every description slowly barged through the heaving flotsam and jetsam of the New York dockside to tie up at the quay in South Street Seaport for disembarkation. Sometimes, when ten or more ships had tied up in one day, immigration authorities were unable to cope with the rising tide of humanity which continued to roll in from the other side of the Atlantic. On those frequent occasions there were long, anxious delays.

Eventually, the bedraggled passengers spilled out into the busy streets around the bustling piers and shadowy wharves. Wide-eyed and weary they took in the lively sights and sounds of New York, a robust mother of a city, which constantly and unfailingly gave birth to embryonic American dreams of promise and prosperity. With a population approaching half a million at that time, more than a quarter of New Yorkers were Irish. Newcomers soon felt at ease with the constant and familiar sounds of the Irish brogue in the air. But not all the Irish voices they heard were as friendly and well intentioned as they sounded.

New overseas arrivals in mid-19th century New York were targeted by tricksters and con-men eager to cash in on their naiveté and big-city innocence. Quay side loiterers invariably included pickpockets and thieves ready to run off with almost any bundle of rags they could lay hands on. There were shifty-eyed boarding house runners touting for trade and dubious 'agents' dressed in eye-catching coats of emerald, green, with a ready line in blarney selling cheap tickets for non-existent onward journeys to unsuspecting anxious hopefuls. Anyone staggering down a gangplank was fair game.

Those who managed to escape the attentions of such welcoming predators still needed to look for paying employment to survive, and many newcomers soon discovered that work was not as easy to find as they had imagined. Some employers saw the sudden influx of eager and desperately willing hands from across the sea as a threat to the economy.

Consequently, offers of employment often bore the legend N.I.N.A. (no Irish need apply). Fortunately for the Russell family they had an address to go to and an established 'American' relative to see them through.

Manhattan Island was largely undeveloped at that time and consisted mainly of farmland and wooded hills. However, the skyline of mid-nineteenth century New York City was silhouetted with church steeples, with most other city buildings being no more than three or four stories high. Handsome brownstone houses lined the broader streets while cheap hotels and shabby lodging houses ringed the sprawling dockside areas of the city where pigs freely roamed, and packs of ravenous dogs could sometimes be seen scavenging for food in the litter of the side streets.

Horse-drawn buses passed by shops and stores of every description with window displays of unimaginable delight and temptation. There were restaurants, bars, and imposing commercial premises the like of which few of the immigrant Irish would have seen before. There was plenty to gawk at, no end of wonders. It was a thriving city which was good and bad all at the same time and promised whatever the imagination could conjure up. To newcomers almost anything seemed possible in New York, particularly to those with nothing.

Charles Tays Russell, the pioneer of the family, was now a respected businessman and his social connections enabled him to help those closest to him to assimilate into the American/Irish community more readily, and perhaps a little less painfully, than most. His favourite was his younger brother Joseph with whom he shared a loyal interest in the brotherhood of Freemasonry.

Joseph soon found himself happily working as an assistant Dry Goods Broker. Painful memories of a hungry childhood back in Ireland and the sickness and death which had constantly stalked his homeland gradually faded; the sting had gone but a measure of sadness and longing would always remain. It was time to look to the future and in that respect the past was the spur. He worked hard in his brother's store and three years later, on October 26, 1848, he became a naturalised American citizen.

The Russell family worshipped at one of New York's Presbyterian churches and it was here that Joseph struck up an acquaintance with Ann Eliza Birney, an attractive Irish colleen of Scottish extraction. As immigrant refugees from a famine-stricken Ireland they had much in common and could often be seen chatting outside the church where they shared sad memories of their homeland and inspired each other with bright and optimistic hopes for the future. Joseph's dutiful church attendance increased, noticeably so, especially when he started turning up twice on Sundays. Miss Birney was impressed. She took her religion very seriously she told her suitor. One-day Ann Eliza Birney became Joseph's 'Liza' and now that he had moved up in the world, he felt confident enough to ask her to be his wife.

Chapter Three

A CHILD IS BORN

Pittsburgh at the beginning of the 19th century was a small riverside town with a sleepy population of little more than a thousand souls who were largely unaware of the rich deposits of iron ore and gleaming coal seams which lay beneath their feet. The coming of the railroads changed all that and by the middle of the century the discovery and exploitation of this mineral wealth had attracted more than 150,000 workers to the area, among them newlyweds, Joseph, and Eliza Russell.

Many of those who toiled in the industrious development of the mines, the rolling mills and the grim factories that characterised the thriving town, lived close to their places of employment in modest homes or cheap lodging houses. Miners and other manual workers at the bottom of the economic scale had to make-do with humble shacks or makeshift huts in the sooty downside and general squalor of shantytown sprawl.

Following a tentative spell as a street market trader in Allegheny Joseph Russell took the plunge and, with generous help from his brother Charles in New York, opened his first shop – Russell's Haberdashers – in premises on the north-east corner of Federal Street and Robinson Street. Initially, life was good for the young couple and with Joseph's New York experience and Irish charm the shop went from strength to strength as the business expanded. Stock was changed regularly as new lines were introduced to meet the demands of the customers who lived and worked in the thriving town. From the start trade was lively and it was not too long before they moved from their lodgings to a house in the favoured suburb of Allegheny.

More than fifty lodges of various orders of Freemasons and Odd Fellows were dotted about the Pittsburgh-Allegheny area in Russell's day and Joseph soon found his way to the Masonic Hall in Water Street which was home to the Allegheny Lodge (No 223) and the Jefferson Lodge (No 288). Although the Roman Catholic Church traditionally opposed Freemasonry numerous ministers of the Presbyterian churches that dominated western Pennsylvania at that time were active Freemasons and it was primarily through this network of predominately Protestant-Irish migrants in the town that the young couple soon established themselves as respectable traders, Christians you could do business with, decent people you could trust. Their little shop thrived.

Their first child was born in 1850 and they called him Thomas, after his grandfather. Less than two years later a second son was born. This time the child was named after his adventurous uncle, Charles Tays (Americanised as Taze) Russell. The two little boys soon had a sister, Margaret, who was born in 1854. Joseph and Liza were so happy. They had everything they had always dreamed about; plenty to eat, proper clothes to wear, a small but sound profitable business of their own, and three noisy and lively children into the bargain. They were happy days. Then disaster struck.

On September 11, 1855, baby Thomas died (from whooping cough) when he was just five and a half years old. Eliza Russell went on to bear two more children, only to lose them also through cruel infant deaths; Lucinda died (from scrofula) on the 21st of July 1858, in her first year and her brother Joseph junior died (from croup) on 25th April 1860, before he was six months old. Although infant deaths were commonplace in those days the loss of three children within the space of five years left its mark.

During that anxious period of sickness and death in the Russell household church attendance subsequently increased as attention focused on the survival of the two remaining children, especially Charles, now the only son in a passionately religious household. The youngster was thus instructed on a relentless daily basis by his strict mother who subjected him to a punishing programme of learning and acceptance. Bible in one hand, whip (tawers) in the other, she took her Christian duties as a mother very seriously, particularly the advice found in the Bible: 'Foolishness *is* bound in the heart of a child, *but* the rod of correction shall drive it far from him.'[41] Regarding those religiously inspired beatings Charles Russell recalls:

'I was about five, as near as I can remember. Of course, I may have gotten some spankings when I was so small, I did not know about it, but when I was about five, I remember I got one. My mother taught me to the best of her knowledge. She had a pair of leather tawers that would bite at the end but do no real harm. There were about six or eight tails to them – their hurt was in their tails.[42] She said, "Charles, bring the

---

[41] Proverbs 22:15, KJV.

[42] Cat-o-nine tails. A multi-tailed flail used officially by the Royal Navy and the Army for administering severe physical punishment in 19th century Britain. Also

tawers and come upstairs." So, I carried the tawers upstairs. She said, "Now sit down here and I will read to you out of the Bible." She thought that I had prevaricated, had twisted the truth; not that I had told a point-blank lie, but twisted the truth a little, as most children are inclined to do, especially if some older folks laugh at them and think they are smart; but I did not have anyone to laugh at me and think I was smart if I should do anything of that kind. I learned that that was not the way to do. So she read to me from Revelation – "but the fearful, and unbelieving, and the abominable, and murderers, and whoremongers, and sorcerers, and idolaters, and all liars, shall have their part in the lake which burneth with fire and brimstone: which is the second death"[43] – and she said, "Charles, I do not want you to have your portion with those in the lake that burneth with fire and brimstone, and it is my duty, as your mother, to give you chastisement and I must do it. I do not want to whip you, but I must do it for your good. This is the teaching of the Lord's Word, and this is what will happen if you should grow up to be a liar, and if you should grow up to become a bad man." You see how much impression that made on my mind, that little suggestion from the Scriptures. The fact that God has no use for liars can very easily be impressed on the mind of a child.'[44]

Ann Eliza Russell was thirty-six years old when she died from consumption on January 25, 1861, just three weeks before Charles was to celebrate his ninth birthday. Soon after the funeral Joseph Russell took on more staff for his busy shop and increased the domestic help at home. Haunted by creeping memories of the ignorance and deprivation which had plagued him in his youth the determined widower vowed that his own son would never be similarly handicapped. Nonetheless young Charles was profoundly affected by his mother's legacy of hellfire indoctrination; so much so that for some years after her death, up until the age of fourteen, he took to chalking scriptural passages on sidewalks and walls, urging people to *'repent and believe!'*.

An unusually keen and studious boy, Charles Russell was reportedly a bright and inquisitive pupil at the local public school. Supplementary private tuition led to school attendance becoming sporadic until eventually all lessons were taken at home. The young pupil blossomed and by

---

implemented as a judicial punishment in both Britain and the USA. The practice in America was abolished by State legislature in 1848.

[43] Revelation 21:8, KJV.

[44] What Pastor Russel Said – Dr L W Jones, 1917.

the time he was ten years old Charles, who took an uncommon interest in commerce for a boy of his age, was helping with basic tasks in the administration of the family business. As a result, in the early years following the death of his wife, Joseph came to rely on the sharper mind of his son who was often found in the office at the shop checking figures and accounts, much to the delight of his proud father. Trade continued to grow, with clothing for men proving particularly popular and profitable.

In the year that saw President Lincoln sign the final Emancipation Proclamation eleven-years old Charles became a partner with his doting father in the family business, even helping write up a deed of agreement and responsibility between them. There was plenty to look forward to and with God's help things were going to get even better, Joseph assured his young business associate. Over the next few years, church attendance slackened in the Russell household until one unmentionable day when it stopped altogether. Joseph concluded that he was just as much a Christian in the Brotherhood as he had been in the church while young Charles decided to try the local Congregationalist Church as it seemed more liberal in outlook. He even joined the YMCA at the suggestion of his father who felt it might fill something of a social void in his somewhat lonely young life.

Curiously enough it was an exchange with a fellow member that caused him to question the very foundations of his Christian belief. The young sceptic pointed out that if God is perfect in wisdom, justice, love, and power, he would never have predestined humanity to eternal torment in the fires of hell as taught by the church in general. Charles was left speechless by such candour. It was this moment of irrefutable truth that led to his outright rejection of mainstream Christianity.

By the summer of 1869 Charles Russell appeared to have finally laid the ghost of his religious past when he declared: 'I'm just going to forget the whole thing and give all my attention to business. If I make some money, I can use that to help suffering humanity, even though I cannot help them any good spiritually.' Now that he was 17 years old, he felt it was time to put the misery of his religious childhood behind him. He started travelling away on business trips and whenever he was in New York he would look in on his uncle Charles.

An additional retail store was acquired, and a third shop was scheduled to open soon. It was the beginning of a trend that would result in the establishment of a chain of thriving retail stores throughout Pennsylvania – Russell & Son, Men's Furnishing Store. Within three years there were no less than five stores in the family business, a phenomenal growth which Joseph Russell put down to his own hard work and the intellectual input and managerial skills of his bright son, and a little bit of Irish luck, perhaps. Indeed, everything was just dandy.

Strolling home one night after working late, Charles Russell heard religious singing coming from a basement hall. Now a well-dressed and immaculately groomed twenty-year old, the dapper young man presented an unlikely figure as he hesitated under the gaslight at the open doorway of Quincy Hall, in Laycock Street. It was only two blocks from the principal store, but Charles had never noticed it before. As he strained forward to catch a little of the sermon being delivered, he fancied he could hear his mother's voice echoing the pleadings and the pledges of the impassioned speaker. Torn between commercial success and the unresolved spiritual void which beckoned from his forgotten past he slid unnoticed into the back of the hall. It was a poignant turning point in the life of the curious eavesdropper, an alluring experience he would always remember:

'Seemingly by accident, one evening I dropped into a dusty, dingy hall, where I heard religious services were held, to see if the handful who met there had anything more sensible to offer than the creeds of the great churches. There for the first time, I heard something of the views of Second Adventists, the preacher being Mr. Jonas Wendell . . . it was sufficient, under God, to re-establish my wavering faith in the divine inspiration of the Bible, and to show that the records of the apostles and prophets are indissolubly linked.'[45]

For quite some time afterwards, Charles Russell was troubled by doubts over the wisdom of his earlier rejection of Christianity and plagued by feelings of guilt whenever his mother came to mind. His father suggested that he might find satisfaction and fulfilment with the local fraternity of, largely Irish, Protestants. They were decent men, sworn to mutual aid, brotherly love, and the relief of others. As an organisation of men in pursuit of good works and spiritual illumination, Freemasonry was not perceived as being in any way contradictory toward organised religion in general. Indeed, candidates for initiation must profess a belief in a Supreme Being, and membership is open to all faiths. Perhaps the Brotherhood, with its fraternity of benevolent and charitable men of goodwill from different religious persuasions might be the very thing he was looking for.

---

[45] Jehovah's Witnesses – Proclaimers of God's Kingdom, WTBTS 1993.

Religiously inclined but spiritually rootless, Charles Russell decided to look to Freemasonry for the answers he sought; answers of profundity to questions yet to be formulated by the young thinker. He was subsequently inducted into the movement and after the cloak and dagger ceremony those present sang The Entered Apprentice's Song:

The world is in pain, our secrets to gain,
And still let them wonder and gaze on;
They ne'er can divine, the Word or the Sign,
Of a Free and an Accepted Mason.[46]

The young initiate was impressed with the Masonic belief that at the root of all religion there was just one supreme and indefinable being who was referred to within Masonic circles as The Great Architect of the Universe, which was encoded by the initials T. G. A. O. T. U. He learned to think of God as Jehovah and was fascinated with the Masonic hope for a Golden Age for all mankind. He was introduced to the wonders of Ancient Egypt and, according to Masonic legend, the mysterious drama surrounding the building of Solomon's Temple. He was intrigued when he read, in the very latest Masonic publication of the day:

'Freemasonry . . . is progressive. Knowledge of it can only be attained by time, patience, and application. In the first degree, we are taught the duties we owe to God, our neighbour, and ourselves. In the second, we are more thoroughly inducted into the mysteries of moral science and learn to trace the goodness and majesty of the creator, by minutely analysing his works. But the third degree is the cement of the whole. It is calculated to bind men together by mystic points of fellowship, as in a bond of fraternal affection and brotherly love.'[47]

The third degree of Freemasonry confers the status of Master Mason on suitable candidates who are then introduced to a mysterious character, whose name is dramatically revealed during a dimly lit cloak and dagger ceremony, when the Worshipful Master leans forward and whispers in the ear of the initiate: 'Death has no terror equal to that of the stain of falsehood and dishonour. Of this grand truth, the annals of Freemasonry afford a glorious example in the unshaken fidelity and untimely death of our Grand Master, Hiram Abif, who lost his life just

---

[46] Composed by Mathew Birkhead, first published in Constitution of the Freemasons, Dr James Anderson 1723.

[47] The General Ahiman Rezon and Freemason's Guide (1871) – D. Sickels 33°.

before the completion of King Solomon's Temple, the construction of which, as you are doubtless aware, he was the principal architect.'[48]

Although the vaguely assumed link between the mythological Hiram Abif and King Solomon's Temple is based largely on supposition, it is always assumed that third degree candidates are aware of this character from their knowledge of the Bible. According to the Scriptures,[49] King David's royal palace was constructed by skilled Tyrian workmen with cedar timber sent by Hyram the king of Tyre. However, apart from the fact that they appear to share the same name, there is no biblical link and certainly no mention of a named architect for Solomon's Temple. Had the name of the master builder been known to the scribes who recorded events detailed in the Old Testament why would the murder of such an important key figure in the story not even be mentioned in the Bible? Such questions fascinated and intrigued the young seeker after truth. He would dig a little deeper.

During this period Hiram is understood to have meant noble or kingly in Hebrew, while Abif is thought to be old French for lost one. Who could this lost king be? He was certainly not Tyrian. Tyre became one of the great sea powers of the ancient world. Solomon and the King of Tyre co-operated in a joint shipping venture importing precious things including gold from Ophir, as recorded in the Bible.[50] However, there is no indication in the Scriptures that the Tyrians were involved in the worship of Jehovah; their association with the Israelites was strictly commercial. Racially they were Canaanites who practised a form of Baal worship, their chief deities being Melkarte and Astarte (Ashtoreth). According to the Bible, when Ethbaal was king of the Sidonians (including Tyre), his daughter Jezebel married Ahab the king of the northern kingdom of Israel. Jezebel was infamous in her determination to end the worship of the Israelite God, Jehovah.[51]

Fascinated by the sweeping drama of biblical history and the role played by the Ancient Egyptians in the formulation of Jewish tradition, Charles Russell, intrigued by the legendary Masonic link with the building of Solomon's Temple, began to see the Hebrew Scriptures in a new and revealing light. No longer haunted by guilt whenever memories of his mother came to mind, he began to sense a feeling of spiritual déjà

---

48 The Hiram Key – Chris Knight and Robert Lomas, Century, 1996.

49 2 Samuel 5: 11; 1 Chronicles 14:1.

50 1 Ki 9:26-28; 10: 11, 22; 2 Chron 9: 21.

51 1 Ki 16:29,31; 18: 4, 13, 19.

vu as he recalled his earlier fascination with John Taylor's curious little book The Great Pyramid of Giza. Could it really be that this far away wonder of the world had been built under God's guidance as a physical template of divine revelation?

Swept along by an irresistible feeling of beckoning enlightenment Charles Russell sensed he was being handed the key to interpreting Bible prophecy, the recondite calculating method of deciphering the riddle of the Great Pyramid, already believed by many Christians to be physically encoded within the dark stillness of that ancient tomb. Perhaps Hiram Abif did not belong in the past after all, he pondered. Perhaps in God's timelessness this 'lost noble one' had yet to figuratively complete his original commission with the building of a *spiritual* temple at some future appointed time. It was a fascinating train of thought and one that evidently led the young researcher to conclude that he, Charles Taze Russell, was the born-again antitypical Hiram Abif.

Russell's obsession with the Great Pyramid of Giza is evidenced by the Ancient Egyptian (Pagan) symbolism adorning his books and literature in the form of a winged globe, a stylised etching of the sun god Ra. He also featured the Knights Templar cross and crown symbol on the front cover of his journal, Zion's Watch Tower. Most notable of all, the brick-built façade of the Jehovah's Witness Assembly Hall in Queens, New York has a frontage decorated with an eye-catching relief of the sun god symbol flanked by warriors after the style of an ancient Egyptian Temple.

Freemasonry demands solemn initiation and members of the Brotherhood are bound for life to demonstrate their allegiance to the fraternity by their deeds rather than by meeting attendance. For his part Charles Russell became increasingly preoccupied with his spiritual temple-building project and eventually drifted away from the physical bonhomie of lodge functions. He did however remain loyal to the Craft throughout his life and often secretly introduced himself as a member of the Brotherhood whenever the occasion arose, often utilising Masonic symbolism in posters and handbills to make known his affiliation. Indeed, many of his early lectures were purposely delivered in Masonic Halls. On one such occasion, he appeared to transcend the secrets of Freemasonry when, somewhat ambiguously, he talked about what he called Bible Masonry:

'I am a Free Mason. I am a free and accepted Mason, but not after the style of our Masonic brethren . . . they have said, how do you know about these things? We thought nobody knew anything about these things except those who had access to our very highest logic, our order is so secret . . . Masons shake hands with me, and I give them what I know is their grip; I don't know anything about it except just a few grips that have come to me naturally . . . Not everybody has the hearing ear and the seeing eye. It is only those who have come into this divine masonry that have this spiritual guidance . . . if any man will be a living stone in the Temple, if any man will be a member of this High, Free and Accepted Masonry . . . let him deny himself and take up his cross and follow me.'[52]

[52] Bible Students Souvenir Convention Report, 1913 – People's Pulpit Association of New York.

Chapter Four

A MARRIAGE IS ARRANGED

Having tentatively embraced the basic tenets of the Brotherhood young Charles Russell was somewhat surprised and disappointed to learn that although Freemasons were obliged to profess a belief in a Supreme Being, discussions of a religious nature were not encouraged. However, when he made it known among a small group of acquaintances that he intended to study the Bible open-mindedly, and without reference to divisive and conflicting creeds, he found he was not alone in his search for truth.

From time to time the determined young man organised informal discussion groups of like-minded displaced Christians in the drawing room of the Russell family home at 80 Cedar Avenue, Allegheny. Among those present for the first of what were to become regular monthly Bible-study classes were his father and sister as well as one of his employees, A.D. Jones, a clerk, and two other older men who made up the original half-dozen who gathered in search of enlightenment and truth. A later associate of Russell recalled: 'Someone would raise a question. They would look up all related scriptures on the point and then, when they were satisfied on the harmony of these texts, they would finally state their conclusion and make a record of it.'[53]

Occasionally various travelling preachers would be invited to lecture on 'Christ's Second Coming' at the Cedar Street meetings. One such speaker was George Storrs, founder of the Bible Examiner, a pioneering Adventist periodical of the time. It was from Storrs and other Adventists that the young truth-seeker learnt the doctrine of the restitution of mankind to a re-created paradise earth following the onslaught of Armageddon. 'The study of the Word of God with these dear brethren led, step by step, into greener pastures and brighter hopes for the world,' he once recalled.

Eventually Charles Russell, together with his father and sister Margaret, were baptised into the Adventist movement in June 1874 with George Storrs officiating. The following year, when he was on a business trip to Philadelphia, Russell came across an Adventist magazine – The Herald of the Morning – in which its editor, Dr Nelson H. Barbour, had written: 'I believe that though the gospel dispensation will end in

---

[53] Jehovah's Witnesses, Proclaimers of God's Kingdom – WTBTS 1993.

1878, the Jews will not be restored to Palestine until 1881; and that the 'times of the Gentiles' – their seven prophetic times of 2,520 or twice 1,260 years, which began where God gave all into the hands of Nebuchadnezzar in 606 B.C. – do not end until A.D. 1914.'[54]

Barbour maintained that Christ had already returned to earth, but invisibly, the year before, the very year of Charles Russell's baptism. This seemed too much of a coincidence to be ignored so he immediately contacted Barbour and offered to pay all his expenses if he would make the journey from Rochester, New York to Philadelphia to explain 'fully and scripturally' that the prophecies indicated 1874 as the date at which the Lord's 'presence' and the 'harvest' began. Barbour agreed to make the trip but only if a public lecture could be arranged so the determined young merchant bowed to his wishes and hired the St. Georges Hall in the city for the occasion. 'He came, and the evidence satisfied me,' Russell later recalled.

Nelson H. Barbour was an American adventurer having journeyed to Australia in search of his fortune after experiencing the 'great disappointment' of 1844 as a twenty-year-old disillusioned follower of William Miller. However, during a long sea voyage back to his homeland in 1859, his interest in Bible prophecy was rekindled in Britain. London was a port of call on his return journey and it was there, in 1860, that Barbour acquired numerous journals and books devoted to Second Advent Truth. With his faith thus restored he returned to America determined to spread the word.

It was from Barbour that Charles Russell learnt how the Greek word Parousia – usually translated in the Bible as 'coming' or 'advent' – could also be rendered more meaningfully as 'presence' according to a new translation of the original Greek text of the New Testament.[55] He was also taught the predictive technique of parallel analogy (type and anti-type) whereby scriptural events of long ago are interpreted as having foreshadowed worldly events in the future.

Thus, Barbour reasoned that as Christ's ministry had lasted just three and a half years from his baptism the period of his second coming would be of similar duration. Therefore, since the Lord had already returned (invisibly) to earth in the autumn of 1874, he was presently shepherding

[54] The Herald of the Morning – Dr Nelson H. Barbour, September 1875.

[55] The Emphatic Diaglot – Benjamin Wilson. An interlinear word for word English translation of Vatican manuscript 1209, published today exclusively by the Watchtower Society.

his 'little flock' of sheep-like ones and would take them back to heaven with him at the time of his glorification in the spring of 1878. The Jews would not be restored to Palestine until 1881 and the Gentile times would end in A. D. 1914', exactly forty years after Christ's (invisible) return to earth.

The future looked so promising to Charles Russell that certain business responsibilities were delegated to trusty employees as he busied himself as Assistant Editor (unpaid) of The Herald of the Morning. During the summer of 1877 he set out on a preaching tour with John H, Paton, a close associate of Barbour. With just over a year to go before the expected 'heavenly glorification' of the last of Christ's earth-bound 'little flock', every Protestant minister in Pittsburgh received a personal invitation to attend a lecture – The Imminence of Armageddon – and to receive a complimentary copy of Three Worlds or Plan of Redemption, a book which detailed a succession of biblically significant dates in an anti-typical parallel history of the world which would end in 1914. Ostensibly it was presented as a joint work, but Russell's only contribution was to finance the project.

Evidently none of the reverend gentlemen who turned up at the Quincy Hall to listen to Barbour's fiery delivery agreed with what they heard and the book itself had little impact. Russell was disappointed but undeterred. To counteract what he considered to be inaccuracies in Nelson Barbour's text he published The Object and Manner of Our Lord's Return, a pamphlet in which he set out his own understanding of Bible prophecy. It was favourably reviewed in The Bible Examiner of February 1878 by Advent Unionist George Storrs: 'The author is one of my very dear friends and a sincere lover of truth.' Russell was greatly encouraged by this gesture and began to distance himself from Dr Barbour.

Notwithstanding such unspoken differences of opinion, the young proselyte and his mentor continued working together, somewhat uneasily, as their pious liaison became increasingly strained. In Rochester, a small town, some 25 miles northwest of Pennsylvania, Barbour was giving talks that attracted upwards of fifty listeners at a time. Back in Allegheny attendance at Russell's home Bible-study group had increased to thirty hopefuls as word spread of the imminence of the 'second coming' of Christ.

In the spring of 1878, Pittsburgh newspapers reported that on the night of the anniversary of Christ's death a group of Russell's followers assembled on the Sixth Street Bridge freshly bathed and dressed in white robes waiting to be transferred bodily up to heaven. A second group, similarly attired, was said to have waited in an upstairs room somewhere in Allegheny. 'Some of the more radical ones might have been there but I was not,' Russell told reporters the following day. For the calculating young prophet, it was back to the drawing room in Cedar Street.

Throughout an acrimonious summer truce Russell continued to finance Barbour's magazine but by the autumn of that year he openly rejected the so-called Trinity. Jesus Christ the Son was created by God the Father and therefore could not logically be the Creator, argued Russell. Barbour, who felt he had nothing to learn from his wealthy young patron, began to see Russell, who was almost thirty years his junior, as something of an upstart with more money than spirituality.

Charles Russell shared his Arian understanding of the Bible with his co-worker and fellow Adventist John H. Paton and together they plotted to split from Barbour. In the following months Russell and Barbour each penned a series of conflicting articles in which they openly disagreed on several doctrinal points. To make matters worse Russell accused his business partner of withdrawing funds from the business bank account in New York for his personal use. Barbour ignored the accusation of 'financial misappropriation' and simply carried on as before.

***

In January 1879 Maria Frances Ackley and her younger sister Emma responded to a Public Appeal advertised in the local Allegheny press inviting those interested to take part in a weekly Independent Bible Study and Quest for Truth at the home of respected local businessman Charles T. Russell. The Ackley sisters were particularly welcomed by Joseph Russell who fussed over them, delighted at seeing his son in the company of such intelligent and attractive young women.

Charles had never shown much interest in the opposite sex and the few friends he had were no more than acquaintances, business associates and fellow Bible students. This had always worried his father who took to engineering the seating arrangements for the meetings so that Maria was next to Charles while Joseph, who could still lay on the Irish charm, felt drawn to young Emma. Her encouraging response to the effusive attention of Mr Russell did not go unnoticed by the widower. When heads were down as Bibles were consulted, flickering lamp-lit glances were exchanged between the handsome old man and the flirtatious new interest in his life. Maria and Emma became regular attendees, sometimes staying behind after meetings for refreshments and a chat.

Mr Russell and his son Charles were such good Christian people, they told their mother.

Maria and Charles soon discovered they shared a deeply complex and cherished understanding of God's purposes. Drawn together by the intimacy of their shared beliefs, the young couple mutually confessed to having previously entertained hopes of a future heavenly existence with the Lord. Sometimes their imaginings would transcend earthly time and space as they peeled through their Bibles while trawling through secular history. It was as if they were peering back and forth through time itself; almost as though they were seeing things through the eyes of God.

Within weeks Charles Russell, who would never develop the ability to look beyond the limits of his own predictions, suggested that given the increasingly long periods they were spending together studying the Bible, it might be more convenient and outwardly respectable if he and Maria were marriage partners in the service of the Lord. Spending all their time together as man and wife during this temporary earthly stage of their lives in mutual pursuit of 'the Truth' seemed so fitting, so right, and proper, they told each other. Joseph Russell was delighted with the news.

There were frequent invitations for the Ackley sisters to dine at the Russell family home and afterwards the two girls would be escorted home by the twinkle-eyed Irishman and his dutiful son. When the blossoming relationship between Charles and Maria was made known Emma confided in her older sister that she too was finding herself entertaining similar prospects. There were return invitations to dine at the Ackley home.

Mahlon F. Ackley had died some five years previously and since then it had been a bit of a struggle for his widow Selena. Proudly, she told Joseph Russell that her eldest son, Lemuel, was an attorney in Chicago; but her four daughters remained at home. Laura, the eldest, and Selena, the youngest of the family, expressed a polite but passive interest in the business of Bible-study to their visitors while Maria and Emma declared they would never give up their study of the Scriptures.

Less than ten weeks after their first meeting, during the month of March 1879, Charles Russell and Maria Ackley were married, by fellow Adventist John H. Paton, an ordained minister of the Advent Christian Church in Almont, Michigan. Paton shared Russell's fascination with chronological calculations and the belief that 'the Bible was based on mathematics'. The wedding ceremony was little more than a marriage of minds. Convinced they were destined for spiritual immortality as androgynous members of the Biblical collective 'bride of Christ' – the 'hundred and forty and four thousand . . . redeemed from the earth'[56] – both bride and groom felt that a spiritual rather than physical relationship would best suit their temporary earthly relationship in the 'short time remaining' before Armageddon.

In deference to the ways of the world they could now respectably spend all their time together in the service of the Lord. Having mutually agreed to a none-physical partnership, Charles Taze Russell and Maria Frances Ackley became spiritually united in anticipation of a rapturous fulfilment of their heavenly expectations. This would take place on or before October 1881, a date which had been 'set in stone' by God, the groom had assured his studious bride.

Charles had recently acquired a large house overlooking the park on nearby Clifton Avenue and it was there the newly-weds set up their temporary earthly home together. Believing they were born to be with Jesus in heaven, physical intimacy was never considered. This suited the young couple perfectly because both felt strongly that the spiritual world which beckoned from beyond the veil – that wisp of consciousness that separates the living from the dead – was their rightful place and it was where they would really come to life. At least, that was their mutual intent according to the Bible-thin paper it was written on.

Charles Russell subsequently convinced himself that he was in love with Jesus and would remain so throughout his life. It was only when facing death that he confessed as much to Menta Sturgeon, his personal assistant and travelling companion: 'I have had such a longing desire to be embraced by the Lord Jesus, to think of myself as the woman, or bride, and to have the Master press me to his bosom. I have prayed earnestly to the Lord that I might experience this sweet relationship, and he has given me this assurance that I do enjoy that sweet relationship.'[57]

***

Some three months after the marriage of Charles and Maria another smart wedding took place. Twenty-three-year-old Emma Ackley was the bride and Joseph Russell, now 66 years old, was the groom. They continued holding the Allegheny Ecclesia in their home, but it would not be long before young Emma began to show signs of laxity in attending the weekly Bible classes. It soon became apparent that Joseph's young wife seemed rather more interested in bombazines than Bibles,

---

[56] Revelation 7:4.

[57] Watchtower – December 1, 1916.

preferring to talk about her newest taffetas and trinkets rather than the Holy Scriptures. She felt she was already in paradise. Heaven could wait.

Reinvigorated by the pace of developments in his personal life Charles Russell decided to withdraw his financial support from The Herald of the Morning as he no longer wanted to be involved with Dr Barbour. In a letter dated May 3, 1879, he explained to his former friend: 'There has arisen a difference of view between us as to the teaching of our Father's word. I must be guided by my own understanding . . . and consequently think you to be in error . . . I feel that our relationship should cease.'

Some three weeks later, encouraged and emboldened by his articulate and opinionated wife, he wrote to Barbour again: 'I leave the Herald with you. I withdraw entirely from it, asking nothing from you . . . Please announce in the Herald of the dissolution and withdraw my name.' Charles and Maria then set about launching their own monthly publication – Zion's Watchtower and Herald of Christ's Presence – enterprisingly referring to Barbour's mailing list to solicit readers. With contributions from Adventist John H. Paton and additional material written by Maria Russell, the first give-away issue of 6,000 copies appeared in July 1879.

To the religiously disillusioned it was a hopeful carrot of unimaginable promise and delight: 'This is the first number of the first volume of ZION'S WATCHTOWER, and it may not be amiss to state the object of its publication. That we are living 'in the last days' – 'the day of the Lord' – 'the end' of the Gospel age, and consequently, in the dawn of the 'new' age, are facts not only discernible by the close student of the Word, led by the spirit, but by the outward signs recognisable by the world.'

In the second issue, also distributed free toward the end of July, Russell stated: 'We have sent out about 6,000 copies each of the July and August editions of Zion's Watch Tower, as samples. This we cannot continue to do . . . and unless a good large list of subscribers is had, fifty cents [per annum] will fall far short of paying for printing . . . Do not suppose these remarks to be an appeal for money. No. Zion's Watch Tower has, we believe, JEHOVAH for its backer, and while this is the case it will never neither beg nor petition men for support. Do not put off until tomorrow what you can do today.'

The disappointment of 1878 was soon forgotten as attention was focused on the year in which the churches of the world would fall, and the ‘rapture’ would take place. During spring of 1881 – the year promising fulfilment – Russell offered his readers an opportunity to buy into the ‘high calling’ with a last-minute cash donation to his publishing enterprise: ‘Dear friends we are not going to pass around the contribution box now, but . . . this is the acceptable (receivable) year of the Lord, and we are close to the day of vengeance of our God . . . if you want a chance in the high calling, you need to be quick and prompt about it; we expect the quota (144,000 according to the apostle John’s biblical Revelation) under the call will soon be filled and hope you will not be among [those for whom] it will be forever too late. Again, we ask, how much will you give?’

Those who were persuaded by the young preacher took out magazine subscriptions and made cash donations to the cause. A month later, with no sign of the fall of the churches heralding the onset of Armageddon, Russell played for time: ‘We have not attempted to say when but have repeatedly said [Armageddon] could not take place before the fall of 1881 – about October 2nd. Our expectations then, relative to this year are different from those of others . . . the teachings of THE GREAT PYRAMID are quite different. It has well been called ‘A Miracle in Stone’ and it commends itself to us as a work of God . . . for it seems in every respect to be in perfect accord with God’s plan as we are finding written in His Word. Just what we should look for from October 1881 onward we can scarcely say.’

A few weeks before the pivotal date of October 2nd, 1881, readers of Zion’s Watch Tower, were again invited to indulge themselves. This time, the guilt-inducing text was in italicised and a touch more insistent: ‘*Dear friends, How much will you give for the gospel of Christ? But do you say is it not a free gospel? Does not the prophet say, ‘. . . everyone that thirsteth come to the waters, and he that has no money come ye, buy, and eat; yea, buy wine and milk without money and without price?’ Yes, that is a correct quotation but there is nothing in the passage quoted to indicate that a man who has money can have the gospel and still, keep his money . . . Now if you have some faint idea of its value, perhaps you will be willing to make some offer for it.*’

Charles Russell’s emotive cold-selling technique proved irresistible to some as circulation of Zion’s Watch Tower increased considerably. Later in the year, he canvassed for ‘a thousand preachers’ and the 400 or so readers who answered the call were sent forth as Colporteurs (evangelists) ‘to labour in God’s vineyard . . . to find in every place Christians . . . giving them tracts; and as a work of kindness and love to them, endeavour to sell them a subscription for ZION'S WATCH TOWER'.

Those who were persuaded to devote at least half their time so employed were supplied with free literature and encouraged to support themselves with the proceeds of their door-to-door sales. They were to 'spend no more than two or three minutes,' persuading reluctant householders to part with a relatively 'paltry sum' in exchange for the priceless reading matter on offer. Trusty schoolchildren ('girls would generally succeed best') could be employed on a commission basis in obtaining magazine subscriptions.

Circulation grew and in the October 1881 edition Charles Russell claimed there were now '7,000 [subscribers] who no longer worshipped the Papal Beast or the Protestant Image'. During those early days of the movement there was no suggestion of forming an organisation of Watch Tower readers. The young preacher originally intended to initiate an interdenominational enlightenment and to create a 'brotherhood of understanding' as opposed to an insular sect. Such visible organisations were 'wholly unnecessary and out of harmony with God's divine plan,' he declared. However, it was inevitable those drawn together by a common interest would naturally want to congregate for discussion and mutual encouragement.

Within a year Zion's Watch Tower readers had spontaneously organised themselves into more than thirty independent Bible-study groups across the states of Pennsylvania, New Jersey, Massachusetts, Delaware, Ohio, and Michigan. Each group, or ecclesia, organised their own local congregational matters and elected their own leaders autonomously. Charles Russell took to visiting these groups whenever he was invited to enlarge upon his published articles in person. He referred to these sermons, as 'the truths I present as God's mouthpiece'. On such occasions some of his followers would address him as 'Pastor Russell'. It seemed apt under the circumstances, and the visiting speaker saw no reason to object.

Much encouraged by the increasing circulation of Zion's Watch Tower and his growing success as a public speaker, he began to feel it was time now to reach out even further. He turned his thoughts to Great Britain. At that time, the British Empire occupied one-fifth of the land surface of the earth and Queen Victoria reigned over a population of 400 million souls – all of them subject to the rule of Britannia and the attention of her emboldened Christian missionaries.

In the shadow of this commercial pomp and ceremony ordinary working-class people in Britain suffered appalling poverty and deprivation, particularly those doomed to live out their wretched, sometimes brutally short, lives in London's overcrowded festering slums. The smoky noisy industrial revolution had brought with it an advancement and prosperity which enhanced the lives of the ruling classes but eluded those at its heart – the operatives and labourers from the 'lower orders' who toiled to make it a success. Great Britain was a class-ridden society with a shameful history of inequality and social division which was officially sustained right down through the ranks of Christian church-going worshippers.

When Pastor Russell made known his intentions toward Great Britain two newly converted pioneering colporteurs – J. C. Sunderlin and J. J. Bender – volunteered to take the first steps in spreading 'the Truth' abroad and financing the trip themselves. The American evangelists sailed into Southampton in the late autumn of 1881 bringing with them Pastor Russell's message of hope. The travellers then made their way to London where they were to carry out their mandate: to print a further three hundred thousand copies of Russell's booklet – Food for Thinking Christians – and to distribute them, free of charge, in principle cities throughout the land. In London alone 100,000 copies were handed out by the boys of the National Messenger Service who stationed themselves outside churches all over the sprawling metropolis after the Sunday evening service. There were no immediate results.

The following year, in June 1882, a dozen or so people in the Scottish city of Glasgow organised the first ever Bible Students meeting in the British Isles. Soon afterwards, in East Kirkby, a Nottinghamshire mining village, Thomas Smedley, the local chemist, put a notice in his shop window – 'Bible Class held here' – and almost immediately a study group was formed, such was the impact of this new and alluring interpretation of the Scriptures. A similar discussion group was started in north London. For the Pastor this was yet another convincing sign of God's blessing on his work in Britain, a country he was destined to visit no less than seven times during his wandering ministry.

There were now some three hundred individuals dotted around Britain all of whom were assiduous readers of Zion's Watch Tower. One of these was northerner Jesse Hemery, a baker and confectioner by trade, from the Lancashire town of Eccles. He was so moved by Russell's 'enlightening interpretation' of the Scriptures that he wrote and told him so. The Pastor's response to Hemery's 'sincere and complimentary letter' initiated a regular correspondence between the two men which scripted a close personal friendship that would span some thirty-two years. Meanwhile, on the home front, expectations of an altogether different kind were announced when Mr and Mrs Joseph Russell made known they were about to become parents.

Taken aback somewhat, Charles dutifully shared the happy anticipation of his father and young stepmother as best he could, but his mind was elsewhere. Maria, who had always been close to her younger sister, reacted somewhat differently, and visited Emma regularly throughout her pregnancy. Once the baby had arrived, she would often look in on her happy sister to fuss over her little girl, Mabel.

Following those excursions into the domestic reality of motherhood Maria would find her longings in a state of flux; feelings of emptiness and anxiety she felt unable to share with husband Charles. Their earthly relationship was something they never talked about. Sometimes Maria's wandering thoughts would take her far, far away from the somewhat vague heavenly destiny she had once longed for.

Chapter Five

TROUBLE AND STRIFE

As circulation of Zion's Watch Tower continued to grow Charles Russell became less focused on the retail business he had inherited. Eventually he sold his chain of menswear stores for a total of $260,000 (today's equivalent of 6.5 million dollars) and set himself up as president of a legal corporation: Zion's Watch Tower Bible and Tract Society. According to Article Two of the charter, which was recorded on December 15, 1884, 'The purpose for which the corporation is formed is the dissemination of Bible truths in various languages by means of the publication of tracts, pamphlets, papers and other religious documents.'

With a sure eye on the future and a tentative grip on reality, the young preacher made his wife Secretary-Treasurer then appointed a Board of Directors from a small group of his most patronising followers. Those who could donate cash to this promising enterprise could buy themselves limited voting rights. Ten dollars bought one vote and a sense of controlling participation in the selection of the directors and officers of the Society. Numerous investors purchased blocks of voting rights in good faith, not realising their contributions would be dwarfed by Russell's huge personal cash input which automatically made him controlling shareholder for the next 32 years.

With all the faith he could muster – and with the remainder of his fortune safely invested in stocks and shares – including a substantial interest in the anthracite mines of Pennsylvania – he then set out to promote his 'approaching Armageddon' in a business-like way. The retailing acumen and administrational skills of draper Charles Russell ensured his Christian publishing enterprise was founded on sound commercial principles. The Pastor and his wife considered their work as 'publishers of the Good News of the Kingdom' to be a direct commission from God.

Today the term publisher identifies those Jehovah's Witnesses who are approved by the Watchtower Society to participate in field service and for whom a Publisher's Record Card is held on file. These I.D. cards, verifying the individual's name, address, telephone number, date of birth etc., are used for recording the number of hours he or she spends 'on the work' (promoting Watchtower beliefs and literature) each month. Also noted on the card are details of any pioneering activity or disciplinary action taken against the holder. Upon moving to a different area or congregation the holder must produce this card before being accepted into the new fold.

Russell's book-selling colporteurs were soon joined by a supporting group of pioneering preachers who came to be known as Pilgrims. Their role was to regularly visit each congregation to boost morale and establish a pattern of cohesion and unification among Russell's followers. As attendance at the Wednesday meetings held at the Cedar Street home of Joseph and Emma Russell increased Charles organised additional Sunday gatherings at a more accommodating venue, the Curry Institute Hall. This led to a series of Bible Student Conventions being held at the Carnegie Music Hall.

It was in this burlesque theatre that Charles Russell first honed his skills as a public speaker with his dramatically staged sermons. Bible Student Ralph Leffler, who heard Russell speak, recalls: 'When before an audience he always wore a long black cloak and a white necktie. His voice was not loud; yet, somehow [it] always carried to the most distant part of the auditorium . . . He spoke from the heart and in a manner, that was very convincing.'[58]

In 1886 Charles Russell published The Divine Plan of the Ages, the first in a series of six books, released over an eighteen-year period, which collectively came to be known as Studies in the Scriptures. During the autumn of 1888, when Charles and Maria were working on the second book in the series, a young boy appeared among the regulars who attended the Wednesday meeting. Apart from giving his name and telling the Pastor he was fourteen years old, Charles Ball had little to say. Maria fussed over the boy, found him a seat next to hers and made sure he had a Bible to hand. The following week young Charles showed up again, but this time with his older sister, Rose, who turned out to be much more forthcoming than her brother.

Upon learning that consumption had recently claimed the life of their widowed mother Pastor Russell sympathised with the newcomers and echoed his feelings in his opening prayer. Throughout the meeting reassuring glances and unspoken expressions of kindness and compassion were exchanged, particularly when God's promise of a resurrection and an afterlife came up for discussion. Indeed, the subject seemed to come alive in the welcoming arms of bereavement.

---

[58] Jehovah's Witnesses, Proclaimers of God's Kingdom – WTBTS 1993.

Thereafter and throughout a grindingly cold winter, Charles and Rose would turn up at the Cedar Street meeting every Wednesday and every Sunday afternoon at the Curry Hall. They never missed a meeting. Pastor Russell was impressed with their youthful zeal. Maria sometimes wondered if they were getting enough to eat.

Early in 1889, Russell built his Bible House on Archer Street, Allegheny, at a personal cost of $34,000 ($900,000 today). With its own meeting hall, adjoining bookstore, warehouse, and office complex, it would be Pastor Russell's headquarters for the next twenty years. The Allegheny Ecclesia would in future hold all their meetings at the Bible House Tabernacle. The freehold of the large four-story building was legally held in title by the Tower Publishing Company, Russell's private holding company which initially published the literature for Zion's Watch Tower Society. Those who volunteered to work full-time at the Bible House received a nominal $10 a month for basic personal expenses while married men having a wife at home were paid $15 a month for their efforts.

With future expansion in mind, much of the fourth floor initially remained empty and unused, but not for long. Moved by the plight of Rose Ball and her brother, the Pastor and his wife tactfully suggested they might like to consider living in the Bible House. When it was put to them that they would have a permanent roof over their heads with regular meals and would never have to return to the lodging house they once called home, the orphaned siblings jumped at the chance.

Rose worked in the main office and the bookstore while her brother was kept busy in the warehouse and running errands. However young Charles Ball would not see the approaching summer for soon afterwards he succumbed to the same disease which had taken his mother. Grief-stricken Rose was comforted by the Pastor and his wife who arranged for the bereaved girl to stay at home with them.

A semblance of family life for Charles and Maria thus ensued bringing with it, to a certain degree, a sense of fulfilment in an otherwise vacuous marriage. Shortly afterwards Charles and Maria Russell let it be known at the Bible House that sister Rose thereafter should be considered and treated as their adopted daughter. Rose would spend her evenings with the studious couple in the large study and reading room at Clifton Avenue before retiring to bed, usually around 9 pm. Maria would then kiss her good-night and, with a glance at her remote husband, tell her to 'pass the kiss along to Mr Russell also'. For the next two years Charles and Maria continued walking with God in this way, charting the future of mankind in anticipation of their own heavenly reward, blissfully unaware that they were being stalked by reality.

***

With the publication in 1890 of Thy Kingdom Come, the third book in the Studies in the Scriptures series, Pastor Russell raised the hopes and expectations of his followers considerably when he spelled out for them in no uncertain terms just how close they were to realising their apocalyptic dreams: 'THE "Time of the End," a period of one hundred and fifteen (115) years from A. D. 1799 to A. D. 1914 is particularly marked in the Scriptures. The Great Pyramid is Jehovah's Witness . . . prophetic and chronological teachings co-exist in it.'

The following year the Pastor and his wife set out on a preaching and fact-finding tour of the world that included a visit to Great Britain. When they docked in the port of Liverpool they were met by Jessie Hemery, his transatlantic correspondent since 1882. Russell's first speaking engagement on British soil took place in the Kensington district of Liverpool. As he stood before a large canvas back-drop of his Chart of the Ages, the cloaked preacher talked about The Hidden Mystery. Then it was on to the Stratford East district of London for a repeat performance. Both gatherings each drew about 150 curious listeners from the deprived communities in which they took place.

Charles and Maria then set off on the next stage of their travels which took them on to Palestine and a trip to Giza. This would be the first time Charles Russell could see the Great Pyramid for himself. For him it was a strangely emotive experience, a private moment of privileged enlightenment and wonder. As for Maria, she could only see the Ancient Egyptian tourist attraction for what it was.

Despite their evangelistic success the Pastor and his wife were far from happy with each other. There had been worrying incidents in their private life that disturbed Maria. At first, she was inclined to dismiss her growing suspicions about her husband's personal behaviour and tended to think it was because they were both susceptible to the attention of Satan and his demons, but uncertainty had taken root.

When they returned to Allegheny the sense of foreboding and unease that Maria thought she had left in the past returned almost as soon as she set foot in the house that she and her husband shared with Rose Ball. The homecoming preacher saw things quite differently. He was so pleased with the way Rose had looked after things at the Bible House during his absence that he proposed her election to the board of directors at the very next meeting. At just 22 years old, Rose Ball became the youngest ever director of the Watch Tower Society. Her dedication was plain for all to see as she often stayed late at the office helping Pastor Russell with his growing workload.

Matters came to a head one day when Maria caught her husband in the room of their live-in servant girl with the door locked from the inside. Flustered, Charles explained that he had locked young Emily Sheesly's door for just a couple of minutes so that he could properly hear what the young girl was saying because she was so sick. Maria, who had heard this 'ministering to the sick' story on several previous occasions, was not convinced. 'We have a great work on our hands,' she sobbed. 'In this work you and I must walk very circumspectly before the world, and if you are going to do things like this, what will happen? Don't you suppose people will talk about things like this?'

The Pastor stood his ground and said he was not going to be ruled by his wife; she was his helpmate, not his spiritual superior, he insisted. Maria's growing suspicions about her husband's relationship with their adopted daughter, Rose, were similarly dismissed as wild imaginings. It was all a terrible misunderstanding; the whole thing must be seen for what it is – a cunning satanic attack on their work, Charles pleaded. He then suggested he could move out and into the Bible House while Maria continued living at home with Rose. Exasperated, Maria left the room in a huff.

A short time later she returned to face her husband again, the business partner she had grown to love. In deference to their great work in the service to the Lord, Maria conceded, she would endeavour to look at matters from his standpoint in future. Charles then asked his tearful wife if she would shake hands. 'Now, will you kiss me, dear, as a token of the degree of change of mind which you have indicated?' Within days, Mr. and Mrs. Russell and their 'adopted daughter' vacated their Clifton Avenue home and re-located to the top floor of the Bible House. It was a bold move that was intended to thwart Satan and quell the rumours. Rose Ball soon found herself back in her old room once more as Charles and Maria settled into the daily routine of communal living.

One day, a new full-time volunteer started work at the Bible House. With more than two years' experience on the road as a colporteur to his credit, young Earnest Charles Henninges was a welcome addition to the dedicated workforce. The Pastor recognised his deep sincerity from the start. Rose Ball quite liked him too.

***

In 1894 Charles Russell found he was facing a conspiracy when some of his closest associates, who worked alongside him at the Bible House, began to question the wisdom of certain aspects his doomsday theology. Three of his more outspoken critics accused him of financial double-dealing and voiced their disquiet and anxiety over the rumoured domestic problems in the Russell household with Maria often found weeping 'bitter tears over brother Russell's sins'.

According to his accusers, the Pastor was attempting to 'lord it' over those who worked for him, including his wife, who, they alleged, felt 'compelled by force of circumstances' to lie and cover-up his alleged misdemeanours for 'the sake of the truth'. To wrest control of the organisation, a proposed vote of no confidence by the board of directors was briefly considered, but when it was realised that Russell's overwhelming majority shareholding would nullify any board decision or collective opinion, the detractors gave up and walked out of the Bible House for good.

Soon afterwards they circulated their doubts and opinions in an eight-page leaflet, defaming Russell in the process, and inviting subscriptions to a new religious journal they intended to produce. Disappointed by a poor response to their exposé, the dissenters eventually went their separate ways and were soon forgotten, but not before Russell's father and stepmother had each received a copy of the defamatory leaflet in the mail. Joseph Russell's health had lately begun to fail, and he rarely left his home now. As for his young wife Emma, she no longer attended her stepson's meetings and barely gave the Bible House literature a glance.

Surprisingly, and to the Pastor's great satisfaction, his wife reacted with impassioned indignity to this latest 'unhappy marriage' gossip. She would have none of it. With the help of her anxious husband, arrangements were made for Maria to visit numerous congregations of Bible Students in ten cities across territory that stretched from New York to Chicago, and without delay.

It was unusual for Russell's followers to be addressed by a woman but the Pastor's reputation and his credibility as 'God's messenger' had been called into question. The 'malicious rumours' had to be stopped and who better to stop them than the one best placed to do it, the wife of the man in question. If anyone knew the truth it would be her. The solemn and the sympathetic turned up in record numbers to hear what Mrs Russell had to say:

'I take this opportunity to speak in defence of my husband and against the bold attack of our enemies in maligning his character and misrepresenting our domestic relations. Our household is composed only of ourselves and our esteemed and beloved helpers in the Watch Tower office, all of whom gladly bear witness to the tranquillity and happiness of our home, save the intrusions of false brethren and busybodies occasionally disturb it. Our home, so far from being a discordant one, is the very reverse. We agree that the Lord is now present, that he assumed his office of King in 1878, and that since that time his household has been richly fed with meat in due season. It seems to me that in dispensing the food to the household the Lord has chosen just *one* servant.'

At every gathering Maria forcefully identified her husband as God's chosen mediator, pointing out that as such he was bound to attract the attention of Satan and his demons. The beleaguered preacher was delighted with Maria's convincing support and later recalled: 'I was not aware of it at the time but learned subsequently that the conspirators endeavoured to sow seeds of discord in my wife's heart by flattery, women's rights arguments etcetera. However, she was aroused and proved herself a heroine in her defence of her husband.'

Most of the Bible Students who heard Maria Russell speak up on behalf of her husband were persuaded by the sincerity of her emotional plea. However, upon returning to the Bible House, having left her passionate convictions of her husband's innocence behind with those of his followers who had readily embraced them, she found herself back once more in the arms of reality. For the disillusioned Pastor's wife, it was an unsettling moment of realisation and sad acceptance; their contrived marriage had not been made in heaven, after all.

From the start of her married life Maria Russell had been relatively happy and content playing the role of dutiful 'earthly wife' and spiritual helper to husband Charles, who took all the credit for their joint work. As co-editor of Zion's Watch Tower, she had written anonymously numerous in-depth articles for the journal from its inception. She had also co-authored the first three volumes of Studies in the Scriptures and was now working on the fourth book in the series. Unlike her husband, Maria Russell had graduated from High School having received teacher training at the prestigious Curry Normal School, a somewhat superior level of educational achievement she would bring up whenever Charles was getting above himself. On those fractious occasions she would hint that one day, perhaps she might replace her husband as 'that servant' in dispensing spiritual 'meat in due season' – especially if that 'particular servant' might prove to be out of harmony with God's plan regarding his other half, his 'twain one'.

To pacify his assertive wife, Charles Russell arranged for her to oversee a special weekly meeting of the Allegheny Women's Bible Students – an arrangement that backfired when the group degenerated into a hotbed of gossip. He later recalled, 'I took particular care to shield my wife as much as possible, laying the principal blame on one of her sisters, whose evil influence I could note at almost every turn of my affairs.'

Support for Maria grew causing Russell to announce that 'slanderous relatives and friends' of his wife were no longer welcome at any of his meetings. Convinced that 'women's rights literature and anarchistic ideas' had sown seeds of discontent in his wife's heart, he sent off angry letters to his father and to Maria's sister Laura, instructing them 'not to receive or harbour my wife under your roof under any pretext whatsoever'. But the ailing Joseph Russell was too ill to read his mail. His young wife Emma was running the house now.

One-day Maria complained to her husband that her individuality was not sufficiently prominent in the Watch Tower announcements that she was the Associate Editor. She requested that her name thereafter appear with each article just as she would write them, without corrections or emendations. Charles was dumfounded and after several days of sulky impasse there were angry exchanges about Maria's written contributions to Zion's Watch Tower which led to her formal resignation as co-editor of the journal. Charles Russell was totally unprepared for such bold forthrightness from his wife; it seemed so out of character, so unlike the woman he thought he knew. In fact, he was speechless, and as far as Maria was concerned, he would remain so for quite some time.

From then onwards communication between the unhappy couple was conducted via petty and vindictive letter writing, with Rose Ball acting as the go-between. In a letter to his wife, dated July 8th, 1896, Charles Russell wrote: 'We have made a mistake in getting married, and this conviction has been growing on me for three years . . . I am convinced that our difficulty is a growing one generally; that it is a great mistake for strong-minded men and women to marry.'

A few days later he wrote again: 'To avoid misunderstanding, let me say, under the circumstances it properly devolves upon you to make the advances on the lines of social amenities between us. It would be improper for me to take the initiative in the matter of amenities such as good morning, good night, etc.' This stilted civility continued for several months before a wearisome Charles Russell and the three indignant

Ackley sisters agreed to let bygones be bygones. In future they would treat one another with kindness and respect.

The Pastor thought he would gain the upper hand with this initiative, spelling out the 'terms of responsibility' toward one another in a written agreement which was signed by all four of them on September 13, 1897. This formalising of domestic trivialities seemed to satisfy Charles Russell somewhat but did little to address the persistent feelings of unease and distrust they all shared.

A few weeks later the three Ackley sisters confronted Maria's husband in his office and accused him of conniving with his father in the preparation of a will in which he favoured his son over his wife Emma and their young daughter Mabel. There was no arguing the matter, Emma insisted, for she had seen the will, which had been drawn up by Charles at the request of his dying father and claimed that its minimal provision would leave her and her daughter practically destitute.

Russell denied all knowledge of the will, but when the document was waved under his nose by Laura, he claimed that it was simply a first draft. A few days later he admitted there had been certain oversights in the draft will and assured the three angry sisters that a new and more favourable will had been drawn up and signed by Emma's frail and failing husband.[59] However, Emma was unaware that her husband's property also included a portfolio of industrial shares with a total capitalisation of more than $500,000, all of which were dummy holding companies administered by his son, Charles.

***

Early one November morning, Maria Russell packed her bags, crept out of the Bible House, and fled from Allegheny claiming her life was in danger. Taking refuge with her brother Lemuel and his wife, who lived in Chicago, she told them that Charles, her husband of eighteen years, was plotting to have her locked up in a mental asylum because he believed she was being used as an agent of Satan to undermine his ministry. She feared for her sanity, she feared for her life, she told them.

Some weeks later Maria received a letter from Charles: 'Come back to me, my dear! I promise that I will do all in my power to make you as

[59] Joseph Lytle Russell died on 17th December 1897 aged 84. His 'new will' left about half of a declared $30,000 estate to his wife Emma, $7500 to his daughter Margaret from his first marriage, and $7500 to his young daughter Mabel. Charles Russell was bequeathed a parcel of land in Florida (worth about $8,000 at that time) with a similar bequest to his wife.

happy as you ever were, and as much more so as lies within my power. Think, my dear, that God has already favoured you with a position as my queen and associate helper that, in some respects at least, is second to that of no other lady in the world.'

Eventually, in January 1898, Maria returned to Allegheny, but this time to live with her widowed sister Emma and her young daughter Mabel. For Charles Russell it was not the homecoming he had expected: 'Maria and her sisters and friends, began a campaign of vilification of every kind, regardless of the truth, going hither and thither wherever they could find anyone willing to hear them, bound on injuring me in some manner.' This went on for several months until one-day Maria, flanked by her two sisters, confronted Charles at the Bible House to tell him that she no longer desired to live with him as his 'earthly wife'.

She then gave him her solemn assurance that she would put a stop to all the gossip and suggested that 79, Cedar Street – the empty house next door to Emma which Charles had previously leased to tenants – be turned over to her. Outnumbered, the reluctant landlord agreed to furnish at least some of the empty rooms, but only on the understanding that Maria would henceforth support herself by taking in lodgers. Other than that, he would not give her a cent. This hasty arrangement seemed, on the face of it, to alleviate the situation so the warring couple shook hands on the deal.

Charles Russell later recalled: 'I gave her possession of a house which I owned facing the parks, and furnished it for her in good style – a better home than she ever before had – thinking to myself, I will overcome her evil with good . . . She manifested some appreciation, sat on my knee, and kissed me, and knelt with me in prayer in that house. In the hope that a change of sentiment was in sight I visited her every Thursday evening for some five times, when she said, "Husband, I have been fearful that the neighbours and lodgers would think it strange to see you come here every Thursday." The hint was sufficient; I discontinued attentions.'

Some years later Charles Russell published an article in which he referred to Maria as 'an editor's wife – an illustration of a misguided conscience'.[60] In retaliation Maria published an account of her experiences with her famous husband which included extracts from his personal correspondence she describes as 'full of envy [of her literary superiority] and vainglory'. She defiantly rounds off her twelve-page

[60] Zion's Watch Tower – November 1902

pamphlet: 'Mrs. Russell still resides at No. 79 . . . supporting herself by her own exertions, not receiving a dollar from her husband, nor from [the literary catalogue of Russell's publishing business] so largely hers.'

Maria circulated her written reprisals among as many of Russell's followers as she could. She also sent bundles of her vindictive tract to various churchmen along with a covering note suggesting that they distribute them among those of their flock who may have been influenced away from the church by Pastor Russell. Some of these pamphlets were sent to Britain and Australia. Eventually, during the month of March 1903, a copy of Maria's sniping circular landed on the desk of her estranged husband. Infuriated, he immediately enlisted the help of several of the brawniest workers at the Bible House and marched round to Maria's lodging house on Cedar Street to repossess his property. Using a pass key, he burst into the house to confront his wife.

During a heated exchange, he grabbed her purse, which contained that week's rental money, and told her to 'get out of here, you blasphemer! You are my wife only in a legal sense. A wife has no rights which a husband is bound to respect.' Then, with the help of his cohorts, he entered the rooms of the tenants and set about removing their private property before he was stopped in his tracks by one of the startled lodgers. The resulting tussle saw a fuming Pastor Russell making a swift exit from the scene vowing to lay down the law to his wife.

Maria took refuge with her sister Emma and immediately started proceedings against her husband for non-support. The court subsequently ordered Russell to pay his estranged wife forty dollars a month. He was later sued by two of the outraged tenants while a third charged him with assault. He was acquitted of assault but found guilty of 'violating the terms' of a leasehold agreement on two counts. Eventually at the Court of Common Pleas in Pittsburgh, Pennsylvania, June 1903, Maria filed for divorce on the grounds of her husband's 'conceit, egotism, domination, and improper conduct in relation to other women'. Upon being summoned to court Charles Russell immediately turned his thoughts to his former 'adopted daughter'.

Back in September 1897, Rose Ball had married fellow Bible Student, Earnest Charles Henninges in Buffalo, New York. The event was briefly mentioned in Zion's Watch Tower along with a notation that the newly-weds were 'scheduled to continue in the Lord's service as travelling pilgrims for the Watch Tower Society'. Russell immediately contacted the roving preachers and suggested they might like to now consider the 'privilege of reaching out' by serving the Lord overseas. How did they feel about establishing a Watch Tower branch office in Australia? Before the year was out Rose Ball and her husband had obediently left the shores of America and sailed to the other side of the world. They were never to return.

Chapter Six

TRIALS AND TRIBULATIONS

The 'Maria F. Russell versus Charles T. Russell' case came up for trial in April 1906 before Mr. Justice Collier and a jury selected from the local population. It was one of the most sensational court cases in the history of Allegheny County and attracted the attention of the national press.

Whispers and rumours concerning Pastor Russell's suspected dalliances, which had been lurking in the unfathomable depths of gossip and innuendo for years, were widely expected to surface. What a catch that would be for certain elements of the clergy who had for so long baited and waited. Reporters from as far away as Washington and New York flocked to Pennsylvania, eagle-eyed and hungry for a story.

Scheduled to testify in defence of Charles Russell were farmer J. A. Bohnet, the Pastor's foremost patron and benefactor, and a clutch of his staunchest supporters who had worked alongside Russell and his wife at the Allegheny Bible House. Amongst the witnesses for the prosecution were Mrs. E. H. Russell, the Pastor's widowed stepmother; Mrs. Laura J. Rainer, Maria's now divorced eldest sister and her brother, Lemuel Ackley, a respected lawyer whose presence as a witness promised to lend an air of respectability and propriety to the proceedings.

When he arrived at the court on the first day of the trial Charles Russell smiled benignly as he and his entourage eased their way through a sizeable cluster of gawping onlookers waiting outside. Meanwhile, inside the courthouse, the opposing attorneys were conferring with the presiding judge. Under last-minute discussion was the touchy subject of 'physical intimacy' – or the lack of it – between the couple throughout the entire period of their marriage.

Mrs Russell's bill of complaint admitted that there had been no cohabitation between herself, and her husband and her attorney was seeking to tell the court that she had been 'deprived of one of the chief pleasures of life' for the entire duration of her married life. However, Charles Russell's attorney saw things differently: 'The fact of the matter was in Mrs. Russell's own control. She did understand that her husband preferred to live a celibate life, but she agreed and expressed the same as her preference. She knew his teachings on the subject – that neither the husband nor the wife may 'defraud' the other of reasonable marital rights.' The Judge decided to side-step the issue and refused to permit such a personal matter to be aired in a court of law, or any reference or allusion to it whatsoever.

'The court will rise,' announced the usher as Mr. Justice Collier entered the lively courtroom. Once the preliminaries had been dealt with, the hearing got under way. Heads turned when 'Maria Frances Russell' was called against a rising surge of murmuring from the public gallery as she took the stand. Order and silence were called for as her attorney, Mr. S. G. Porter, set the scene and opened a biographical chapter in the private life of Pastor Russell that would prove to be manna from heaven for his detractors.

***

'What was the name of the girl?'

'Rose Ball.'

'I want you to tell us what your husband did in company with this woman Rose, in your presence and in your home. Tell us what you saw and what he said and what was done.'

'Our library and bedrooms were next to each other upstairs on the second floor but I spent the evening downstairs reading on one occasion, and I went upstairs about ten o'clock to my room, and I supposed that he was either in the library or had retired, and when I went up there I found that he was in neither place, and I stepped out in the hall and I found that he was in his night robe, sitting beside Miss Ball's bed and she was in bed. On other occasions I found him going in there and I found she called him in and said she wasn't well and wanted him in, and I objected to this, and I said it was highly improper, and I said, "We have people about the house, and what kind of name will be attached to this house if you do that kind of thing," and he got angry.'

'You state that you found him doing this at other times. How often after that?'

'I found him several times; I don't remember how often.'

'In her room?'

'Yes sir. And I found him in the servant girl's room as well and I found him locked in the servant girl's room.'

'Did he make any explanation why he was in the girl's room?'

'No, he did not; he just got angry.'

'What did Rose do at the Watchtower?'

'She attended to the correspondence.'

'Where was her desk with reference to the desk of Mr. Russell in the Watchtower Society?'
'It was not near his; it was in the office . . . She came home with him in the evenings, and they came about eleven o'clock, and the young men that were in the office – she was the only girl – and the young men would go home, and he wouldn't allow her to go home with them, and she must wait and always go with him.'
'State to the Court and Jury what talk, if any, you had with this girl Rose, regarding her relations with your husband, which you communicated to your husband.'

The Pastor's attorney immediately leapt to his feet and objected at length to what he considered unverifiable, and therefore, inadmissible evidence, given the absence of Rose Ball. Mr. Justice Collier then addressed Mr. Porter: 'The objection is sustained unless you show what you propose to prove.'
'We propose to prove by the witness upon the stand that the plaintiff after observing the conduct as stated by her, of her husband with Rose Ball, she went to the girl and secured from her the statement that Mr. Russell at various times embraced her and kissed her; that he called her his little wife and jelly-fish, and told her that a man's heart was so big he could love a dozen women, but a woman's heart was so small she could only love properly one man; that after receiving this statement from Rose Ball, the plaintiff told her husband that, and he admitted that it was true.'

Once again, the Pastor's attorney was back on his feet, but the judge ruled: 'We will not permit you to show what Rose Ball told her. We will permit you to show that she went to her husband and told him that Rose Ball had told her that he was keeping her and telling her she was his dear little wife, and that he said it was true.' Mr Porter then turned to Maria: 'You understood the ruling of the Court? You are to tell what you stated to your husband what Rose had said, and his reply to you.'
'I told him that I had learned something that was so serious, and that I didn't tell him right away. I let a day elapse, until I felt I had control of myself and I could talk, and then I told him that I had something very serious to tell him about this matter, and he said, What is it? and I said, Rose has told me that you have been very intimate with her, that you have been in the habit of hugging and kissing her and having her sit on your knee and fondling each other, and she tells me you bid her under no account to tell me, but she couldn't keep it any longer. She said if I

were distressed about it, she felt she would have to come and make a confession to me, and she had done that.'

'What did he say?'

'He tried to make light of it at first, and I said to him, Husband you can't do that. I know the whole thing. She has told me straight, and I know it to be true. Well, he said he was sorry: it was true, but he was sorry. He said he did not mean any harm. I said, I don't see how you could do an act like that without meaning harm.'

'What year was that?'

'In the fall of 1894.'

'Did you state to your husband at this meeting any endearing terms?'

'Yes, sir.'

'What were they?'

'I said, she tells me that one evening when you came home – I asked her when these things occurred. I said to him, she says they occurred down at the office, when she stayed down there with him in the evenings after the rest had gone, and at home at any time when I was not around. She said one evening when she came home with him, just as she got inside the hall, it was late in the evening, about eleven o'clock, he put his arms around her and kissed her. This was in the vestibule before they entered the hall, and he called her his little wife, but she said, I am not your wife, and he said, I will call you daughter, and a daughter has nearly all the privileges of a wife.'

'And what other terms were used?'

'Then he said, 'I am like a jellyfish. I float around here and there. I touch this one and that one, and if she responds, I take her to me, and if not, I float on to others', and she wrote that out so that I could remember it for sure when I would speak to him about it. And he confessed that he said those things.' Pastor Russell's attorney then stepped forward to cross-examine Maria: 'Without going into any question whatever, about the disputes over that young lady whose name I forget – Rose Ball – I merely wish to know when she went to Australia, or wherever she went?'

'Just after this suit was entered, in 1903.'

'What age was the girl at the time of her marriage?'

'She was about nineteen or twenty when she came to us, and this was twelve years afterwards. It would make her about thirty-two – past thirty; I suppose about thirty-two.' Later in the trial Charles Russell gave his version of events when his lawyer, Mr. J. F Carpenter, questioned him about the alleged trysts with Rose Ball:

'Did you ever at any time undertake to humiliate, or did you ever do any act or say any words, such as using the expression 'jellyfish', or anything that would hurt Mrs. Russell's feelings in any way?'

'Nothing intentional, sir, if I might I would like to explain. We had in our family this Miss Ball that was referred to. Might I mention that? This Miss Ball one evening came to me in the front room – or rather I heard someone sobbing, and I turned around to see and she was crying at her desk, and I inquired what was the matter, and she didn't answer for a while, and finally she jumped up and came over and sat down on my knee and was still crying, and I inquired what was the matter. She said Mrs. Russell had been overworking her or something, and I tried to show her that she was mistaken, and I tried to allay her feelings. Another time she came and sat on my knee when there was some young man who was giving her attention more than she liked and had been making himself unpleasant and she was worked up and was crying. But she merely came to me as a father.'

'You treated her as a daughter in your home?'

'Yes, sir. She looked to be about thirteen. I don't know how old she was. I heard someone say that she was only ten. She was a very young-looking woman.'[61]

'They have mentioned that matter when you were found in her room.'

'I don't remember the occurrence, but it is likely it would be true that Mrs. Russell might have come in and found me by the bedside with her hand in mine. I suppose I was feeling her pulse. I don't know anything else. It would be a common occurrence; I gave medicine in the family. I used to be the family physician. I happened to have some knowledge of medicine. But if anybody would get bad, we would send for a regular physician.'

'Anything of that kind that occurred was just in the interest of family health?'

'Yes, sir. Another matter Mrs. Russell mentioned to me years ago when she was intimating that she might bring a suit. This was in 1896, ten years ago. She said, It would look very badly for you if I would tell in Court that I found you once in the room with Emily . . . I can't think of the name, Mathews, since married . . . and that the door was locked. I

---

[61] Rose Ball joined the Russell household in 1888. Her Australian Certificate of Registration states: 'Born in the Unites States of America 19th March 1869 . . . wife of Earnest Charles Henninges'. Rose died in 1950 in her 82nd year, her husband having predeceased her 3rd February 1934.

said, Dear, that was the morning that Emily Mathews was sick, and you told me of it and asked me to go up and see her, and when they were running in and out with water in the pails, I turned the key for half a minute until I would have a chance to hear quietly what she had to say. There was not the slightest impropriety in anything that was done. I would just as soon that everybody in this room would be present.'

'There were some expressions used here about a jellyfish.'

'No sir, I never made use of such an expression. I hope I don't look idiotic enough to say that. In my opinion any man that claims to be a jellyfish would have no sense at all. I would like to be given credit for having some backbone.'

'I ask you again whether you can recall any instance at all in your experience with Mrs. Russell, that you consciously attempted to wound or hurt her in any way, or humble her?'

'I never did.'

Maria's attorney then stepped forward: 'Did you or did you not tell the plaintiff that her sickness was the judgement of God on her for her failure to obey you?'

'I did not.'

'What did you say?'

'Miss Ball, who was her special friend, and who I knew would tell her, I told her in my opinion, this was a judgement from the Lord on her.'

'And you intended Miss Ball to tell her that?'

'Yes, sir. I wished her to. I thought she ought to know it.'

'Was that the time she had erysipelas? [a febrile streptococcal infection of the skin and subcutaneous tissue].

'Yes, sir.'

'Did you believe that it was the judgement of the Almighty?'

'I think so . . . I think the Almighty does choose sickness as a means of correcting people at times.'

'When she was on her sick bed?'

'Yes sir.'

'That is your idea of good treatment?'

'That was my idea.'

***

Maria won the day when the jury found in her favour. She had instructed her attorney to secure for her a 'partial' or 'qualified' decree which would effectively style the couple as 'in divorce'. Maria's brother, Lemuel, had advised her that a limited divorce of this type carried with it financial support while an absolute divorce, which could have been won on the same evidence, did not. To avoid the social stigma of an absolute divorce Charles Russell readily complied with the Court Order without hesitation. The ambiguity of a 'qualified divorce' seemed to imply something far less damaging and distasteful.

Maria celebrated her victory by self-publishing her own thoughts on women's rights – The Twain One – A Cup of Cold Water for a Thirsty Soul – a leaflet in which she declared: 'If any apology is needed for the publication of this small work, it is the very general misconception of the teaching of the Word of God [regarding] the social standing of [women].'

With his credibility now in question Charles Russell portrayed himself as a victim of a 'malicious and slanderous' press and sued the Washington Post for reporting the legal proceedings against him in a 'defamatory manner'. The Washington Post was subsequently judged to have reported certain personal aspects of the divorce case in a derogatory – as opposed to defamatory – manner; a technical point of law which was found in Russell's favour. The Brooklyn Eagle duly informed its readers that the 'phoney Pastor' had been thus awarded 'a derisory one- dollar damages'.

In the aftermath of the court proceedings a whiff of scandal and suspicion hung in the air. Some Bible Students began to question Russell's private life as half-forgotten rumours from the past were reconsidered in the light that doubt affords. They wondered if indeed anything untoward had taken place between the handsome charismatic preacher and certain of his adoring female followers in those earlier formative days of naïve fleshly confusion and groping spiritual intent.

More questions were raised when the somewhat chastened preacher published his defensive observations on the 'weakness of the flesh': 'The Apostle forewarns us that we must not forget that, although we are reckoned by the Lord as dead according to the flesh and alive according to the spirit, nevertheless we have this treasure of the new life in the earthen vessel, which is only reckoned dead, but which is very much alive and constitutes our chief enemy. Meantime the conflict is on between the new will (which has no body of its own kind) and the old flesh (which has no will of its own kind). To be a conqueror the new will must struggle with the old flesh, and by the Lord's assistance keep it under, in subjection until the end of the course, until literally dead.'[62]

---

[62] Zion's Watch Tower – January 15, 1907.

Notwithstanding such moralising it soon became apparent that something more had to be done to quell the lingering gossip. Eventually, in the pages of Zion's Watch Tower, Pastor Russell vowed: 'to conduct myself toward those of the opposite sex in private exactly as I would do with them in public . . . and, so far as reasonably possible, I will avoid being in the same room with any female alone, unless the door to the room stands wide open.' He then went on to promote his Vow to the Lord – 'one of the best safeguards that you can set up' – as a model of intent for all male Bible Students. Those who did so would have their names published in future editions: 'Advise us, if you please, when you take the vow. We will preserve an alphabetical list which may be of use some time.'

The more obsequious among his followers put pen to paper without hesitation while others took exception feeling they were being coerced into publicly confessing that they too shared the Pastor's suspected tendencies. Eventually a trickle of resentment and resistance turned into a disturbing riptide of unease and discontent as some Bible Students began to openly question his motives in formulating the Vow. Among these were some of Charles Russell's closest associates of many years standing including his sister Margaret.

Sifting through his mail one day, Pastor Russell found himself wandering through haunting shadows of the past as he reluctantly read between the lines of a letter from Australia; it was from brother Henninges. The disillusioned emigrant and his wife, Rose, no longer shared Russell's view that his followers were on a par with Jesus Christ as a collective mediator for all mankind. Consequently, they wished now to disassociate themselves from the organisation. Furthermore, a growing number of Bible Students in Melbourne were openly refusing to sign up to the now infamous Vow amid growing suspicions about the Pastor's alleged moral laxity.

The tell-tale letter was widely circulated among Bible Students throughout America and Great Britain. A notable recipient was Margaret Russell who consequently publicly disowned her brother and abandoned his teachings altogether. Soon afterwards several hundred Australian defectors organised themselves into the New Covenant Believers, the first of numerous splinter groups who would separate themselves from Russell's International Bible Students. Despite this setback many believers stayed loyal to the errant preacher. As far as they were concerned Pastor Russell was innocent. The Lord's chosen envoy immoral? The very idea was unthinkable. Such thoughts would never even have entered his head, they reasoned. How on earth could they?

***

In the late Middle Ages Satan and his demons were widely believed to be able to assume the appearance of either a man or a woman to tempt the unwary. To do their work the demons would assume a human form, known as incubus or succubus, sometimes even taking on the appearance of the victim's marriage partner or lover. Demonologists of the period further promoted the belief that a she-devil (succubus) could materialize as a woman and copulate with a man and later transform itself into a male-oriented devil (incubus) with the ability to impregnate its often-unwilling female victim with the human sperm it had received as a succubus.

This serpentine belief was often used to explain away a forbidden sexual liaison or even an unwanted pregnancy. Enough numbers of medieval nuns lent credence to this myth by claiming they had been raped by incubi. Those who claimed to have been compromised in this way invariably cited their Christian piety as the reason for having been attacked by these lecherous devils.

In a dubious 17th century incident, a noble woman claimed she had been visited by her absent husband in a dream and made pregnant by him. There was much speculation as to whether she might have been the victim of an incubus as her husband had been away for more than three years. So compelling were such beliefs, the woman's ingenuity was never questioned, publicly at least. Other women were not so fortunate. Those thought to be witches or necromancers were invariably accused of the sin of having unnatural sex with devils and were severely punished for it.

Today the notion of unsuspecting humans being coerced into participating in wanton and unbridled sexual activity by malevolent forces of evil is interpreted by some psychologists as 'reaction formation', a defence mechanism subconsciously dreamed up to block urges and impulses which, although occurring naturally, have become deeply offensive to the individuals concerned. Only in this way can sexual activity – normal and innocuous in the everyday lives of others – be rendered acceptable to those who harbour such beguiling thoughts.

Periodically the experiences of Jehovah's Witnesses who claim to have fallen victim to similarly unwanted attentions of satanic forces in the form of phantom sex-partners are published by the Watchtower

Society. Typical is the following account: 'After showing interest in the Watchtower Bible message a young woman who worked as a 'spirit healer' soon discovered that she had become a helpless puppet of evil unseen forces. Under spirit command she was forced to arrange for immoral women to entice her husband away from home [to] commit adultery with them. The spirits then demanded that sex relations form part of the healing rituals that she performed in her home. The explanation was that by this means the sick person would be 'unloaded' or cured, the sickness being transferred, by means of sexual intercourse, to the medium. The spirits also ordered that the women patients be treated by performing acts of lesbianism with them. In the case of young people, the spirits encouraged 'sex control', in reality; masturbation . . . the sexual depravity of these wicked angels is still very evident.'[63]

During the 1970's the Watchtower Society's preoccupation with the furtive evils of sex climaxed when it was argued that when Jesus cited fornication as grounds for divorce, he was actually referring to all forms of illicit sexual intercourse. Furthermore, fornication could even take place within the marital union where a whole range of 'unnatural acts' could so easily slip between the sheets. Presentations about 'porneia' were frequently included in the programme at large conventions and local elders the world over were required to deliver explicit talks on the subject based on graphically detailed outlines provided by the Watchtower Society. Sodomy, oral sex and masturbation topped the convoluted list of 'depraved activities' to be avoided in the marital bed. As a result, many Witness couples became paranoid about sex in general while others sought guidance from the elders on just what was permissible as foreplay in the bedroom.

Special judicial hearings were held as confessions of forbidden sexual activity were investigated by local elders. Married women suffered excruciating embarrassment when they were required to respond, with graphic honesty, to probing questions about their sex lives. Elders who were considered too moderate or lenient in their handling of such matters were reported to the Governing Body who then issued a letter of guidance:

'Dear Brothers, please let us know if any of the elders in the congregation have been giving incorrect advice regarding matters involving oral sex. If any of the elders in the congregation have advised married persons that it would not be improper for them to engage in oral sex,

---

[63] *Awake!* – September 8, 1976.

then on what basis was such counsel given? If wrong counsel was given, then let us know if appropriate steps have been taken to correct any misunderstanding on the part of the individuals who were given the wrong counsel and let us know if the elders concerned agree with what has been stated in the Society's publications about oral sex. If any of the brothers as elders have been advising individuals that oral sex would be permissible as foreplay prior to having actual sex relations, then such advice was not correct.'

In a desperate effort to save her marriage, one woman wrote to Ray Franz, a member of the Governing Body, for personal advice saying that she and her husband loved each other deeply but were accustomed to [a certain type of foreplay] which was frowned upon by the Society: *'I believe it's a matter of conscience, but I'm writing you to be sure . . . I am scared, I am hurt, and I am more worried now about* [her non-believing husband's] *feeling for the truth . . . I know you will tell me what to do.'*[64]

Some unhappily married women took advantage of the new ruling and reported their Witness husbands to the elders for forcing them to commit acts of a 'lewd or gross nature', the Watchtower Society having decreed that such married men were guilty of 'fornicating' with their own wives. In some cases, divorce soon followed. Young Witnesses, particularly those who had been persuaded to put off their marriage plans until after Armageddon (at that time forecast for 1975), developed damaging guilt complexes about masturbation and forbidden 'lewd thoughts' while hormone-hyped adolescents were continually pressured into not even thinking about sex. It was an intolerable situation which threatened to divide and destabilise the world-wide community of Jehovah's Witnesses.

Eventually, after six tumultuous years of sex-policing, the Governing Body reversed its unpopular reading of the words of Jesus with a flash of 'new light' on the subject which appeared out of the blue in the Watchtower magazine: 'The Bible does not give any specific rules or limitations about the way in which husband and wife engage in sexual relations.'[65] There was no explanation, regret or apology and the matter was never referred to again.

According to Pastor Russell's edict – 'There is no distinction of sex among the angels and . . . such will also be the future condition of

---

[64] Crisis of Conscience – Raymond Franz, Commentary Press 1992.

[65] Watchtower – February 15, 1978.

humanity.'[66] – sexual activity will one day be a thing of the past for Jehovah's Witnesses, not only for those who entertain heavenly hopes but also for those believers who look forward to an everlasting physical life on a paradise earth.

Noted British Bible Student Albert O Hudson (1899-2000), a former Watchtower Society elder who served under both Pastor Russell and Judge Rutherford, goes a step further when he conjures up a graphic portrayal of sexless immortality in a post-Armageddon paradise where there will be no place or purpose for genitalia: '. . . the further propagation of the human species will cease . . . the purpose of God in endowing human beings with procreative powers is revealed in the Book of Genesis to be entirely and solely for the adequate peopling of the earth, and when that object has been achieved it is but reasonable to expect that those powers will atrophy and disappear.'[67]

---

[66] Watchtower – January 15, 1912.

[67] God Has a Plan – Albert O Hudson, Bible Fellowship Union (5th edition), 2014.

Chapter Seven

THE CHRISTIAN ZIONIST

Charles Russell was summoned to attend an Alimony Hearing in April 1907. In an affidavit the Pastor's ex-wife stated that she and her former husband had written most of the material for their Watch Tower journal between them. She also claimed she had written 50% of the contents of each of the first three volumes in the Studies in the Scriptures series and all but the last chapter of the fourth volume. She also pointed out the books were printed at a cost of 25 cents each – 'but they sell them for $1.00 each.'

When asked whether Maria had helped in the writing of the chapter on the Great Pyramid in the third volume of Studies in the Scriptures Charles Russell replied, 'No, sir. She co-laboured in the arrangement, she read the proof and examined my manuscripts . . . she had no knowledge of the subject . . . her assistance was one of amanuensis.' When he was asked why he had failed to deny that Maria had written over half the material in the Studies in the Scriptures in the divorce trial he replied, 'I was not asked anything about it . . . I do not care who wrote the books, it is the matter I am anxious to get before the public'.

When questioned about his mail-order clothing and household goods catalogue – The Solon Society Journal – which was posted to American Watch Tower subscribers each month throughout 1905, he said he could not remember anything about it. However, Christine Weir, a former Bible Student, testified that she 'saw [the mail-order catalogue] being wrapped in the same packages as the Watch Tower magazine and taken over to the post office'.

Maria's affidavit further stated: 'Mr. Russell is profiting from the Watchtower Society personally' and claimed that in 1906 he had made a profit of $20,000 from the publication of the Watchtower magazine and $31,300 from book sales, in addition to $65,261 in donations and 'at least $5,000 profit on the bookstore'. This was on top of an unspecified gain from investments in his holding company, the U.S.I.C.

Unconvinced by Charles Russell's counter claims of poor memory and financial naivety, the Court awarded Maria alimony of $100 a month. The Pastor was totally unprepared for such check-mate financial humiliation, so sure was he of his own probity. When he realised that he had been financially compromised by the 'qualified divorce' he immediately launched an appeal before setting off on a speaking tour.

Upon his return to Allegheny toward the end of the summer, he was going through his mail bag when a letter from New York caught his attention. The correspondent was a member of the legal profession – one Judge Joseph F. Rutherford – who described himself as a Bible Student of some twelve years standing having been formally 'baptised into the truth' the previous year along with his wife and young son. All three of them were now looking to serve the Lord full-time. Would the Pastor be so gracious as to suggest in what capacity their various abilities and talents could best be employed in this regard? Pastor Russell replied at once, inviting Rutherford to visit him at the Allegheny Bible House at a mutually convenient time.

Judge Rutherford's personal recollections of his initial encounter with Pastor Russell were originally published in The Springfield Press, Missouri and later reprinted in the Bible Students Souvenir Convention Report, 1913. Thus, we can eavesdrop, word for word (according to Rutherford), on that meeting of minds and of men.

From the start a firm handshake would have signalled an unspoken affinity between the two. The Judge mentioned he had once given up on religion altogether just a few weeks after getting married because his Baptist minister had told him that his future wife would be going to hell because she had not been immersed, and that he would be going to heaven because he had been. 'It all but swept my reverence for religion into oblivion.' he confessed. 'My logical mind revolted, and I became an atheist. I felt that my wife was, in many ways, better than me, and worthier of the love of God and men and the reward of heaven.'

'It is seldom a man is found who has drifted into agnosticism or atheism from religion and who then regains his confidence in religion' replied the Pastor. 'Religion should not be and really is not a matter of sentiment, but a matter of reason, specially is this true when the individual concerned has a mathematical and logical mind instead of the sentimental mind peculiar to most religionists.'

'I owe my present knowledge of the Bible and love for the Lord to you, and I thank you for it,' the Judge replied. 'If you had presented religion as a mere theory, I would have had nothing to do with it. I was satisfied long before I ever read any of your writings that that which cannot satisfy the mind has no right to satisfy the heart. I was determined to ascertain if you, whose pen has made clear the reasonableness of the highest standards I have ever read, were as the Scribes and Pharisees of olden times. I was determined to know whether you were a doer of what you teach or whether you were merely a preacher of it.'

'My private investigation was not made hastily. I have spent some years at it. I dug up every record I could find. Some of these records were made by your enemies – and I've never known any great man who had true friends and did not have some enemies – and as I investigated every charge or complaint made by them, they yielded the same testimony when sifted to the bottom. No sane mind could therefore doubt the truth thereof – that you surely must be one of the cleanest men, both morally and intellectually it has been my pleasure to encounter.'

'We are not trying to convert the world,' replied the Pastor. 'We do not believe the Scriptures teach the conversion of the world . . . On the other hand, it is quite evident that there are men and women of all nations who are so thoroughly consecrated to their Lord that they are willing to give up all things to obtain the promises set forth in the Scriptures. It is to these we appeal.' As a lawyer, and as a man,' said Rutherford, 'it seems to me that the association of brothers which is now stretching around the world, using as its textbooks the Studies in the Scriptures, must constitute the greatest theological school the world at present knows.'

The Judge's favourable summing up evidently went down well with the Pastor for some weeks later the persuasive lawyer, along with his wife Mary and son Malcolm – who would later become Russell's personal stenographer – moved into the Allegheny Bible House. Once they had settled in enthusiastic introductions were exchanged in the communal dining room when it was announced that Judge Rutherford had been appointed as Legal Advisor to the Watch Tower Society.

The advocate and the preacher got on well together, the brusque analytical approach of one complementing the somewhat gentler polemic of the other. They enjoyed their regular dining-table discussions and the two became close friends, crusaders for truth in a world of sceptics, evolutionists and religionists who had lost hope. Judge Rutherford immersed himself in his new brief – representing righteousness itself – and soon afterwards began giving public talks. He also penned Man's Salvation from a Lawyer's Viewpoint, which found its way into print courtesy of Pastor Russell who subsequently convinced himself that spiritual forces were at work in his choice of associates. Indeed, he came to rely rather too much on the worldly wisdom of his trusted advocate.

***

The Russell v Russell appeal was argued on May 7th, 1908. A propensity for letter writing and methodically documenting almost any trivial event in his life, even to the extent of publishing his domestic marital problems in the pages of Zion's Watch Tower, was to be Charles Russell's downfall. Judgement was made by the Superior Court of Pennsylvania on October 12th, 1908, when Mr. Justice Orlady summed up:

'After a careful review of the 150 pages of testimony in this case, we are satisfied that the verdict was fully warranted, and was rightly sustained by refusing the defendant's motion . . . In an analysis of the testimony, it is quite difficult to understand the view of the respondent regarding his duty as a husband . . . From his whole testimony, he was right in reaching the conclusion stated by him in a letter to his wife, to wit: "I conclude that I am adapted to no one, and that no one is adapted to me, except the Lord. I am thankful that [we] understand each other and have confidence in each other."'

The Court once again ruled in Maria's favour and the original judgement was upheld. Determined not to pay a cent more than he was already paying, the Pastor turned to Judge Rutherford for advice. The legal sophist then hatched a plan of financial consolidation whereby Charles Russell would donate all his property holdings and personal assets to the Watchtower Society then legally declare himself to be a penniless $10 a month live-in Bible Student. As such he would be rendered lawfully incapable of paying his ex-wife the increase in alimony.

The Pastor's hollow plea was subsequently ignored by the Pennsylvanian authorities who informed the recalcitrant divorcee that he could be jailed for failing to comply with the Court Order. Judge Rutherford then came up with what the beleaguered Pastor thought was an inspired solution to the problem: relocation. The entire Watchtower enterprise would move to another State out of the jurisdiction of the Pennsylvanian courts.

Alternative accommodation for Pastor Russell and his live-in staff of 30 was soon located in New York City. Home was now 124 Columbia Heights, the former parsonage of Congregationalist clergyman and writer Henry Ward Beecher who, in 1874, had also faced a charge of adultery, but which was not proven. The Watchtower Society also acquired Beecher's Plymouth Congregational Church in Brooklyn which was subsequently renamed the Brooklyn Tabernacle. No sooner had he settled in when a reporter from the Brooklyn Eagle appeared on his doorstep.

When he was asked whether the removal of the headquarters of the Watchtower Society to Brooklyn was coincident with the hearing, before Judges Brown and Ford in Pittsburgh, to have him jailed, Russell replied: 'I did not leave because I was afraid to be put in jail. I told the court I could not pay it and, so they are now trying to put me in jail for contempt. Well, I am not afraid. If they want me back in Pittsburgh, I will go. But I do not intend to pay more than the $40 a month. The decree was granted in her favour, not so much because I was cruel, it was only that the jury believed that we could not live together happily anymore anyway. All men are influenced by a pretty woman's charms. Since then, she has been persecuting me in every possible way . . . Ah, it is too bad . . . before she became a suffragist, she was an ideal wife. I might say she was as perfect as it is possible for anyone to be.'

The April 15th, 1909, issue of Zion's Watch Tower was the first to carry the new address of Russell's organisation. A copy soon fell into Maria's hands, and it was not long before the Brooklyn Eagle, hungry for a story, was once again perched outside 124 Columbia Heights. 'If I were to die tomorrow, I think my former wife would soon follow me, for she could not live long unless she had me to nag,'[68] said the runaway preacher.

***

Following his second visit to the Great Pyramid of Giza in 1910 Pastor Russell journeyed on to England. With the scandal of his divorce now behind him, a politically restrained Fleet Street press and a socially blinkered British society, still confined to Victorian attitudes, afforded the American preacher a God-given opportunity to re-establish himself as an unblemished spiritual messenger to the British public.

A London office – The Pastor Russell Lecture Bureau (Thanet House, 231 The Strand, London W.C.) – had been set up to syndicate his sermons to British newspapers and periodicals on a quid pro quo arrangement, advertising space being taken on the understanding that favourable reviews (puffs) of his activities would appear as spontaneous editorial comment. Within a year no less than 300 national dailies and provincial weeklies throughout the British Isles expediently increased their advertising revenues in this way. A typical example appeared in Christian Globe, an independent weekly journal: 'Pastor Russell is now on his way to London having just revisited the Pyramids and Palestine. It is expected that his recent investigations will have much to do in still

---

[68] Brooklyn Eagle – May 4, 1909.

further unsealing the mysteries which for centuries have been kept secret by that "Stone Witness" . . . having been to Jerusalem during the recent Passover week, Mr Russell will now be in position to speak with added knowledge regarding the work of the Zionists.'

Huge numbers of nominal Christians in Britain at that time wanted to know more and from the moment the doors opened on the 8th of May 1910, the cavernous Royal Albert Hall began to fill up. At 7.30 p.m. Pastor Russell appeared to sustained applause as he took his seat on the platform where he was flanked by his American entourage and a group of elders representing the London Bible Students. The subject for Russell's talk was The Great Hereafter and the mood of the 7,500-capacity crowd was to listen intently for King Edward VII had died the previous day.

A commanding chord from the great organ then set the tone of the gathering when everyone fell silent as the Chairman, brother Sawyer (an old soldier, nick-named 'the colonel') stepped forward. 'I have much pleasure in introducing to you tonight Pastor Russell of Brooklyn Tabernacle, New York. He is a well-known preacher of the Gospel and author of that great work known as Studies in the Scriptures. It is a work that has been translated into seventeen different languages and read by thousands in different parts of the Empire with gratitude . . . Pastor Russell will now address you on the subject already announced, The Great Hereafter:'

'It was in Germany that I heard of the death of your esteemed monarch, Edward VII. I realised that not only your nation, but all Christendom had lost an unobtrusive but wise counsellor, a power for peace and goodwill among men. I take this opportunity to express to this great audience my sympathy, which, I assure you, is shared by many of my American countrymen. There is, thank God, a 'hereafter' for kings as well as for peasants, and royal mourners and a mourning nation need the message from God's Word, particularly now. And since no more representative audience will probably assemble in this capitol of the Empire, I have a suggestion to offer which I trust will meet with your approval. It is that before offering prayer we show our sympathy for the royal family in their bereavement by standing.'

With that, the great organ pealed out the opening chords of what was said to be the deceased King's favourite hymn – Nearer my God to Thee – as the entire concourse rose to the comforting sounds of the familiar sacred music. The sombre crowd then sang along earnestly with the assembled choir. This was followed by a brief prayer in which the Pastor mentioned the Royal Family. His sentiments were endorsed by an emotional 'Amen' from everyone present. Thus primed, the vast audience listened with rapt attention to the visiting savant as he paced about the platform embracing the whole audience with his candour and sincerity.

Eloquent and gentle in his reasoning, but not averse to keen and cutting directness when commenting on the Catholic and Lutheran churches, the out-spoken Pastor spelled out his objections to church creeds in general with a slew of biblical quotations to argue his point: 'While the Bible shows, and all the creeds confess, that only a 'little flock' will be joint-heirs in the Kingdom with Christ, nevertheless there is another salvation which is for the world, an earthly salvation in contrast with the heavenly one, a restitution to mental, moral and physical perfection, to be attained during the thousand years of Messiah's reign in glory, for which we pray, thy kingdom come, thy will be done on earth as it is in heaven.'

With just four years to go before Armageddon was expected to strike, there were now some five thousand active Bible Students in Britain. The majority were concentrated in the London area with numerous smaller 'classes' of believers scattered throughout the land, most particularly in the coal-mining communities of South Wales. In those desperate days, almost every Welsh town and village had its own local community of International Bible Students. Impoverished families who were struggling against economic odds would sometimes take to the hills where they held open-air meetings to pray for the 'new heavens and new earth' that would sweep away the cruel poverty that plagued their hungry lives.

Throughout Britain Russell's itinerant colporteurs had now sold more than 130,000 volumes in the Studies in the Scriptures series. Just like their American counterparts and others elsewhere in the world, they undertook this work voluntarily as and when they could, travelling from town to town calling on householders with the Watchtower – a godsend of a magazine they so wanted to share with others. They were compared to the Lollards – followers of Wycliffe in the Middle-Ages who were known as God's Glee-men – because they went about with happy faces singing praises to God as they trudged from door to door with their message of hope.

***

Flushed with the success of his campaign in Britain Pastor Russell returned to New York claiming, 'a person would go into darkness after two years of reading the Bible alone [but] would be in the light reading the Studies in the Scriptures alone'. Judging by the huge numbers of agreeable letters in his postbag, his enchanted followers thought so too. However, it was an entirely unexpected letter among them that caught his attention.

Dear Sir: Your sympathetic interest in the Jewish people for years past has not escaped our notice. You may well understand how surprised we are to find a Christian minister acknowledging that there are prophecies of the Bible still unfulfilled, which belong to the Jew and not the Christian, and that these prophecies, according to your studies, are nearing a fulfilment of momentous interest to our Jewish race and, through us as a people, to the nations of the world . . .These things, Pastor Russell, have led to the formation of a Jewish Mass Meeting Committee, which, by this letter, requests you to give a public discourse, especially to our people. We suggest Sunday afternoon at 3 o'clock, October 9. We have secured an option on the Hippodrome, New York's largest and finest auditorium, for that date, and we hope that this date and the place will be agreeable to your convenience. We assure you also of a large audience of deeply interested Hebrews, besides the public.

During the week preceding Russell's agreed appearance at the Hippodrome Theatre thousands of copies of a special promotional newspaper, printed in both English and Yiddish, appeared on the news-stands claiming, 'Pastor Russell is going to try to convert the Jews to Christianity'. When the time came an inquisitive crowd of, mainly Jews, filtered into the opera house. Among them were scores of rabbis and teachers who had come to hear what a Gentile might have to say to them during Rosh Hashanah, their week of feasting and celebration when, they believed, the fate of every Jew would be decided for the coming year. Then there were the sceptics and doubters; hostile and simmering, ready to boil over should Pastor Russell seek to convert them. Many prominent figures from the Hebrew literary world were also present, some of whom had escorted the controversial preacher to the theatre in a head-turning 'automobile' before taking their places in the auditorium.

No symbol of any religion greeted the curious assembly when they gazed beyond the silent orchestra pit which lined the Hippodrome's deserted stage, now temporarily stripped of its operatic grandeur. With the house lights fully up there was a stark and dusty bareness about the place. A small round table stood on a patch of carpeting toward the front of the proscenium arch from which hung three peace flags. There were no preliminaries and without introduction Pastor Russell, tall, erect, and white-bearded, strode purposefully across the stage and placed a Bible on the table. Moments later a double quartet from the Brooklyn Tabernacle filed on-stage and sang, quite unexpectedly, the Jewish hymn Zion's Glad Day before leaving the stage in silence.

Undaunted by the alienating atmosphere Russell picked up the Bible from the table: 'I will read in your hearing from the Holy Scriptures, Leeser's translation, the Hebrew version.' After reading a selection of familiar verses from the Old Testament Prophets,[69] the Pastor launched into his talk: 'My Jewish friends and others: I have pleasure in being before you today. I am here because of your invitation, for which I thank you. I am pleased to have an opportunity of speaking to my Jewish friends and neighbours in this city.' He then referred to the Russian pogroms and described in macabre detail the 'recent demonic conduct of the so-called Christians of Rumania', emphasising that such atrocities were inconsistent with his brand of Christianity.

'When we come to see what our God is doing, then there is a great sympathetic bond I believe between every intelligent Jew and every intelligent Christian. We have one God, the Father of all, and we have one hope in his glorious plan, and the glorious hope of this plan is all centred in the Messiah that has been promised to the Jews these 3,500 years since the day of Abraham. To my understanding, dear friends, the Scriptures are very clear in their statement that this New Covenant will be for Israel only and that all the nations of the world, if they desire to receive the blessings of that covenant, must come to Israel, so that during the reign of Messiah, which will be for a thousand years, all nations will eventually come to be part of Israel . . . I stand for the Bible, and the Bible stands for Israel, and therefore I stand for Israel . . .'

A ripple of applause was heard as glances were exchanged throughout the auditorium. Soon, everyone was applauding. Russell then talked about Theodor Herzl (1860-1904) who advocated the formation of a Jewish state and convened the first Zionist Congress at Basel in 1897: 'God has raised up for you [this] great leader. Through his efforts the attention of the whole world has been attracted to Palestine, and to the Jews, and to the original covenant. It is not necessary for me to tell you that the Zionist movement has reached practically its limit. What then? Should you feel discouraged? I say that this is NOT the time for discouragement. This is the very time for encouragement!'

---

[69] Micah 3: 1-7; Ezekiel 16: 60-63; Isaiah 40: 1,2.

This drew sustained applause punctuated by agreeable shouts of approval. From that moment on the enraptured audience hung on to every word as the famous orator hailed the Jews as one of the bravest races on earth and boldly predicted that before long, they – God's Chosen People, Israel – would come to the fore in world affairs. He then explained his interpretation of Nebuchadnezzar's dream, as described by the prophet Daniel:

'The seven Times, or years, of Gentile domination, reckoned on the basis suggested in the Scriptures themselves, should be interpreted a day for a year, lunar time. Seven years in lunar time would represent 2,520 days; and these symbolically interpreted, would mean 2,520 years . . . so far as I have been able to determine, the year of Zedekiah's dethronement was 606 B.C. Thus calculated, the 2,520 years Gentile lease of power will expire in October 1914. When that time of trouble comes over Christendom, over the civilised world, a great many of the wealthy Jews will go back to Palestine . . . At that time, according to the Scriptures, your ancient Worthies, your saintly ones, Abraham, Isaac, Jacob, David . . . will appear as perfect men . . .'

At the end of his talk Russell acknowledged the prolonged applause as the Tabernacle Choir filed on-stage once more. 'It has been suggested,' he said, 'and I think it a good plan my dear friends, that we close this service by the singing of a hymn: Hatikva – Our Hope, which I understand you are well acquainted with. For a moment or two the audience remained impassive. Then a great cheer went up as the tearfully delighted Jewish assembly began to sing along with the Gentile choir:

So long the ancient fires blaze, In ev'ry staunch Jewish soul,
And Eastward we longingly gaze, Toward Zion, beloved goal
Not lost is our hope of old, Graven in our hearts so deep,
To return to that land foretold, where our loved sires sleep.

As the emotional singing enthusiasm was at its height, and before the anthem had ended, Charles Russell quietly left the stage to stunning effect, his timing perfect. Afterwards he was warmly congratulated by many of those who had come to carp and to criticise; he had made a friend, they all declared, of everyone who had heard him that day.

***

Three days later Russell left New York for a nation-wide tour of the British Isles beginning with another series of appearances at London's Royal Albert Hall where, for three Sundays in succession, thousands crowded in to hear him speak on God's Message to the Jews and God's Message to Christendom. He then toured the country prior to sailing across the Irish Sea to Belfast and Dublin before returning to London to address a Bible Students convention which was held in Whitefield's Old Tabernacle in City Road, where George Whitefield and John Wesley had preached in the 18th century.

Charles Russell now felt the time had come to raise the profile of his Watch Tower Society in Great Britain. Perhaps the eight mutually independent self-governing groups of Bible Students located in the metropolis at the time could now unite to form a much larger and more conspicuous congregation, he suggested to Jesse Hemery. What was needed was an appropriate building located in an area 'of good tone' in central London.

In the autumn of 1910, Craven Hill Congregational Chapel, a Nonconformist place of worship dating from the late 18th century, came up for sale. A viewing was arranged. The building was situated in Bayswater, a favoured residential area adjacent to Hyde Park. Russell looked no further and made an immediate decision to buy the empty 1200 seat chapel. He also purchased a fifty-year leasehold on the adjoining Mansion House (34, Craven Terrace, Bayswater) which later became the London headquarters of the International Bible Students Association. Additionally, Jesse Hemery was granted the right to live in designated 'bed and board' quarters in the Mansion House 'in perpetuity'. There were no conditions attached to the enduring legality of the document to which the Pastor and his grateful disciple put their hand.

Following a winter of renovation and redecoration the old chapel, now renamed the London Tabernacle, was ready for use with the inaugural meeting being held on April 3rd, 1911, with Pastor Russell officiating. It soon attracted regular gatherings of about 800 worshippers at a time. Attendance continued to increase until it peaked, when the Great War was at its height in 1916, with almost 1,500 worshippers at a time packed into the church every Sunday. During those dark days of the conflict, it was the biggest congregation of Bible Students in the world having 19 elders and more than 50 deacons serving the varied interests and undertakings of an active and expectant British Bible Student community.

From 1910 onwards, Russell's followers the world over were identified as associates of the London-based International Bible Students Association, not the American Watchtower Bible & Tract Society. However, it was not until June 30, 1914, that the IBSA was formally incorporated in London under the Companies Act of 1908 with Charles Taze Russell as its President and Jesse Hemery as Vice-president. Two other trustees – H.J. Shearn (Secretary) and W. Crawford (Treasurer) – completed the board of directors. This, in effect, put the entire work in Britain under the direct control of the British Bible Students subject to the paternal oversight of Pastor Russell who provided the literature (at a price).

With British autonomy in sight, all four men were close associates strongly united in purpose. William Crawford was a well-respected Bible Student of nearly thirty years standing while Henry Shearn was a London businessman who had first read the Divine Plan of the Ages in 1906 and consequently initiated a close correspondence with Pastor Russell, entertaining him at his London home in 1909.

Because of that intimate meeting, Shearn sold up his business, donated a substantial sum of money to the Watchtower Society and settled his family in a cottage in Somerset while he took up the colporteur service travelling the country and spreading Russell's message. In March 1911 he returned to London with his wife to reside at the Mansion House living and working alongside bachelor Jesse Hemery and Scotsman William Crawford and his wife.

Shortly after the inauguration of the London Tabernacle the Lord Mayor of London, Sir T. Vezey Strong, donned his official robes of purple and gold to preside over a widely publicised Peace Meeting at the Guildhall in the city. There were speeches by Mr. Asquith the Premier and A. J. Balfour, leader of the opposition, welcoming the proposal of the President of the United States in favour of a general treaty between that country and the British Empire to promote peace in the world.

Among the distinguished guests who accepted invitations to attend were the Archbishop of Canterbury, the Chief Rabbi, and the President of the Free Church Council. In addition to the 800 or so 'men only' members of the public witnessing the proceedings, more than forty dignitaries, including Pastor Russell, sat beneath the British and American flags to hear and applaud the speakers.

Prior to the commencement of the meeting, Russell had mingled freely with the high and the mighty of the day and, with a discreet handshake, was warmly greeted by those who were members of the

Brotherhood, among them, Rabbi Bramwell Booth, who introduced the 'Christian Zionist' to Mr. Balfour. Russell was delighted to learn that the Scottish statesman and philosopher shared his belief in the inevitability of a national home in Palestine for the world's Jews.

'I am proud to think,' said Mayor Strong in opening the meeting, 'that this great assembly not only represents our ancient city in all its greatness of commercial developments and civic achievements but is also graced with the presence of leaders of the statesmanship and religious sentiment of the land, and the active encouragement of responsible and duly accredited representatives of every portion of the Empire.'[70] It was a showcase moment of civilised debate in a politically unstable world already divided by ancient religious demarcations. For Pastor Russell, rubbing shoulders with some of the most influential political and religious leaders of the time, it was a sure sign that God's blessing was upon his work in Great Britain.

---

[70] Daily Mirror, April 29, 1911.

Chapter Eight

MIRACLES AND ORACLES

Upon his return to New York, in the spring of 1911, Pastor Russell learned, to his dismay, that a change of address two years earlier had not placed him outside the parameters of the American Constitution after all. The law finally caught up with the Brooklyn resident when Judge Macfarlane of the Court of Common Pleas in Pennsylvania ruled yet again in Maria's favour. In his summing up, he concluded that Charles Russell's course of conduct toward his wife evidenced 'such insistent egotism, extravagant self-praise and continual arrogant domination that would necessarily render the life of any sensitive Christian woman a burden and make her condition intolerable. No error being found in the record, the assignments of error are overruled, and the judgement is affirmed.'

Charles Russell was now obliged to comply with the original court order to support his ex-wife with a monthly allowance of one-hundred dollars, which was backdated more than two years. Under Pennsylvanian Law, Maria Russell was also granted an attachment against some of their jointly owned property which was transferred by her ex-husband to the Watchtower Bible and Tract Society 'for the purpose, as charged, of defrauding his wife'. Taking the attachment ruling into consideration, the court awarded Maria an immediate cash payment of $9,000.

Commenting on the case, the Brooklyn Eagle reported: '. . . extracts from the minute books of this society, which were obtained by court order, show "Pastor" Russell's success in getting liberal donations from his women followers . . . his business has expanded to an extent that is little less than marvellous, and clearly shows the enormous earning power of this extraordinary preacher. He has extended his operations until they cover every State in the Union as well as most countries in Europe. His employees are now numbered by the hundred and the output of his advertising plant on Hicks Street exceeds that of the largest business institutions in Brooklyn.'

Russell ignored his critics and launched an advertising campaign for Miracle Wheat, a biological curiosity which had been discovered back in 1904 by a farmer in Fincastle, Virginia. It was claimed that a single stalk of this remarkable plant could produce an abundance of up to 142 heads of grain. To the Pastor, it was a sign from Jehovah: 'In this natural way God is preparing for the Millennium, when the earth shall yield her increase.'[71]

One of Russell's followers – J. A. Bohnet, a farmer – had subsequently acquired thirty bushels of the grain at his own expense and donated them to the Watchtower Society. The Miracle Wheat was then sold on as seed grain at 'a dollar a pound' through the columns of the Watchtower magazine throughout the summer of 1911. At that time regular wheat usually sold for less than a dollar a bushel but Watchtower readers, eager for a taste of what was to come in the approaching New World, were more than happy to pay sixty times the market price for a commodity that eventually proved to be nothing more than a mutant strain of wheat that soon lost its alleged potential. By then the Watchtower Society had netted a profit of $1,800.

The Brooklyn Eagle seized upon the miracle wheat claim as a preposterous moneymaking scam, an absurd story without a grain of truth in it. In a sarcastic press report that cast doubts on his morality Charles Russell was ridiculed as the 'phoney Pastor' and criticised as a sharp businessman of dubious intent. On Judge Rutherford's advice Russell promptly sued the editor and the proprietors of the Brooklyn Eagle for libel, demanding $100,000 in damages. He then lodged a written declaration of his innocence with the Commissioner of Deeds in New York:

'In view of my soon departure for a foreign shore, and in view of the increasing virulence and threats of my enemies, and under the assumption that they may await my absence to make a fresh attack, by advice of my counsel I make under oath the following sweeping statement; namely, 'That I never was guilty of immorality toward any person. Furthermore, I never cohabited with any person at any time and, furthermore, I have never desired to do so.'

***

Cold November was in the air when Pastor Russell, refreshed and invigorated after yet another lecture tour of Britain, returned to New York. He felt even more pleased with himself when he learned that Judge Rutherford had persuaded a coterie of wealthy female Bible Students to meet his domestic obligations toward his ex-wife without compromising the finances of the Watchtower Society. However, while he had been abroad, lecturing the British on their future, the Brooklyn Eagle had been busy digging up his past.

---

[71] Watchtower. – October 1, 1908.

Some years previously the entrepreneurial Pastor came up with the idea of selling burial plots to the faithful when an attractive parcel of land, just beyond the city limits, came up for sale. Russell paid $27,000 to acquire the property for the Peoples Pulpit Association, a separate publishing corporation affiliated to the Watchtower Society, before selling it on to the United States Investment Company (a dummy corporation within the Watchtower Society conglomerate) for $30,000.

Charles Russell then created another company – Rosemount Hope and Evergreen United Cemeteries – and appointed one of his low-profile followers, J.C. Messner, as president of its Board of Trustees. In some way not clearly explained, Russell's new cemetery was supposed to benefit poor people, a somewhat nebulous intent which encouraged some of his followers to mislead and persuade four eminent Pittsburgh clergymen into lending their names to the project.

A front page report in the Brooklyn Eagle described in detail how Russell managed to dupe the clerics into 'advocating a dubious business venture involving a variety of dummy transactions that would do credit to a Wall Street banking expert: So cleverly did Russell manipulate the deal that the clergymen, who represented the Episcopalian and Presbyterian churches, and who were bitterly opposed to Russell's teaching and methods accepted positions as trustees on the Russell cemetery before they found out'.

Among the impressive Board of Trustees featured on the official stationery was a Mr. C. T. Russell (minus his assumed clerical status), Also listed were nine Bible Students (unidentified as such) along with Bishop Cortland Whitehead; the Rev. S. Edward Young; Dr B. F. Woodburn and the Rev. J. W. Witherspoon, thereby adding a touch of mainstream religious acceptability to the enterprise.

Brother Messner's presidency of Rosemount was short lived; so was his faith in the Watchtower Society: 'Russell told me to act as Treasurer and President to the board of trustees. The business was all done somewhere else. Then one-day Russell telephoned me: "Messner," he said, "I know you're a busy man, I've got a girl in the office here who can handle the money . . . just send me a cheque for what money you have on hand, and I'll take care of the business from now on." I sent him a cheque for several hundred dollars.'

According to the Eagle report it was this telephone call that helped open the whistle-blower's eyes. When asked what had become of the property, the former Bible Student replied: 'I believe it is being run by some of Russell's local representatives. I understand they are selling many lots and doing quite a business. It has a beautiful location and probably was a good investment.'

Russell's personal interest in the enterprise amounted to 990 one-dollar shares of the $1,000 capital with two of his followers holding the other $10 worth. Upon being shown a dispatch of the Eagle investigation into Russell's affairs prior to its publication the Rev. S. Edward Young, Pastor of the Bedford Presbyterian Church in New York City, promptly wrote out a statement of disassociation:

'I recall that several years ago I was asked to serve as trustee of a new cemetery, the Rosemount Hope and Evergreen United cemeteries, and that Bishop Whitehead of the Protestant Episcopal Church, diocese of Pittsburgh, Dr Woodburn, Pastor of the First Baptist Church, Allegheny and other ministers and laymen well known to me, were to be fellow trustees. Upon being persuaded the enterprise was hardly the sort of one I had been assured it would be I served notice that my name should be dropped from the list of trustees.'[72]

Two weeks before Christmas the Brooklyn Eagle filed its answer to Russell's bill of complaint and publicly accused him of persuading 'great numbers of persons' to donate their property to the Watchtower Society in anticipation of the end of the material world: 'Much of the money that has been received in this way has been invested in real estate, mining stocks and various speculative enterprises, the investments having been made in the name of dummy corporations, partnerships and associations, or through other persons acting as secret representatives of 'dummies' for the plaintiff [whose] operations have extended until they cover every State in the United States as well as many countries in Europe . . . the religious cult is nothing more than a money-making scheme.'[73]

On Boxing Day, the Brooklyn Eagle continued its rant against Russell with a selection of letters from readers, including one from a Mr A.C. Bull of 25, Fairland Road, Stratford, London, England.

'Pastor Russell has a good following in this country and has deluded thousands of followers into believing that Christ returned to this earth in 1874 . . . many have gone so far as to sell up their homes over here, expecting to die before 1914 . . . I was related with his movement for twelve years, but my eyes, thank God, have been opened. When one

[72] Brooklyn Eagle – November 10, 1911.

[73] Brooklyn Eagle – December 9, 1911.

leaves their society, because of enlightenment, Mr. Russell at once advises his followers to shun such a one and counsels his followers never to read anything emanating from any other source but his own pen! I could write you for a week telling of the bitterness and sorrow that this man Russell has left in many a Christian home here in England.'[74]

When a reader challenged the newspaper to account for Pastor Russell's phenomenal success, despite all the criticism, the editor replied: 'That is easy. P.T. Barnum said that people liked to be fooled; and he knew, because he had fooled them for many years and in many ways. Barnum was only a showman and fooling people was his business . . . they enjoyed it. But it is a very evil thing if the man who is fooling the people in that way believes his own teachings, as Mr. Russell presumably does, that makes him only the more dangerous.'

Russell ignored the press criticism of his Miracle Wheat and a couple of weeks later he was offering Watchtower readers 'prolific beans' for seed: 'Sister Smith, of Nebraska, recently discovered one stalk of beans which she declares yielded so prolifically that she calls it the Millennial Bean. She desires to get the beans into the hands of others, and at the same time donate to our Tract Fund for the sending forth of free spiritual food to the hungry. Accordingly, the beans have been sent to our office. We believe the project quite a proper one, and if the beans be as prolific elsewhere as in Nebraska, we would be glad to purchase them at the rate of five beans for one dollar. (We have heard of seed wheat selling at one dollar per grain.) However, in view of unfriendly criticism of enemies, we think it best not to sell these beans, but to give them free to our subscribers who have gardens, and who will request them – five beans each.'[75]

The determined preacher then set out on a tour of the Far East. But on this occasion advance purchasing of advertising space on the usual quid pro quo basis did not always go to plan, especially if the Brooklyn Eagle had swooped in first. Despite extensive local billboard postings and press advertising the turnout for his public address at the Manila Opera House was disappointingly low. The following day the Manila Times accused Russell of 'accumulating wealth at the expense of the ignorant,' and justified its stance with an account of its dealings with Russell's press agent: '. . . money was deposited along with several

[74] Brooklyn Eagle – December 26, 1911.
[75] Watch Tower – January 15, 1912.

laudatory articles ('puffs') for publication as editorial comment. After the advance agent had left the city the attention of this paper was called to the fact that there was another side to "Pastor" Russell's propaganda.'

Upon his return to New York the roving preacher was accused of 'delivering sermons to imaginary audiences on tropical islands' and undertaking 'searching investigations into the missions of China and Japan by spending a few hours in each country.' He was also greeted with the news that his libel action against the Brooklyn Eagle had come to nothing. Judge Rutherford blamed the 'letter-writing clergy, atheist journalists and certain known Catholics' who were involved in the court proceedings.

Impervious to criticism, Russell continued promoting his millennial products and miraculous cures in his magazine: 'Once we put into The Watchtower a notice about Miracle Wheat. We believe we did right in putting that notice in. We also put in a notice about beans. Last year we offered our readers a few grains each from a wonderful stalk of cotton seven feet high, bearing hundreds of bolls. The only conditions were that they should send us one-half the seed of their crop, keeping the remainder for their own use. As a result, we have received some sixty or seventy pounds of cotton seed. We will be pleased to send this to cotton-growers, giving a preference to those whose names are found on the Watchtower mailing lists. We also put in a notice recently about a cure for cancer . . . and a great many have reported good results. People saw that we were not trying to get their money, saw that we were trying to do them good.'

Chapter Nine

IMAGES OF PARADISE

Tension was mounting in Europe in 1912. In response to a continuing German naval build-up Britain had withdrawn her battleships from the Mediterranean and placed them on patrol in the North Sea. The action followed the breakdown of Anglo-German talks aimed at slowing down the rate of expansion of the two countries' navies. Germany had suggested a 'mutual declaration of neutrality' but Britain turned the proposal down fearing it would endanger relations with France and Russia. Meanwhile the Russians, alarmed by the situation in the Balkans, were busy mobilising troops in Warsaw.

In Britain militant suffragettes, led by Emmeline Pankhurst, continued their struggle for equality as they rampaged through the streets of London smashing windows of smart West-End stores. Groups of women struck simultaneously and without warning, leaving behind a trail of destruction that stretched across the city centre. Number 10, Downing Street was targeted by Mrs. Pankhurst who threw stones at the Prime minister's residence and broke windows on both sides of the famous front door.

Following a transport strike, which had brought the United Kingdom to a standstill in May, the government was also beset with problems in Ireland where 120,000 Protestant members of Ulster's Orange Order rallied protesting against Home Rule for Catholic Ireland. On the domestic front, an official report by Sir George Newman, Chief Medical Officer for schools, showed that 500,000 British children were 'ill-fed, diseased and un-hygienically dirty'.

The following year in London a peace treaty, dated May 30, 1913, was signed at St. James's Palace by Turkey and her erstwhile enemies of the Balkan League only to be torn up just two months later when Bulgaria turned on her allies in their war with Turkey and marched against Serbia. The Greeks, also attacked by the Bulgarians, allied themselves with the Serbs and Romanians. Montenegrin forces were then expected to join the battle against the Bulgarians. Then Turkey became involved as the Czar of Russia attempted to bring the warring countries to arbitration. Convinced they were living through the 'great tribulation' prior to Armageddon, Russell's Bible Students on both sides of the Atlantic took heart at such depressing news.

***

The growing popularity of 'motion-pictures' as an entertainment form fascinated Charles Russell and he was intrigued when he read press reports of immigrants learning English by reading subtitles out loud in the movie-showing arcades in Manhattan's Lower East Side. He also noted that as in Europe the audiences for these Vaudeville's of Motion Pictures were predominantly working-class people – the very ones he wanted to reach out to. At that time there were an estimated 10,000 'Nickelodeons' (arcades where movies could be seen for a nickel) across America attracting 26 million people each week, about 20 percent of the population at that time.

Thomas Edison had joined forces in 1908 with the Biograph Company to form the Motion Picture Patents Company to centralise control of the fledgling industry. However, following a court decision early in 1912 which disallowed one of its key patent holdings, it was subsequently declared a monopoly and eventually disbanded. This opened the market and Russell, forever on the lookout for new and innovative ways to reach out and communicate with the masses, seized the moment.

He was intrigued when he read reports in the New York press of a 'demonstration of talking motion pictures' to be given by inventor Thomas Alva Edison at his West Orange, New Jersey laboratory. The process reportedly utilised a device which was 'part camera and part phonograph enabling picture and sound to be recorded simultaneously while actors moved about freely'. Edison had been working on his latest project for two years and stated that he hoped it would be in use in theatres in another two. Pastor Russell wrote to the famous inventor expressing his admiration and great interest.

Motion picture production was at that time largely based in New York, so the entrepreneurial preacher did not have far to go to locate such pioneering movers and shakers as G.W. (Billy) Bitzer, who went on to become cameraman for legendary filmmaker D.W. Griffiths, and W.K.L Dickson, a former employee of Edison, who was among the first to produce outdoor scenes – 'actualities' – in America and abroad.

It was during a convention of Bible Students in Little Rock, Arkansas in July 1913, that Pastor Russell announced his intended foray into the alien world of show-business. Previously he had condemned the 'prostitution of the ministry of the Gospel' by the established Church which, in his estimation, condoned theatre going (except on Sundays) as an 'uplifting institution' and teaching that 'card playing, novel reading and dancing were not inconsistent with Christian life'. Consequently, delegates at the convention, unaccustomed to whiling away valuable preaching time playing card games, novel reading, going to the theatre or, heaven forbid, patronising the local nickelodeon, were quite taken aback when Pastor Russell explained just how this increasingly popular entertainment form could be viewed as a teaching aid.

After revealing that he had been working on the idea for some years, he quoted from an official report by the National Board of Censorship: 'The motion picture is a form of book, a form of art museum, a method of propaganda, and a method of scientific instruction. It appeals to the interests, where a book may only appeal to the abstract faculties of the mind.' A resolution was then proposed which stated, in part: 'The time has come for the use of moving pictures in teaching Bible truths. The Lord sanctioned this in his use of parables and in the symbols of Revelation, which are word pictures.

The Photo Drama of Creation would feature lantern slides accompanied by specially recorded music and commentary and, most sensational of all, coloured motion pictures with synchronised sound. It is not known who agreed to co-produce and direct the motion-picture segments of Russell's ambitious project, but the allure of an open-ended budget was evidently recognised by an anonymous expert in the field as an opportunity to further experiment in the new art-form without personal risk. It was a reckless financial arrangement on Russell's part and one that would bring the preaching movie producer to his knees.

***

A month later, Pastor Russell set out on what was to be his last overseas tour. He was in conference with his close friend Jesse Hemery, along with William Crawford and Henry Shearn, co-managers of the London Tabernacle when, during a lunchtime meeting in the adjoining mansion house, he appeared to lose the thread of what he was talking about, not once but several times. At first, the interludes of rambling incomprehension were politely and stoically borne by the anxious elders when Russell rose to his feet as if to make a point then slumped to the floor unconscious.

The dead-weight preacher was heaved onto a sofa. Upon coming to he was assured he had just had a dizzy spell. Soon afterwards however, Jessie Hemery arranged a visit to a small private clinic in Harley Street as a precautionary measure, where Russell lapsed into incoherence, once again, before his condition appeared to stabilise.

The patient was confined to his bed for two days before returning to Harley Street with his trusted friend once again where a consultant urologist administered a mercury-based medication as a 'precautionary treatment' for a 'suspected infection' of the urinary tract. Additionally, plenty of rest and a meatless diet were recommended to 'cleanse the blood and address a general physical malaise and attendant mental exhaustion'.[76] Within days a decision was taken to cut short his stay in London and a much-subdued Pastor Russell sailed back home to New York.

As for Jesse Hemery, his allegiance to Russell was tested to the limit and beyond as all kinds of thoughts flashed through his mind. Long forgotten rumours of scandal in the private life of Pastor Russell began to take on a retrospective significance in the light of recent events. Some forty years would pass before he shared his disquiet with the breakaway Bible Students of Britain, recalling how the stricken Pastor had been prescribed laudanum (a tincture of opium), a commonly used remedy of the day 'to ease headaches and general discomfort' and cocaine for his 'general well-being'.[77] Charles Russell, a lifelong teetotaller, followed the doctor's orders religiously, never ate meat again and trustingly took his intoxicating medicine in ever-increasing doses until the day he died.

A Brooklyn Heights doctor was not quite so discreet about the Pastor's rumoured condition. The loose-tongued nonagenarian GP told writer and former Jehovah's Witness Barbara Grizzuti-Harrison that when he was a practising physician, he had prescribed the treatment of the day for suspected syphilis for many of his patients, Charles Taze Russell among them.[78] A London surgeon notes: 'Venereal disease has been no respecter of persons, or religion for that matter. Members of the church have not been immune from venereal disease. Cardinal Wolsey contracted syphilis and it was probably conducive to his death. There were three syphilitic Popes: Alexander vi, Julius ii, and Leo x.'[79]

Commenting on the Pastor Russell affair Dr Michael Waugh, President of the International Union Against Sexually Transmitted

---

[76] From the recollections of Pastor Russell's former close friend and ally in Britain, Jesse Hemery, as recounted by Albert Hudson and William (Bill) Simmons.

[77] Cocaine was a popular pick-me-up and appetite suppresser (slimming aid) for the middle-classes in Britain and America for years before it was banned in the former in 1925. Popes Pius x and Leo xii both drank wine which was laced with Cocaine while Queen Victoria was said to have been quite addicted to the drug, ordering large quantities from her Balmoral pharmacist. In its white powder form, it was usually taken as snuff, perfectly acceptable then, even in the best of circles.

[78] An Accidental Autobiography – Barbara Grizzuti-Harrison, Haughton-Miffin, 1996.

[79] British Journal of Venereal Diseases (1971) – A. Dickson Wright.

Infections, posited: 'The Scottish expression 'not proven' is the phrase to keep in mind with the history of all well-known and not so well-known persons who are alleged to have had syphilis before the present scientific era when we have been able to confirm it with laboratory tests. That is basically for clinical practice from about the time of the first World War onwards. I do realise however, obviously the serology for syphilis came into being in 1906 but there is always a lag period. It is only too easy to implicate the spectrum of venereal diseases on any historical character without always proof . . . the history of Charles Russell is interesting. However, I would not presume to make a diagnosis from that.'[80]

Some doctors' familiar with the history of this disease, which was distressingly common in the 19th century, have noted that high aims and an attendant forcefulness of personality were often characteristic of many disease-driven achievers. Medical opinion has often recognised that in resisting disease sufferers often exert powers they never knew they possessed. In its more advanced stage, the sexually transmitted disease affects the mind, with sufferers experiencing delusory visions of grandeur prior to descending into a condition known as G P I – General Paralysis of the Insane.

The unresolved case of Sir Winston Churchill's father, Lord Randolph Churchill, bears a striking similarity to that of Pastor Russell. In the 19th century Lord Randolph transformed British politics when he created Tory Democracy and became the Chancellor of the Exchequer. He then rocketed to fame before succumbing to an unspecified mental condition which gnawed away at his lucidity and reduced the once articulate and persuasive orator to embarrassing incoherence as a public speaker who insisted on making speeches in the House of Commons although his faculties, unknown to him, were clearly gone. Like Watchtower Society apologists, the Churchill family has always denied that Lord Randolph had contracted syphilis on his stag-night but, as in the case of the controversial 'Pastor', a dark condemning doubt stubbornly lingers.

***

When the New Year of 1914 finally arrived, Charles Russell launched his ambitious Hollywood production in New York's theatre-land. It was to be his swansong, his final presentation of God's plan before the world met its apocalyptic end 'sometime during the autumn' of that very year.

[80] Dr Michael Waugh in correspondence with the author.

Some twelve months earlier he had taken over New York's half-built Playhouse Theatre, which was originally intended to be a permanent home for a stock company headed by actress Mary Shaw (1854-1929) under the direction of actor-manager Butler Davenport (1871-1958). However, after running into financial difficulties, the project was abandoned, and the theatre remained unfinished – until Pastor Russell came on the scene. His off-Broadway screen debut was duly announced in The New York Times: 'The International Bible Students Association will begin to spread the gospel in New York with the aid of moving pictures next Sunday afternoon and from that day on will give two performances daily, free of charge, at The Temple (formally the Playhouse Theatre), West Sixty-Third Street on January 11, 1914.'

It was a crisp and cold winter morning when lengthy queues began filing into New York's newest movie-theatre. Charles Russell's controversial futuristic visions of glory for mankind were about to enter a new and exciting phase. No expense had been spared in renovating the once forlorn and unfinished theatre where Butler Davenport's ambitious dreams of slick productions of the revolutionary plays of Henrik Ibsen and the like had faded into bankruptcy.

Behind the scenes a team of anxious volunteers, trained in the operation of hand-cranked cinematographs, magic-lantern slide projectors and clockwork phonographs with enormous speaker-horns, stood by ready to perform their individual tasks with well-rehearsed co-ordinated precision. As the magnificent auditorium chandelier dimmed promisingly the capacity crowd gaped at the beckoning screen in open-mouthed silence.

Two projectionists to the rear of the balcony and two phonograph operators stationed each side of the stage endeavoured to ensure a continuously synchronised commentary and musical accompaniment to the images appearing on the screen, but the results were not always entirely satisfactory. Indeed, by later standards it was crude and less than perfect but in 1914 it was an unrivalled and miraculous display of ingenuity. Better still, it was free to anyone who cared to turn up, and they did – in ever increasing droves.

More than a decade before Al Jolson sang Mammy to wide-eyed cinema audiences in 1929, a sepia-tinted Pastor Russell flickered onto the silver screen and spoke to captivated New Yorkers who were witnessing a faltering but historic step in the early development of motion pictures with synchronised sound, the first 'talkie' ever. Some sixty years later former Bible Student Alice Hoffman recalled: 'As he would appear on the screen and his lips began to move a phonograph would be started at the precise moment and we would enjoy listening to his voice.'

Innovative time-lapse photography was used in the first scenes to show the unfolding of a flower and the hatching of a chick. Karl F. Klein, also present at that first showing, commented: 'At the same time that these pictures were being shown there was an accompaniment of fine music – such gems as Narcissus and Humoresque.' Martha Meredith, another former Bible Student who later identified with the Jehovah's Witnesses sect, also looked back to her first movie experience: 'I see Noah and his family walking into the ark with the animals [and] Abraham and Isaac walking to mount Moriah. When I saw Abraham put his son on the altar – this son he dearly loved – I shed tears.'[81]

The Photo-Drama presentations were the first colour films ever to be seen and they were regarded at the time as sensational. In addition to the motion pictures there were the 'talking coloured-slides'. These were orthodox three-inch square optical lantern slides of the day, specially manufactured in France, to specifications drawn up by Russell from existing illustrated scientific data depicting the evolution of the earth from its original formless state through various geological ages to the appearance of man.

Hundreds of specially commissioned fine art engravings and watercolour illustrations were used in the manufacture of many of the lantern slides depicting some of the early biblical events recorded in Genesis, the story of the Garden of Eden, the Flood, and the Tower of Babel for example. Some of the pictures were painted in London and Paris, while the majority were done in Philadelphia and New York. There were just under 1500 of these stereopticon slides and the accompanying voice-over commentary and appropriate music was contained on ninety-six 12-inch (80 rpm) gramophone records specially manufactured by the Columbia Record Company.

The movie film segments were among the first to be professionally produced in Hollywood – then a little-known suburb of Los Angeles – from detailed scripts furnished by Russell. Professional actors and actresses played their parts on specially constructed studio sets while outdoor crowd scenes, featuring Bible Students who volunteered as extras, were shot in the Californian sunshine. Other scenes were filmed in New York with animals from the Brooklyn Zoo adding a touch of realism to the story of Noah and the Ark.

---

[81] 1975 Yearbook of Jehovah's Witnesses.

The post-production work of hand tinting the black and white film positives, frame by frame, was undertaken by a small team of specially trained Bible Students based in New York. This was a colossal task which involved the individual treatment of almost a quarter million celluloid pictures, each measuring just one inch by one and a quarter. The complete Photo Drama occupied a marathon eight-hour performance (5 hours of lantern slides and 3 hours of motion pictures) and was necessarily divided into four screenings of up to two hours each. More than one visit to the theatre was needed to see the whole production with each segment of the epic telling a complete story.

Part one gave an account of the creation and development of the earth and the coming of man and events in the Garden of Eden. Part two continued the Bible story to the time of Moses and the exodus, while the third part dealt with the coming of Christ, his life, death and resurrection. The fourth and concluding segment of this cinematic marathon featured a potted history of Christianity from Pentecost and the early church through almost two thousand years of sectarian strife and misunderstanding to the late 19th century, the period when Charles Russell formulated his countdown to Armageddon which, he believed, was corroborated by selected lineal measurements – 'correspondencies' [sic] – of the Great Pyramid of Giza, the mammoth stony calendar that he surely believed it was.

The final scenes in this early epic of celluloid make-believe purported to offer a glimpse of the paradise-like conditions which, according to Pastor Russell, would soon prevail on earth. Coloured images of Californian blue skies and palm trees waving gently in the coastal breeze transported audiences into another world. Animated street scenes and sunny aspects of New York City flashed onto the screen showing the latest in modern buildings, automobiles and aeroplanes which often drew audible expressions of admiration and wonder.

Upon leaving the theatre patrons were handed 'Pax – Sons of Peace' pin-badges and impressive newspaper broadsheets of the pictures and dialogue featured in the production. Hailed by the press and the public as the most ambitious pictorial presentation of the Bible story ever seen, the Photo Drama was more than two years in the making at a cost of $315,000 which was more than three times the amount D.W. Griffiths would spend on his masterpiece The Birth of a Nation in 1915.

Press coverage was favourable: 'Though the main object of the Bible Students Association in this production is to spread the Gospel through moving pictures, the Photo Drama is not didactic, and it tells an interesting story. Five thousand persons attended the initial performances and many more were turned away. The film, in which 500 hundred performers take part, will be shown all over the country free.'[82]

The show then went on the road with a travelling company of more than one hundred volunteers who staged the film show across America wherever a suitable theatre could be hired. Sometimes there were screenings in prisons and, on rare occasions, in places of worship. In Cincinnati priests and nuns frequently sat among audiences along with Sunday school teachers who attended afternoon performances with their classes. However, in some other cities militant clergymen made efforts to prevent the movie being shown at all.

A Methodist minister who caught sight of billboard posters advertising the Photo Drama outside the Opera House in the city of Laurel, Mississippi, confronted the owner of the theatre and threatened to close the place down if the show went on. Enraged, he shook his fist at the Watchtower official who had hired the theatre and exclaimed, 'You try to show these things here, and you will have the biggest fight on your hands. Better get out of town, and quick!'

When the angry clergyman was silently ignored, he convened an emergency meeting of the Ministerial Union which passed resolutions against the Photo Drama and Pastor Russell, calling upon the Mayor of the city and the Chief of Police to enforce its rulings. The Electric Light Company was then persuaded to cut off the power to the theatre and the owner was subsequently pressured into tearing down the huge colourful posters advertising the 'Forthcoming Attraction!'

The Watchtower tour manager then approached one Judge Beavours, the leading attorney in town, and appealed to him for assistance. Within the hour the lawyer had informed the Electric Light Company, the Ministerial Union and other officials who had been drawn into the fray, that unless they backed off, he would apply to the courts for an injunction, restraining them from 'unlawfully exercising' their power. Eventually, common sense ruled the day and the Photo Drama played to packed houses for a fortnight.[83]

Back in New York, packed houses soon became divided houses when the issue of segregation cast a jarring shadow over the silver-screen. Russell apparently felt that his white patrons were in danger of paling into insignificance as New York's blacks queued up outside the Temple

---

[82] The New York Times – January 12, 1914.

[83] Jehovah's Witnesses in the Divine Purpose – WTBTS, 1959.

theatre in ever increasing numbers to see the free movie show. Russell, who had long harboured eccentric – sometimes extreme – racist views, tackled the touchy problem with patronising ambiguity, worthy of many a vote-seeking politician, when he put his thoughts down in black and white:

'We might have anticipated that many coloured people would be deeply interested in the Drama. Of course, we were glad to see them, but whereas the coloured people of New York are about five percent of the population, in our audiences they are about twenty five percent, and the number is increasing. As the attendance of the coloured people would increase, proportionately the number of whites would decrease; for explain it how we will, most whites prefer not to intermingle closely with other races . . . If nature favours the coloured brethren and sisters in the exercise of humility it is that much to their advantage . . . those who have been faithful will be granted new bodies, spiritual, beyond the veil, where colour and sex distinctions will be no more. Some who were still tenacious and quarrelsome we merely reminded them of our Lord's declaration that in inviting visitors into the house it is the place of the host to say where they shall sit.'[84]

Conscious of his elevation to film-star status because of his off-Broadway movie-theatre appearances, Russell evidently felt obliged to explain it all away, characteristically, in the third person: 'The personality has been permitted to come before the people regarding the Drama, because newspaper people assure us that without the personality the Drama would be taken for some ordinary church entertainment. The personality necessary for advertising the Drama and the Sermon is quite distasteful to us but is submitted to in the interest of the cause. Not only have we lectures that are interesting and profitable, but they are delivered by a Talking Machine combination peculiarly our own, which is, we believe, superior to anything which has ever been produced. The horn talks with the volume and tone of an orator, and no one recognises that the words come from a machine.'

By April, Russell's travelling road show was being mounted simultaneously in thirty-one theatres throughout the United States with an average daily attendance of 35,000. In Russell's home state praise was lavish and aptly non-sectarian: '. . . now it is the 'movies' that are teaching us the story of the Bible. Whether we will be any better morally is quite another story. But it is at least worthwhile considering the indelible

[84] Watchtower – April 1, 1914.

impression that these free bible pictures are making upon a thoughtless world.'[85] That same month, the S.S. Lusitania pulled away from her New York moorings, bound for the British port of Southampton. She was carrying several large wooden crates, marked Industrial Equipment, for delivery to 34 Craven Terrace, Bayswater, London. On board, a small team of Bible Students checked their itinerary and prepared a training programme for their British brothers.

Prior to the London opening of the Photo Drama, an ambitious publicity campaign was mounted in which hundreds of thousands of leaflets were dutifully distributed throughout the great metropolis. Advertisements appeared in newspapers and popular journals as eye-catching posters appeared on huge street hoardings across the city while many shops and places of business in the suburbs were persuaded to display small placards detailing the 'Coming Attraction!'

On the Sunday afternoon of June 14, 1914, lengthy queues formed outside the Princes Theatre, on Shaftesbury Avenue. The theatre was packed out for a week after which the show transferred to the London Opera House where it ran for a further five weeks with continuous afternoon and evening performances. From then until the end of the year the Photo Drama was shown in many cities and towns of Great Britain and Ireland to great acclaim. Twenty male Bible Students, who were able to take time out from their normal occupations, toured the country in five teams of four operators with the necessary equipment to set up and stage each performance.

Following the London premier small groups of Russell's followers in Norway, Sweden, Finland, Denmark, Germany, Switzerland, and France made their way to Britain to take part in a specially devised training programme before returning home with the equipment needed to put on a show. Russell's followers could now be found in more than 1,200 congregations in many lands across the globe avidly reading his Studies in the Scriptures and eagerly scanning the latest editions of the Watch Tower magazine for encouraging clues and hints about the coming apocalypse. Meanwhile the pivotal 1914 doomsday month of October loomed ever closer.

With one eye on the calendar, and the other on the current issue of Russell's iconic magazine, expectant believers were persuaded to give themselves a little more leeway when the Pastor declared: 'Armageddon may begin next spring, yet it is purely speculation to attempt to say just

[85] The Reading Herald – April 1914

when.'[86] This newly introduced nebulous aspect took the edge off things as faith-powered biological clocks were self-consciously reset to accommodate the unexpected delay. Nonetheless there was much disappointment all round as clouds of doubt began to form.

During the run at the London Opera House, events which were to alter the course of history were unfolding in the Balkans. With just two shots from his Browning automatic pistol Gavirilo Princip, a nineteen-year-old student, assassinated both the heir to the Austro-Hungarian throne, the Archduke Franz Ferdinand, and his morganatic wife, the Duchess of Hohenburg. A tidal wave of horror and indignation swept over Europe in the wake of the murder of the royal couple. In London, *The Times* declared, 'It shakes the conscience of the world', while in Rome Pope Pius x was said to have fainted on hearing the news.

As the nations of the world braced themselves and prepared for war additional presentations of the Photo Drama of Creation were hurriedly staged with a seven-day stint at the Royal Albert Hall and another seven days at the London Opera House. During this fortnight of previously unscheduled performances more than forty-two thousand Londoners attended the free film show. A further tour of the provinces took in even more towns and villages. Attendance figures, collated between June 1914 and late 1915, revealed that close to two million Britons had attended a screening of the Photo Drama of Creation.

Free admission to the movie ensured its world-wide success which proved to be more of an attraction than the alleged message it carried. In the end Pastor Russell's costly epic was no more than a spectacular novelty – although much literature was sold on the back of it. The film ran for two years off-Broadway in New York and was eventually seen by curious millions the world over. Today Russell's Photo Drama of Creation – a landmark production in which both Thomas Edison and D.W. Griffiths may well have had a hand, if only in an advisory capacity – remains largely forgotten in the 21st century.

---

[86] Watch Tower – September 1, 1914.

Chapter Ten

THE BLACK SHEEP OF THE WATCHTOWER FAMILY

Although not widely known, the Watchtower Society has traditionally portrayed blacks, indeed, anyone who is not white, as examples of human inferiority and degradation. This deeply ingrained corporate attitude can be traced back to the racial inequality which was politically instituted in America in 1857 when the Supreme Court of the United States, sitting in judgement on one Dred Scott, a slave who had audaciously petitioned for his freedom, ruled that no one of African descent could have any rights of citizenship. Two years later, in 1859, abolitionist John Brown defiantly challenged the ruling when he attempted to free and arm slaves at Harpers Ferry, Virginia. He was subsequently captured, executed, and immortalised as a martyr for the cause in the hymn John Brown's Body.

Not surprisingly, the Watchtower Society, with its perennially Caucasian majority leadership, stands accused by some commentators of having been institutionally racist since its inception. The segregation of blacks within their ranks for much of the 20th century was officially perceived as being morally justified. It was a temporary aspect of mankind's physical imperfection according to Pastor Russell's interpretation of events detailed in Genesis: 'Noah had foreseen that Ham's characteristics, which had led him to unseemly conduct, would be inherited by his son [whose] degeneracy would mark the posterity of Canaan, degrading him, making him servile. We are not able to determine to a certainty that the sons of Ham and Canaan are Negroes; but we consider that general view as probable as any other.'

Charles Russell spelled out his white supremacy theories thus: 'White people living in China eventually produce Chinese offspring – without intermarrying – due to the influence of soil and climate. The secret of greater intelligence and aptitude of the Caucasian is to be attributed to the co-mingling of blood among its various branches; and this was evidently forced in large measure by circumstances under divine control. It remains to be proven that the similar co-mingling of the various tribes of Chinese for several centuries would not equally brighten their intellects; and the same with the peoples of India and Africa.'[87]

The door-to-door preaching work of the Bible Students was from the start restricted to white Protestant believers. On one occasion when more than a hundred 'coloured brethren' responded to a call for volunteers they were all turned down by Pastor Russell: 'They rightly realised that we have not the slightest of race prejudice, and that we love the coloured brethren with just the same warmth of heart that we love the white, and they queried therefore why such a distinction should be made in the call. The reason is coloured people have less education than whites – many of them quite insufficient to permit them to profit by such readings. Reading matter distributed to a coloured congregation would more than half of it be utterly wasted, with a small percentage indeed likely to yield good results.'[88]

On a later occasion Russell held out the compromising hope that those he had previously labelled 'degenerate' could one day, through the power of prayer, become acceptably white: 'Rev. William Draper gave a living affirmative answer to the famous Biblical question, Can the Ethiopian change his skin or the leopard his spots? Though once as black as charcoal, the Rev. Mr. Draper is now white. His people say that his colour was changed in answer to a prayer. Many years ago, Draper was employed by a fair skinned man, and he was often heard to remark that if he could only be white like his employer, he would be happy. From that day forward, he prayed constantly and fervently that he might become white. He first experienced a prickling sensation on his face and upon close investigation found several white spots scarcely larger than the point of a pin. Gradually the white spots became larger and extended, until now, after the change has been in progress for over 30 years, Draper has not a single dark spot on his body.'[89]

Russell evidently interpreted such phenomena as premonitory signs of the restitution of God's allegedly original white-skin standard for the entire human race. A few years later he brought the subject up again when he declared: 'God can change the [black man's] skin in his due time. Julius Jackson, of New Frankfort, Montana, a Negro boy of nine years, began to grow white in September 1901, and is now fully nine-

---

[87] Zion's Watch Tower – July 15, 1902.
[88] Zion's Watch Tower – April 15, 1900.
[89] Zion's Watch Tower – Oct. 10, 1900.

tenths white.'[90] Today we know he was simply describing a medical condition known as vitiligo (leukoderma), a colour-changing loss of cells, producing melanin in the epidermal skin, which generates black or dark brown pigmentation resulting in dark skin turning strikingly pale.

In his day Judge Rutherford drew attention to the fact that the nations of the British Empire were all ruled by whites, having 'superior mental, moral, or physical force' and patronisingly kept blacks chained to their biblically designated station in life – for life: 'The curse which Noah pronounced upon Canaan was the origin of the black race. They have been and are a race of servants, but now in the dawn of the twentieth century, we are all coming to see this matter of service in its true light and to find that the only real joy in life is in serving others; not bossing them. There is no servant in the whole world as good as a coloured servant, and the joy that he gets from rendering faithful service is one of the purest joys there is in the world.[91]

During the winter of 1928 a Special Colporteur Bulletin, which offered tips and suggestions on how to sell Watchtower literature more effectively, was issued to Rutherford's travelling preachers. In poorer, predominately black, areas books and Bibles could be traded for chickens or vegetables and fruit: 'They are not the best territory by any means, and some colporteurs who sell well skip the coloured people as a rule.'[92] Alerting Bible Students to the subtle dangers of innocently exposing their children to the devilish ways of the world he condemned a book, sympathetic to blacks, which he called 'the work of Satan'. The book, written by Harriet Beecher Stowe, was Uncle Tom's Cabin, a favourite read of outspoken atheist Mark Twain.

During the early 1950's America's black Jehovah's Witnesses were not allowed to attend regular conventions held by the Watchtower Society, especially in the southern and border states of America where 'alternative arrangements' were put in place. Inexplicably, none of the Witnesses, black or white, seemed to mind – publicly, at least. When other religious groups marched in protest, against ethnic prejudice, during those decades of racial tension, the Watchtower Society referred to them as 'crazed-mobs'. Consequently, both black and white Witnesses dragged their feet to such an extent that they were out of step all the way

[90] Zion's Watch Tower – February 15, 1904.
[91] Golden Age – July 24, 1929.
[92] Golden Age – July 24, 1929.

along the road to integration in the United States of America during the 1950's and 60's.

As recently as February 1952 the Watchtower Society's patronising opinion of blacks at that time noted: 'Our coloured brothers have a great cause for rejoicing. Their race is meek and teachable, and from it comes a high percentage of theocratic increase'. Sociologist Werner Cole later commented: 'In the official 1953 report of their 1952 International Convention, not one African-American is identified as having a position of oversight. Two black Americans are pictured as 'cleaning up the kitchen'. It is difficult indeed to escape the impression that the role which the non-white delegate plays in the Witness organisation is not dissimilar to that traditionally assigned him by the least enlightened sections of white society.'

Since its inception in 1879 the Watchtower Society has held fast to the belief that only Caucasians of Northern European-American descent were fit to serve on the Governing Body. Indeed, on January 25, 1973, the Brooklyn Bethel felt obliged to issue the following statement: 'Membership [of the Governing Body] in the corporation is not something determined by race . . . selecting of men to handle unusual responsibilities is because of spiritual qualifications and not because of racial or national points . . . God is not impartial, but in every nation the man that fears him and works righteousness is acceptable to him.'[93]

In the 1980's former Jehovah's Witness Randy Watters, a prominent critic of the movement who once served at the New York City headquarters, commented: 'While the Watchtower does have a few blacks in high position, including Circuit Overseers and members of the Service Department at Bethel, such ones have been promoted no higher despite their adopting 'white' attitudes . . . a black may be appointed to the Governing Body – time will tell. One thing is for sure, they will have to lose their 'soul' to do so!'

In the closing months of the 20th century, when apocalyptic expectations were once again heightened by the calendar, Samuel Herd, a black Jehovah's Witness of some 50 years who was then a member of the Service Department at the Brooklyn headquarters, was elevated to membership of the Governing Body. Today, it seems that brother Herd's ethnicity is of little or no import, and rightly so. Indeed, hawk-eyed online critics and commentators have been quick to point out how well he now blends in with the rest of the Watchtower Society's elite leadership

---

[93] Acts 10: 34, 35.

when he appears on the JW.org channel sporting a $20,844 Rolex Oyster Submariner Watch.

EXODUS

Chapter Eleven

RAILROAD TO HEAVEN

It was during a Bible Student convention, held in Saratoga Springs, in the last week of September 1914, that one of Russell's lieutenants, A. H. Macmillan, publicly announced: 'I am ready to be offered! This is positively my last discourse on this side of the veil.' The seeds of such hopes and expectations which Pastor Russell had been scattering for forty years had also taken root in the minds of almost 20,000 of his followers and expectations were running high that month. However, the long-awaited first day of October 1914 proved disappointingly uneventful and routine.

The work force at the printing plant had steadily increased over the years and there were now 175 full-time volunteers at the Brooklyn headquarters. As usual the evening meal was taken in the communal dining room where conversation focused awkwardly on anything but the significance of the date. As for Pastor Russell, he remained uncharacteristically silent throughout the day before retiring for the evening.

Decades later Macmillan, who remained earthbound well into the second half of the 20th century as a high-ranking Watchtower official, revealed what happened in the Brooklyn Tabernacle on the following day: 'Friday morning, we were all seated at the breakfast table when Russell came down. As he entered the room he hesitated, as was his custom, and said cheerily, 'Good morning, all.' But this morning, instead of proceeding to his seat as usual, he briskly clapped his hands and happily announced: 'The Gentile times have ended; the kings have had their day.' We all applauded.'[94]

Pastor Russell then sought to dispel any lingering doubts that may have taken root during the night with a cheery 'Anyone disappointed? I'm not. Everything is moving right on schedule.' Some weeks later, emboldened by the respite he had engineered, Russell had the temerity to put forty years of definitive speculation to one side when he declared:

---

[94] Faith on the March – A.H. Macmillan, Prentice-Hall 1957.

'We did not say positively that this would be the year.' However, a more down-to-earth day of factual reckoning was about to dawn.

Production costs for the Photo Drama had been considerable and this latest unscheduled pause on the road to paradise placed an unexpected strain on finances. Cash was haemorrhaging out of the organisation at an alarming rate as magazine subscriptions were cancelled and growing stacks of books remained unsold. Having spent money like there was no tomorrow, Russell's financial security now looked as vulnerable as his credibility. In his annual report he admitted: 'a million dollars has been spent in the service of present truth this year. God kindly veiled our eyes as respects the amount of labour connected with the Drama. Had we foreknown the cost in time and money . . . we would never have begun it.'

The following year the remaining stocks of the book which highlighted the apocalyptic date of October 1914 were withdrawn and replaced with a 'new edition' in which Armageddon was rescheduled to take place 'near the end of A.D. 1915'. Soon afterwards many of the faithful defected in worrying numbers with clergy-led ridicule and negative publicity adding to the encircling gloom. The more resolute among Russell's followers were encouraged to wisely focus on the wartime slaughter and unrest in Europe to keep their Armageddon hopes alive. Eventually the ongoing war came to be understood as a precursor to the apocalyptic end of the world. Nonetheless, there were now almost two hundred mouths to feed at the Brooklyn Bethel.

Early in the New Year Russell started laying-off some of his workforce. By the spring of 1915 more than seventy live-in workers, many of them key personnel, found themselves back in the outside world homeless and unemployed. Meanwhile Judge Rutherford wrote A Great Battle in the Ecclesiastic Heavens – as seen by a lawyer, a sixty-four-page booklet in which he defended Russell's controversial end-time dogma, his allegedly dubious financial deals, and his rumoured sexual dalliances. All of this was executed with pious indignation and a scorching criticism of Roman Catholicism and its offshoot Protestant factions, 'Papal Rome and her mongrel progeny against one man'.

Returning the compliment Russell described the withering diatribe as a 'spicy defence': 'Brother Rutherford, grieved by the various untruthful, slanderous attacks upon the Editor, has prepared a pamphlet in my defence. A copy of it has just been handed to me. I have not read it yet, though, of course I knew of its preparation and in a general way its contents. I prefer not to have anything to do with its publication. It explains Brother Rutherford's views as a lawyer, as a brother, and as a man who most fully understands the entire situation.'[95]

However, despite this mutual backscratching, the relationship between Russell and Rutherford had become strained in recent years, particularly during the anti-climactic period surrounding the non-event of October 1914. There were times when Russell sensed his authority was being challenged, sometimes eclipsed, by his assertive attorney. On one fractious occasion, in the summer of 1915, this undercurrent of disquiet surfaced when Rutherford openly disagreed with Russell on a certain aspect of scriptural interpretation in the presence of others.

A few days later the opinionated lawyer was called into the Pastor's office where he was told that his professional services, although timely and much appreciated over the years, were no longer required at the New York Bethel. The Judge would now be free to serve the Lord wherever he felt the need was greater, he was told. For Rutherford, who had always assumed he was an indispensable member of Russell's inner circle, it was a bombshell of a dismissal. To help him on his way he was awarded $1,000 'relocation expenses'.

So, it was that the redundant attorney, along with his crestfallen wife Mary and their now disillusioned 23-year-old son Malcolm left New York behind and settled in the town of Monrovia, California. Eventually Judge Rutherford joined the staff of the Broadway Department Store in Los Angeles where he was retained as Company Attorney and Legal Adviser.

He continued to speak at Bible Student conventions and, probably to Russell's dismay, organised independently a series of public debates during which he flaunted his commanding presence and aired his persuasive oratory skills. Unfettered by a restrictive accountability to his former employer Judge Rutherford was now free to conduct his own personal battle against Satan's earthly agents. He would never see the Pastor alive again.

***

It was June 20, 1915, when a cash-strapped Pastor Russell wrote to Jesse Hemery suggesting the Bible Students in London might now like to assume responsibility for the outstanding loan on the Tabernacle. Having taken out a mortgage on the massive church building and making no provision for servicing the debt much beyond 1914, he explained that this new arrangement would 'resolve legal questions regarding a

---

[95] Watch Tower – May 1, 1915.

foreigner holding property in Britain'. He would however continue paying the rental on the adjoining mansion house. Russell's proposal was put before the body of elders who were reluctant to finance the acquisition of a property over which they would have no administrative control. Throughout the summer months they remained undecided.

Once October 1915 had arrived without even a hint of the delayed apocalypse Russell immediately sent off another anxious letter to Hemery: 'In respect to the Tabernacle arrangements being turned over to London, we reply that if [the elders] are ready to take up all the obligations of the Society connected with the Tabernacle, including interest payments, we will be very happy indeed to turn over the entire management of the Tabernacle to the congregation.'

Once the new arrangement was under way many in the congregation felt that the affairs of Bible Students in Britain should now be seen to be in the democratic hands of the locally appointed elders and deacons. However, Jesse Hemery argued that such a move would be anti-theocratic and sent off a warning letter to Pastor Russell in New York, accusing Henry Shearn and William Crawford of 'fostering unrest'. It was dated October 23, 1916, and crossed the Atlantic by steamer.

Over in America the presidential campaign was in danger of being eclipsed by events in Europe. With less than a fortnight to go before polling day, President Woodrow Wilson was presenting himself to the people as the 'peace candidate' while his Republican opponent, Charles Evans Hughes, Governor of New York, was calling for 'greater military preparedness' in the shadow of the war raging on the other side of the Atlantic.

Also, on a campaign trail, Pastor Russell – scheduled to address a meeting of his supporters at the Friday Morning Club Auditorium in San Antonio, Los Angeles – was half-way through a whistle-stop tour canvassing prospective supporters of a future heavenly government which would administer its directives through a re-established Jewish Assembly in Palestine. He was accompanied by his secretary, Menta Sturgeon, a middle-aged bachelor who had latterly become more of a personal companion and carer to the ailing preacher.

After the opening prayer Russell took centre stage. He appeared drawn and weak and paused uneasily as he beckoned Sturgeon to remove the lectern and replace it with a chair: 'I regret I am not able to speak with force or power, pardon me for sitting down please. The worldly wise have rejected the Bible, and do not trust it as a Revelation from God. Nevertheless, some of our great thinkers, Mr. Edison, and others, are rapidly seeing that the world is just on the verge of the most wonderful inventions and knowledge. Some few have been calling attention to the fact that we have been in the millennial dawn ever since the year 1874. Bible chronology quite clearly teaches that the six thousand years from Adam's creation have ended . . . six great days of a thousand years each . . .' The pauses grew noticeably longer as Russell's adoring followers strained forward willing him on.

'Forty-two years-ago nearly all the labour of the world was done with the sweat of the face; today it is nearly all accomplished by machinery, the sewing machine was just reaching perfection; today it is everywhere indispensable. So, with all our sanitary and plumbing arrangements. So, with the farm implements, reapers and binders, mowers, automobiles and gas engines . . . all belong to these forty-two years. . . Solomon in all his glory never dreamed of such things as the poorest in America may . . . enjoy . . .'

The speaker trailed into a long staring silence before he was gently helped to his feet and led from the platform by his companion who reappeared alone a few anxious moments later. 'Before we continue brothers let us consider the words of Daniel – Daniel chapter twelve verses one to four.' A swishing of solemn page-turning relieved the tension while backstage a now desperately ill Pastor Russell reached for his medication as Sturgeon filled in with a ponderous reading of the chosen scriptures before leaving the platform once again. Some anxious moments later he reappeared with Russell on his arm and melted into the background once the frail speaker was seated and had signalled with a nod that he was ready to continue with his talk.

'The next phase of the trouble, according to the Bible, is to be the great 'earthquake' such as never was since man was upon the earth – not a literal earthquake, but a symbolic one . . .' As he struggled on groping for words to express his meandering intent an uncomfortably long silence fell upon the assembly as the confused orator was helped to his feet. There were audible murmurs of concern as the speechless and bent preacher shuffled out of sight. Shortly afterwards, primed with a cocktail of medication and leaning heavily on the arm of Menta Sturgeon, Pastor Russell returned to close the meeting.

'I must say good-bye to you all . . . May the Lord's blessing be with you richly. We will now sing song number one: 'Abide, sweet Spirit, Heavenly Dove, with light and comfort from Above; Be thou our guardian, thou our Guide, o'er every thought and step preside.' Isn't this a beautiful thought? Preserve this spirit in your midst. Have perfect confidence in the Lord, and you will be led aright. We were not brought into the Truth by any human catchword, but by the Word of the Lord. I bid you all good-bye.' There were tears as everyone rose to their feet and sang earnestly.

After the meeting, a decision was made to cut short the lecture tour. Eventually a waiting car took Russell and his companion to the station where they boarded the Santa Fe train No. 10 and settled into 'Rose Isle', their private Pullman car (compliments of a grateful patron) complete with its own drawing room. Before the train pulled out of the station there was just time for one of the local brothers to go to the nearest drugstore for extra supplies of the ailing preacher's medication, enough for the five-day journey.

As the train puffed and rumbled its way out of the station Russell clambered into his bunk and drifted into a fitful sleep; he would call if he needed any help during the night, he told his companion. Within a couple of hours, he called out for assistance and an hour later he called out again. His carer describes what then took place: 'I soon discovered that another chill was coming on. He had had his first one two nights before. I put five Pullman blankets upon him and tucked them in close on every side; but he still shook. I remained by his side, lying down at times on the couch beside him. Toward morning he had me make a robe for convenience sake by pinning a sheet inside a blanket, wrapping him in it like a robe and fastening it under his chin. He stood up for this purpose and then lay down on the couch. I therefore sat on his bed while he lay before me.'

'After several hours he stood up again and said, 'Please make me a Roman toga.' I said, 'Brother Russell, I do not understand what you mean'. He said, 'I will show you.' He had me take a clean sheet and turn it down twelve inches from the top; and then a second one the same. Placing his hand on my right shoulder, he said, 'Fasten them together here.' The sheets being fastened with safety pins, as he had directed, he said, 'Now fasten them together on the other shoulder.' This I did. There he stood, one sheet extending from his neck to his feet in front and the other in the back, fastened together on his shoulders and folded together at the sides.'

Without saying a word, Russell then lay down on the couch on his back and closed his eyes. As Sturgeon looked on, he recalled that the toga was worn by Roman officials and priests. Sometimes symbolising victory and peace, and at other times that the one wearing it had fulfilled his vows. The Santa Fe Express swayed and switched its way over the lonely tracks as the day dawned. At one-point Sturgeon tentatively asked about the much anticipated seventh volume of Russell's Studies in the Scriptures – the book that would finally resolve so many unanswered questions. 'Someone else can write that,' sighed Russell.

No meals were taken throughout the entire day and as the evening darkness presented itself the Pastor, still in his toga, lay full stretch in his berth. Sturgeon remained fully dressed and lay down on the nearby couch and was just about to drift off when Russell called out as rigor set in once more. Our eyewitness describes the scene: 'I folded blanket after blanket over him, tucked them in close to him; but still he shook. I therefore lay on him and pressed my face to his until I felt the warmth return to his body. The fact that this was the third chill in four nights deepened the impression in my mind that the end was drawing near. About midnight a great change came over him. He no longer cared for any of his medicine and did not even seem to thirst for water as before, he could no longer lie straight in bed as formerly. He must sit up; and when he would lie down, he would double altogether.'

Russell spent the next seven hours tossing and turning with a skinny arm hooked around the neck of his exhausted companion: 'In the early morning, he surrendered. He was exhausted, and I could now lay him straight in bed and he could at last rest. The calm after the storm had come. He was now to die, and I was to stand by watching him, loving him, and expressing my affection for him by gently stroking his hair and his beard and rubbing his head, his face, his hands, and his feet. I did not seem to be able to do enough for him.'[96]

It was now Tuesday, the last day of October when Sturgeon, red-eyed and worn out, concluded that Pastor Russell would be dead before the day was out. He wrote out a telegram: 'Before October closes our dearly beloved brother Russell will be with the Lord in glory. We are alone in car Rose Isle on Santa Fe train No. 10, due in Kansas City 7.35 Wednesday morning, and he is dying like a hero. After embalming will come home with his remains.' He then called in the conductor who telegraphed ahead for a physician to board the train at Panhandle, the next stop. At mid-day, a doctor duly boarded the train and, after examining the patient, confirmed the death of Charles Taze Russell.

Judge Rutherford had been attending a Bible Student convention at Maryland during that last weekend of October and before returning to California he stopped by in Detroit to have some urgent dental

[96] Watch Tower – December 1, 1916.

treatment. It was there that he received a telephone call from Macmillan in New York telling him that Pastor Russell had died. He also told him that the Society's Vice-president, Alfred I. Ritchie, had apparently assumed control. Furthermore, some of the brothers were already referring to *him* as 'President', he confided. 'Don't do anything 'till I get there,' said the Judge. A twelve-hour train ride through the Halloween night saw Rutherford back in Brooklyn. Large as life, he strode into the Bethel and immediately made his way to the late Pastor's study.

Chapter Twelve

THE PARTING OF THE WATCHTOWER SEE

Joseph Franklin Rutherford, one of eight children raised by James and Lenora Rutherford, was born in 1869 on small farm some three miles north of Versailles, Missouri where the family attended the local Freedom Baptist Church. As a young man Joseph worked on the farm along with the rest of the family but showed little interest in becoming a farmer himself. His disappointed father, who did nothing to encourage his ambitious son in his desire to be a lawyer, grudgingly consented to his attending college to study law at the age of sixteen, so long as he continued as a working member of the family.

Young Joseph was so determined and so persuasive he managed to secure a bank loan, on his own word, to finance his further education. Soon after enrolment at law school he took a part-time job selling encyclopaedias from door to door to help pay a hired hand to take his place on the family farm. On one occasion when he was calling at a farm he fell into an icy stream, ruined his sample books, and almost drowned. On that luckless day he promised himself that when he became a lawyer, he would never turn away a travelling book salesman.

He taught himself the rudiments of shorthand writing and became a trainee court stenographer which brought in the extra money he needed to pay off his bank loan. At the age of eighteen he had completed his academy education and went on to spend two years under the tutorship of Judge E.L. Edwards before being appointed official reporter for the 14th. Judicial Circuit, Missouri. When he was in his twenties, he wrote The Laws of Missouri which was published in conjunction with the Boonville Advertiser as a give-away supplement and financed by the fifty percent advertising content it carried. It was Rutherford's first venture into the commercial world of publishing.

Upon being admitted to the Missouri bar on May 5th, 1892, he secured for himself a position with the firm of Draffen & White, as a trial lawyer, and went on to serve four years as Public Prosecutor in Boonville, Missouri. It was during this period that he was approached by two travelling booksellers (a couple of Pastor Russell's colporteurs) who called at his office one cold January morning in 1894. Mindful of his own bookselling days, he listened politely to their message and bought three volumes from his callers. When they had gone, he flipped through the pages of the books with the practised eye of a wary litigant before putting them to one side. Some weeks later he picked them up again. This time he could not put them down, neither could his wife, Mary. Soon afterwards he wrote to Pastor Russell:

'About two months ago, two young ladies came into my office selling [Studies in the Scriptures] . . . I bought three volumes, thinking that by doing so I was helping them out. I have since concluded that these ladies brought me 'glad tidings of great joy', I took the books home and thought little of them, until a few weeks ago, when I had some spare time, I began reading the first volume, and it was so interesting that I could not stop. The result is, my dear wife and myself have read these books with the keenest interest, and we consider it a God-send and a great blessing . . .'

The following year court-room protocol bestowed upon him the temporary title Judge Rutherford when he presided over two minor trials having been called upon to stand in for a local judge who was incapacitated for a couple of days. Soon afterwards, back in his role as a trial lawyer, he was cited for contempt of court three times; on one occasion allegedly presenting misleading evidence by lying to the court. With his reputation sullied and his pride dented he felt it was time to move on taking with him his, officially temporary title, Judge.

He admired fellow lawyer and politician William J. Bryan, an ardent pacifist and a leading anti-Darwinian campaigner who famously argued: 'It would be better to trust the Rock of Ages than the age of rocks.' When he stood as the Democratic candidate for the presidency, he appointed Rutherford as his election campaign manager. Bryan was heavily defeated by Republican William McKinley in 1896 and again in1900. Once more the ambitious advocate found himself out in the cold. Thereafter the Judge and his wife became increasingly involved with Russell's movement and were eventually baptised as Bible Students in 1906.

In May 1907, Rutherford applied to the New York bar and was admitted to practice before the Supreme Court of the United States in Washington D.C. He was no match for big-city sophisticates and the success he thought he deserved continued to elude him. That same year he sent off a second effusive letter to Pastor Russell who, on this occasion, replied immediately. Some weeks later the self-styled Judge made his way to Allegheny to meet the man himself.

***

The first day of November 1916 was a busy one for Rutherford. Following a quick conference with his informant, Macmillan, the Judge simply took over and assumed control of the organisation. With his customary eyeglass attached to a long black ribbon about his neck, black string bowtie, and silver-tipped cane, the hefty lawyer paced along the corridor. He was known to have a blunt approach, and on this occasion, he was in no mood for diplomacy or compromise.

Vice-president Alfred I. Ritchie, who had gingerly installed himself in the Pastor's study, was asked to leave as Judge Rutherford – 'of commanding appearance, standing six feet two inches tall and weighing 225 pounds'[97] – breezed into the room. There were many and various legal formalities that required his immediate attention, he announced. He would call if he needed any assistance. Thankyou. The slight and inoffensive heir-apparent immediately withdrew and thereafter was no longer referred to as the president by anyone; brother Macmillan saw to that. Within weeks brother Ritchie was replaced by Vice-president Andrew N. Pierson but he too was to suffer the same fate, eventually being forcibly removed from office in 1917.

At the breakfast table, as Macmillan later recalled, Sturgeon's telegram was read out to the Bethel family: 'A moan went up all over the dining room. Some wept audibly. None ate breakfast that morning. All were greatly upset. At the end of the meal period, they met in little groups to talk in whispers: "What's going to happen now?" Little work was done that day.'[98] Meanwhile Rutherford, alone in the study that was once the library of Henry Ward Beecher, methodically searched the floor-to-ceiling walnut bookcases that lined the walls and soon found Russell's Will, a document the Judge himself had drawn up in 1907.

He set to work at once carefully inserting his own name in a list of 'five others' on the editorial committee of the Watchtower magazine whom the Pastor had suggested as suitable replacements in the event of his death or indisposition. Although there were now six names in the will, one of the original five (Dr John Edgar) had died in 1910 and the document had not been updated since it was last sealed and placed in Rutherford's custody that same year. Although Dr John Edgar had already died, his name appears last, making it unlikely Rutherford's name had been substituted at an earlier date. With the late president's ostensibly written codicil naming the Judge as a worthy substitute on the

---

[97] Jehovah's Witnesses – Proclaimers of God's Kingdom, WTBTS, 1993.
[98] Faith on the March – A H McMillan, Prentice-Hall, 1957.

editorial committee Rutherford then turned furtively to the dead man's personal safe-deposit box – and he knew just where to look.

Later that day the shock news of Russell's death was telegraphed around the world to stunned Bible Students everywhere. They had not expected their Pastor to die before the end of the world and the war was far from over; the Jews had not been restored to Palestine and most Bible Students who entertained heavenly hopes were still earthbound. More worrying still, and contrary to what Russell had so convincingly predicted, all the other religions of the world and the nations built around them were still in existence.

There was such a great outpouring of sentimental grief among Russell's mourners that few were aware that within hours of his death Judge Rutherford had hatched a scheme to seize power and gain control of the Brooklyn headquarters and sequester a cash sum of $160,000 into the bargain. According to Alice Banks, one of several Bethel residents who were subsequently evicted by Rutherford in the summer of 1916, several wealthy female Bible Students had made substantial cash donations to the Watchtower Society and moved into the Brooklyn Bethel as residents-in-waiting.

Russell had planned to reinvigorate his flagging fortunes with this cash injection but with his health failing he could no longer cope with the workload. He contacted ex-front man, Robert Hollister, and asked him to come back to the Bethel to help with a restructuring of the organisation as a pre-emptive step into the shoes of the leadership. Hollister accepted Russell's offer and agreed to assume the presidency. However, in the year or so since leaving New York, the Pastor's enterprising disciple had built up a thriving business and he would need two or three months to wind things up before he could come back, he explained.

Before setting out on his final and fatal tour Russell had trustingly revealed his plan to brother Macmillan: 'He asked me if I would like to come back to Brooklyn. He told me at that time that he realised his strength was rapidly ebbing away and that he would not be with us much longer.'[99] Judge Rutherford still had his supporters who saw him as the most likely successor to Pastor Russell, especially his two close friends, A.H. Macmillan and W.E. Van Amburgh, who were often seen drinking with him. They very much wanted him to take over should Russell die. As soon as Russell had embarked on his tour Rutherford was informed of the Pastor's contingency plans. Meanwhile Robert Hollister

---

[99] Faith on the March – A H Macmillan, Prentice-Hall, 1957.

eventually disposed of his business interests and wrote to Pastor Russell telling him he was on his way back to New York. He mailed his letter to the Brooklyn Bethel on the day the ailing preacher died.

***

Eleven days after his death Russell's body finally reached Brooklyn where his remains lay in glorious state for a weekend of intense and protracted mourning. A preponderance of extravagant floral tributes, including a masonic 'broken pillar' of flowers, almost obscured the open coffin as wave after wave of tearful followers flooded into New York to pay their last respects.

During the final afternoon vigil, when the meeting hall was packed to its silent capacity and the service about to begin, a heavily veiled woman arrived alone. Ignoring the ushers, she walked down the centre aisle toward Russell's casket and stood with her head bowed for a moment or two as the curious mourners looked on. To great and gloomy effect, the mysterious woman then turned and slowly made her way to the exit where she disappeared into the crowded street. Nobody seemed to know who she was, so thick was her veiling. Later a small bunch of Lilies of the Valley (the Pastor's favourite flower) was found in the casket with the inscription, 'To my beloved husband'. Today the Watchtower Society maintains that the woman in black was his guilt-ridden and remorseful ex-wife.

Allegations in the Brooklyn Eagle regarding Pastor Russell's 'habit of locking himself into a room with female members of his congregation'[100] went noticeably unchallenged by the preacher who was often stalked by adoring female worshippers. One such woman was sixteen-year-old Sophie Hassan who would occasionally sneak into to the Brooklyn headquarters where she hid in the vestibule to be near her idol. Russell eventually tired of these impromptu visits and reported the matter to the police who removed Sophie to the Kings Park Asylum for observation. The shadowy figure who approached Russell's casket on that mournful day was more likely one such fantasist (perhaps even Sophie herself) who continued to dream on as the late-Pastor's widow. At the time of Russell's death and funeral his ex-wife was living in Tampa, Florida.[101]

---

[100] Brooklyn Eagle – October 28, 1911.

[101] Russell's ex-wife Maria eventually left Tampa and moved to St Petersburg, Florida, to live with her widowed sister Emma, who was being looked after by her daughter Mabel, until her death on Feb 5, 1929. Maria died March 12, 1938.

'I desire to be buried in the plot of ground owned by our Society, in the Rosemount United Cemetery,' Russell had stated in his will. And so, he was. Following a Sunday afternoon funeral service for the Bible Students in New York, and a second service in the evening for the public, his casket was sealed and transported to Allegheny, Pennsylvania at midnight. A third and final service was held by the local congregation in Pittsburgh's Carnegie Music Hall on the Monday afternoon. According to Russell's wishes, interment took place in his private hillside burial ground.

The cemetery lies some four miles north of Allegheny Centre, east of Perrysville Avenue, on the south side of Cemetery Lane and nearby Masonic Way. The farmhouse of J. A. Bohnet was once within view down the hill. Today a headstone designates Charles Russell as The Laodicean Messenger, the last in a succession of seven messengers to God's people. The first six are understood to be Saint Paul, Saint John, Arius, Waldo, Wycliffe, and Luther.

***

On November 19, barely three weeks after Russell's death, his erstwhile personal advisor, Paul S. L. Johnson crossed the Atlantic on 'urgent business'. Jesse Hemery's vindictive letter, accusing Henry Shearn and William Crawford of 'fostering unrest' had landed on the desk of Judge Rutherford who immediately sanctioned Johnson's visit to deal with this insurrection and strengthen ties with London.

Upon arriving at 34 Craven Terrace Johnson announced that he that he had been authorised by the directors of the organisation, as 'minister plenipotentiary', to assume financial control of the Society's funds in London and to dismiss and dispense with the services of Henry Shearn and William Crawford. To their great shock, Hemery readily complied and within forty-eight hours both directors, along with their wives, found themselves in alternative temporary lodgings.

Several telegraphs from all those involved were exchanged with New York and it was not long before Johnson was summoned to 'return at once' to the Brooklyn headquarters while the two ousted directors were hastily re-instated. There had been a misunderstanding, Hemery explained. When confronted with Rutherford's directive to 'return to New York' the errant preacher had claimed he was Pastor Russell's true successor and that he was staying put. However, during the hours of darkness of that day Johnson slipped out of the Mansion House unnoticed.

A few days later news was received from Liverpool that he had sailed for the United States. Before boarding he had written a long and rambling letter to Jesse Hemery in which he predicted a great famine was imminent. The coming disaster would 'reflect an episode in the life of the prophet Elisha,' he wrote, and it was imperative that stores of food be laid up at the Craven Terrace headquarters, 'especially wheat and monkey-nuts'. He signed off, 'Am not at all well, my brain is quite weary, but the Lord will sustain me to finish the work that He has given me to do.'[102] The self-appointed 'minister plenipotentiary', who had suffered a similar mental breakdown (termed 'brain-fag' at the time) some years earlier, had created an unprecedented scene of confusion and misunderstanding among Britain's five thousand or so Bible Students. Upon his return to the Brooklyn Bethel, he was carpeted by Rutherford who resolved to dispense with him at the first opportune moment.

For two months after the death of Russell a caretaker executive committee had oversight of the affairs of the Society. Early in January 1917, during a two-day convention which was held in Pittsburgh, Joseph Franklin Rutherford (48 years old at the time) was elected President of the Watchtower Bible & Tract Society. The chairman at this all-important business meeting was his good friend A.H. Macmillan, who had engineered the nomination of Rutherford for president by Andrew N. Pierson in exchange for his own nomination as vice-president.

On the second day of April 1917 apocalyptic expectations heightened at the Brooklyn Bethel when America entered the war. Bickering differences of opinion were put to one side, but not for long. Treasurer Van Amburgh, who saw democratic business procedure as a threat to theocratic principles, stubbornly refused to let anyone inspect or audit the Society's books. Newly appointed Vice-president Pierson stated: 'We never had a satisfactory report from the treasurer since I have been a director. We do not know how the trust fund is invested. What are the securities? What do they draw?'

Such questions were given an airing in the ensuing pamphlet war in which both camps issued long-winded charges and counter-charges against each other in an effort, on the part of Russell's old guard, to maintain the status quo, and on Rutherford's part, to hold on to power. A week or so later simmering opposition to Rutherford's autocracy threatened to boil over when some of the more determined elders on the

[102] Bible Students in Britain – Albert O. Hudson, Bible Fellowship Union, 1989.

board plotted to unseat him. However, the wily lawyer was one step ahead of them.

The constitution of the Society provided for a majority vote to limit the president's power and four out of the seven directors planned to have the recently introduced by-laws amended at the next board meeting. However, they were summarily dismissed from office on a technical point of law before a vote could even be taken. Having got wind of the plan Rutherford had produced a written 'impartial and independent opinion' of the Watchtower Society's original charter.

The document, which had been favourably drawn up by an equally-crafty Philadelphia lawyer, ruled that as the four dissenting directors – all of whom were 'appointed for life' by Russell – had not been formally re-elected at the January meeting they had no legal right to remain in office. The slender technicality upon which Rutherford's argument hung could easily have been lawfully overturned but the element of surprise and the supporting 'legal document' pushed under the noses of his naive opponents won the day. From that moment on the Brooklyn Bethel was a house divided.

A few days after their dismissal the redundant directors and their supporters were presented with a copy of The Finished Mystery, the late Pastor's seventh volume in the Studies in the Scriptures series. The allegedly posthumous book was, in fact, the work of Clayton J. Woodworth, and George H. Fisher, two of Rutherford's staunchest supporters. It had been secretly printed by an outside firm in Pennsylvania.

Pent-up outrage erupted into fist-shaking rebellion in the communal dining hall as angry supporters of the recently deposed directors protested loudly. Rutherford and his cronies were openly accused of vote-rigging back in January as bread rolls were thrown at the top table. It was this unholy row that brought on the noisy birth of numerous embryonic schisms which had been incubating during the previous nine turbulent months. The meal ended in an atmosphere of whispers, mutterings, and silent eye-balling confrontations.

Ten days after the release of the book things came to a head when, at the close of a conference the Judge challenged his detractors to deliver their ultimatum. When told they had none, he stood tall and boomed out: 'Then, I have one to deliver to you: my authority in this house has got to be obeyed and you will all get out of this house by Monday noon. Brother Johnson will get out today,' he added, with a darting glance in his direction. In the open-mouthed silence that followed Rutherford turned and made his way to the dining room.

A short while later, during the midday meal, the Judge rose to his full height and announced to the entire assembly that the four deposed directors and brother Johnson would be compelled to leave the Bethel home by Monday noon. Objections and pleadings from the accused were silenced when Rutherford left his seat and charged over to Johnson, seized him by the arm and dragged him to his feet shouting, 'You will leave this house before night; if you do not get out you will be put out!' With that he strode out of the dining room with a theatrical flourish that left his nervous audience in no doubt about who was in charge.

After making as dignified an exit from the dining hall as possible Johnson and the four ex-directors left the building and met up at the Society's nearby Hicks Street office to consider their plight. Rutherford's monstrous behaviour flew in the face of everything to which they had dedicated their lives and they would stand their ground, they assured each other. A passing policeman was called. 'Officer put these men out!' cried Macmillan. 'Move on, gentlemen,' said the policeman. 'You have no right to put us out officer,' replied one of the directors, 'we are employed by this society, and we are not disturbing anybody or anything.' The local street-cop, who knew them all by sight, good-naturedly suggested the five accused keep the peace and pursue the matter in a court of law.

Following a hurried visit to Borough Hall to consult with lawyers the reluctant desperadoes returned to Watchtower headquarters to pack their things and prepare to leave. As they approached the Bethel home, they noticed Johnson's clothes and books on the pavement directly in front of the main entrance. Squads of vigilantes had been detailed to stand guard at the various doorways to prevent him from entering the building.

Watchtower shareholders were petitioned with pamphlets in which both sides laid claim to God's favour. Nonetheless the Finished Mystery was widely circulated throughout the world as the organisation campaigned against Christendom's support for the war effort in America, Canada, and Great Britain. Consequently, many young Bible Students in those countries were imprisoned for refusing to serve in the armed forces.

The year ended with a mass distribution of ten million copies of a special edition of The Bible Students Monthly, a supplementary Watchtower publication, containing excerpts from The Finished Mystery purporting to show how Catholic and Protestant religious organisations together formed a modern-day Babylon the Great which would soon be destroyed by God.

Apocalyptic enthusiasm was rekindled among the rank and file when, at a shareholders meeting in January 1918, Rutherford was re-elected as president with his challengers receiving only a small percentage of the votes. Faced with the choice of submitting to the iron hand of the Judge or disassociating themselves from the Watchtower Society altogether the dissidents went their separate ways having been awarded $300 apiece in an out of court settlement.[103]

On the twelfth day of February 1918 the Canadian government issued a public press dispatch: 'The Secretary of State, under the press censorship regulations, has issued warrants forbidding the possession in Canada of several publications, amongst which is the book published by the International Bible Students Association, entitled STUDIES IN THE SCRIPTURES – The Finished Mystery, generally known as the posthumous publication of Pastor Russell. The possession of any prohibited books lays the possessor open to a fine not exceeding $5,000 and five years in prison.'

Meanwhile the New York press carried advertisements inviting its citizens to a 'Free Lecture – Millions Now Living Will Never Die – to be given by the Hon. J. F. Rutherford, member of New York State Bar,' during which he declared: 'The old world legally ended in 1914 and the process of removing the worn-out systems is now progressing. Therefore, we may confidently expect that 1925 will mark the return of Abraham, Isaac, Jacob and the faithful prophets of old as legal representatives of the new order of things on earth.' According to the Judge these 'ancient worthies' (the illustrious King David among them) would appear on earth, in the flesh, sometime in 1925, to oversee the restoration

---

[103] Initially, two splinter groups developed: the Pastoral Bible Institute, organised by the three ousted directors of the Watchtower Society, and the Layman's Home Missionary Movement, which was founded by a determined Paul Samuel Leo Johnson, formerly Levitsky, (1873-1950). He was born in Titusville, Texas of Jewish parents from Poland. He married Emma B. McCloud January 3, 1905, and following a short period as a Lutheran Minister became one of Pastor Russell's Bible Students. He was subsequently disowned by his father, a prominent Hebrew scholar.

On the west coast of America and in Canada another group of Bible Students severed all links with Rutherford's organisation and called themselves the Standfasters. Later still, another separation resulted in the formation of one of the largest groups of dissenting Bible Students – The Dawn Bible Students Association – legally incorporated as The Dawn Publishers (New York) in 1932. Eventually, in 1944, yet another group of vigorous and determined separatists in New Jersey officially styled themselves the Dawn Bible Students Association.

of paradise on earth and the installation of a Zionist administration in Palestine.

In Washington secret agents were instructed to investigate the affairs of the Watchtower Society and to consider the background of its president. To quell public hysteria against pacifism on religious grounds certain members of Congress aired the France Amendment to the Law of Espionage, proposing exemption from prosecution for those who spoke 'what is true, with good motives, and for justifiable ends'. However, according to the Congressional Record, May 4, 1918, the amendment was defeated when the Attorney General observed: 'Experience teaches that such an amendment would to a large degree nullify the value of the law. Human motives are too complicated to be discussed, and the word 'justifiable' is too elastic for practical use. One of the most dangerous examples of [such] propaganda is the book called The Finished Mystery, a work written in extremely religious language and distributed in enormous numbers. The only effect of it is to lead soldiers to discredit our cause and to inspire a feeling at home of resistance to the draft. The International Bible Students Association pretends to the most religious motives, yet we have found that its headquarters have long been reported as the resort of German agents. The passage of this amendment would greatly weaken American efficiency and help none but the enemy.'

On May 7, 1918, warrants for the arrest of Rutherford, Van Amburgh, Macmillan and the five members of the Watchtower magazine editorial committee were issued by the Unites States District Court of New York under the Sedition Act of 1918. In an early morning raid on Watchtower headquarters Federal Agents immobilised the printing facility, dismantled radio equipment and seized books, bank statements, cheque-book stubs, and numerous documents, following a detailed search of the premises. Within the hour the entire leadership of the Watchtower Society were solemnly led away for questioning as police stood guard outside. To the shocked members of the Bethel family left behind it seemed like the end of the world.

Chapter Thirteen

JUDGEMENT DAY

At a preliminary hearing, before Judge Harland B. Howe on May 15, 1918, a grand jury returned an indictment charging Joseph Franklin Rutherford and his seven fellow directors of the Watchtower Society with 'unlawfully, feloniously and wilfully causing insubordination, disloyalty and refusal of duty in the military and naval forces of the United States of America . . . through and by personal solicitations, letters, public speeches, distributing and publicly circulating a certain book called The Finished Mystery and distributing and publicly circulating certain articles printed in pamphlets called Bible Students Monthly, Watchtower, Kingdom News and other pamphlets not named.'

Judge Rutherford, Secretary-treasurer Van Amburgh, and two other directors of the organisation, were additionally charged with violating the 'trading with the enemy' act because a draft for $500 which had been sent to Zurich, Switzerland on November 7, 1917, had ultimately found its way to a payee in Barmen, Germany. The defendants pleaded not guilty to all the charges.

The trial began on June 3, 1918, and after listening to the evidence over a three-week period the jury retired to consider their verdict. Some four hours later they returned to the silence of a hushed courtroom. When the jury foreman announced that the defendants had been found guilty on all four counts of 'conspiring to violate the espionage law, insubordination, disloyalty and resistance of the selective draft act,' Judge Howe remarked that the verdict was 'thoroughly right'.

The following day, before passing sentence, he stated: 'A person preaching religion usually has much influence, and if he is sincere, he is even more effective. It is necessary therefore to make an example of those who sincerely teach this religion, which, like that of the Mennonites and the Quakers and many other sects, forbids the taking up of arms. They have been found guilty, plainly, of having urged men to follow what they consider to be the teachings of the Lord, and to apply literally the commandment, thou shalt not kill. So, the jury could do nothing less than find them guilty, whatever may be the correctness or incorrectness of their attitude toward the moral and religious law.'

Seven of the defendants were sentenced to eighty years imprisonment – twenty years each on four counts, to run concurrently. The eighth defendant, Italian immigrant Giovanni De Cecca, was given forty years – ten years on each of the same four counts, to run concurrently. The charge of 'trading with the enemy' was not proven. The New York Post commented: 'There is no doubt that Judge Howe made his sentences severe enough; they are double those imposed by the Kaiser upon the Socialists who have been trying to upset his wicked regime, and three times longer than many sentences imposed on would-be regicides.'[104]

Throughout the spring and summer of 1918 extensive press coverage of the case fired up patriotic hysteria that threatened to engulf the American heartland. In some parts of the country mob rule took hold with many incidents being reported in the press: In March, at Shattuck, Oklahoma, Bible Student J. B. Siebenlist, a Native American, was arrested when he went to the local mail depot to pick up a package of Watchtower literature. After spending three days in jail, he was released to a mob that tarred and feathered him.

In April, at Walnut Ridge, Arkansas, five men and one woman, all of them Bible Students, were jailed. The jail was then broken into by a cursing mob that whipped, tarred, and feathered their terrified victims before driving them out of town. Respected local businessmen and clergymen were among the angry crowd. In June 1918, at Roanoke, Virginia, Bible Student C. W. Morris was jailed for three months for being 'a strict adherent of the Pastor Russell sect'. In other places some Bible Students were taken to creeks at night and ducked in the cold water as their homes were being trashed.

In Los Angeles clergymen made it their business to persuade owners of apartment houses to consider evicting tenants who were known to be members of the International Bible Students Association. In a raid on Watchtower headquarters in the city all their literature, including Bibles and hymn books was seized and taken away. Twenty-six Bible Students were then arrested for having in their possession copies of The Finished Mystery and the Kingdom News pamphlet. 'We've been trying to get these Russellites for thirty years and now we have them,' said Dr Torrey of the Bible Institute of Los Angeles.[105]

Bible Students in Germany experienced similar treatment, but it was in the United States of America that the worst atrocities occurred. In New York City known Bible Students were spat upon and dragged through the streets because they refused to buy War Bonds. The

---

[104] New York Post – June 21, 1918.
[105] Jehovah's Witnesses in the Divine Purpose – WTBTS, 1959.

situation was desperate and soon all activity at Watchtower headquarters in Brooklyn ceased. Essential supplies – paper, coal, and other commodities – were not so easy to come by anymore. The work of the Bible Students, now too afraid to be seen on the city streets, appeared to be over.

Once a decision had been taken to leave New York the Brooklyn Tabernacle was put up for sale and soon afterwards the much-depleted Bethel family vacated their old familiar brownstone home on Columbia Heights and returned to Pennsylvania. On the twenty-sixth day of August 1918, the old parsonage, now stripped bare and silent, was boarded up and abandoned to the ghosts of Henry Ward Beecher and Charles Taze Russell.

An executive caretaker Board of Directors was appointed to serve largely as an editorial committee to keep the Society's literature in circulation. Within a short time, it was business as usual when modest accommodation was rented in an office building in Pittsburgh from which subsequent limited editions of the Watchtower magazine were produced. These were printed by Bible Student W. B. Conkey, the proprietor of the local printing firm that produced the first editions of the spurious seventh volume of Russell's Studies in the Scriptures.

***

The Great War ended in victory for the democratic Allies on November 11, 1918. The national mood changed and demonstrative opposition to the Bible Students began to wane. In Pittsburgh, Pennsylvania, more than one thousand Bible Students voted unanimously to re-elect Rutherford and his fellow directors to office in their absence. A few weeks later certain newspapers launched a campaign for the release of the 'jailed Christians' which resulted in congressmen, senators and governors receiving thousands of letters pleading for the release of the Watchtower officials. Moreover, a nation-wide petition, calling for a review of the case, was signed by some 700,000 supporters – the largest such an appeal of its time.

Meanwhile, within the walls of the Atlanta Penitentiary, the president of the Watchtower Society and his fellow directors were conducting Bible classes with more than one hundred fellow prisoners. Daily the Judge would fervently pray to Jehovah: 'If you ever get me out of here, I am going to give the old whore [the Catholic Church] the worst licking she ever had.' For Bible Students everywhere it was a time of high hopes and passionate expectations.

On the 21st of March 1919 Justice Lewis B. Brandeis of the Unites States Supreme Court ordered bail for the eight convicts and instructed that they should be given the right to appeal on April 14. The following day the prisoners were transferred from the Atlanta penitentiary to the Raymond Street jail in Brooklyn, New York where, on March 26, 1919, the federal authorities released them on bail of $10,000 each, pending a retrial.

When the day came for their case to be heard Judge Ward stated: 'The defendants in this case did not have the temperate and impartial trial to which they were entitled, and for that reason the judgement is reversed.' It was a majority decision with just one abstention, that of Judge Manton, an eminent Roman Catholic who had previously denied Rutherford and his associates bail for no assigned reason.[106] Upon their release from custody the Watchtower Society president and his fellow directors were feted as conquering heroes in Brooklyn and Pittsburgh.

A few days later the lionised Judge Rutherford returned to his home on the west coast, but to a somewhat different reception. He had not seen his wife for some eighteen months and during that time things had changed, dramatically so. Mary Rutherford, once the Judge's teenage sweetheart, now crippled with arthritis and confined to a wheelchair, had become accustomed to thinking for herself during her husband's absence and told him that she would never compromise her faith in Pastor Russell any more than she would her faith in the Bible. Malcolm Rutherford, who stood tall enough to face up to his domineering father, told him straight that he too wanted nothing more to do with the Watchtower Society. Before the day was out Joseph Rutherford was making plans to return to New York.[107]

Soon after getting back to Brooklyn the Judge installed himself in lofty separation from the rest of the Bethel family in a luxurious Manhattan apartment. Thereafter he plunged himself into his work with a

---

[106] Judge Manton was later made a Knight of the Order of St. Gregory the Great by Pope Pius X1 but his disregard for justice was eventually laid bare when, on June 3, 1939, he was sentenced to the maximum penalty of two years imprisonment plus a fine of $10,000 for accepting bribes totalling $186,000 for six decisions.

[107] Rutherford's wife, Mary, subsequently aligned herself with Pastor Russell's breakaway Bible Students and died a widow in 1962. Her son, Malcolm abandoned religion altogether and never spoke to his father again. After a long working life as a Police Department Bailiff, he died at his home in California (1148 Paloma Drive, Arcadia) on June 22, 1989, in his 97th year. Sometimes former Jehovah's Witnesses who had broken free from the organisation would call at his home, seeking to lay the ghosts of their Watchtower Society experience, but they were always bluntly turned away.

messianic determination that would surpass the efforts of his predecessor. The cabalistic significance of the number forty, which always seems to present itself throughout the Bible whenever there is a test of faith, came to mind. For example: the forty-days Jesus spent in the wilderness; the forty-day fasts of Moses and the prophet Elijah; the forty-day rainfall of Noah's day, and so on.

Rutherford's doomsday mentality provided that recent events in his own life were antitypical of Charles Russell's spiritual awakening in 1874 which climaxed in 1914 with the world at war with itself. Then there was the (invisible) return to earth of Jesus Christ in 1878 and the launch of Zion's Watch Tower in 1879. Such reasoning tied in nicely with his own 'Babylonish captivity' in 1918 and subsequent 'miraculous release' some nine months later in 1919, exactly forty years after the first edition of Zion's Watch Tower had announced the coming of Jehovah's Kingdom.

In the autumn of that year, Rutherford embarked on a major restructuring of the Watchtower Society when operations were relocated back to Brooklyn, New York City. The entire back catalogue of Watchtower magazine was re-issued 'to rouse up and encourage the surviving anointed remnant to resume their open, public service of God in a fearless manner'. Priced at 'just one third the original subscription rate', they were snapped up as a life-saving bargain. At the same time, the colporteur or pioneer service was revived and the 150 Bible Students who initially volunteered as full-time evangelisers soon became more than 500.

In April of that year the news broke that Britain had signed the Treaty of Versailles which incorporated the Balfour Declaration of 1917. This latest political development promised Zionists a national home in Palestine and meant that the Jews could at last begin work to re-establish their ancient homeland. As far as the Judge was concerned, this was irrefutable additional proof that God's plan was unfolding across the world. What he could not understand was why increasing numbers of Bible Students in Great Britain continued to disassociate themselves from the Watchtower Society. In 1920 a brief unofficial private visit was organised.

It was in his London hotel that Rutherford learned first-hand, from Jesse Hemery, just how strong the feelings of resentment toward him were among the British brethren. Nonetheless, before returning to New York he secured a leasehold on an upmarket apartment overlooking Hyde Park in the heart of the great metropolis. Two years later, during the summer of 1922, he returned on his first official visit to the London Tabernacle to consolidate his shaky hold on power in Britain.

Twenty elders donned their traditional English frock coats, de rigueur in those days, and obediently lined up in the dining room at Craven Terrace to meet the new president of the Watchtower Society. Among them was 23-year-old Albert Owen Hudson whose parents were among the first of those in Britain to embrace the teachings of Pastor Russell. Albert was the eldest of four children who were raised as Bible Students in the Forest Gate district of London. He sat and listened to Pastor Russell's sermons as a boy. As a young man, having been excused military service because of his employment in 'communications', he served as an elder at the London Tabernacle during the 1914-18 war. However, young brother Hudson had his doubts about Judge Rutherford.

Jesse Hemery then conducted a kind of military inspection to ensure everyone was presentable. 'I am now going to fetch the Judge, brethren,' he said, before disappearing through a door at the far end of the room. Presently he reappeared with Rutherford at his side. 'These are the elders, brother Rutherford,' said Hemery with a slight wave of his hand. The cane-carrying Judge, looking like the prosperous businessman he was, stayed his distance and solemnly eyed the horseshoe line-up across an unspoken divide. There was an awkward silence before Hemery volunteered a little information about the organisation of the London Tabernacle to which the Judge responded by saying that he would be seeing the elders again. With a curt nod toward the frock-coated Londoners he turned and walked out in silence with Hemery trailing behind. Young Albert was not impressed. 'This man is no successor to Pastor Russell,' he told himself. He later learned that two other dissenters in the line-up were of the same opinion.[108]

Rutherford then set off on a speaking tour of the country but in many places, it soon became clear that many of Pastor Russell's original followers did not take to the Judge at all. Almost immediately the number of British congregations declaring their independence from Rutherford's Watchtower Society grew from 135 to 160. The Judge, conscious of the strength of feeling against him, then took the extraordinary, and entirely unnecessary, step of hiring several personal bodyguards for the remainder of his lecture tour.

---

[108] Bible Students in Britain – Albert O. Hudson. Bible Fellowship Union, 1989.

In Glasgow he faced the second largest congregation of Bible Students in Britain – some 800 strong at the time – augmented on this occasion by curious visiting Bible Students from other parts of Scotland. Upwards of a thousand people were gathered to hear Pastor Russell's controversial successor. Having been tipped off about certain outspoken elders who were opposed to his presidency, Rutherford had prepared his address accordingly. To everyone's astonishment, the visiting Judge, who appeared on the rostrum flanked by several muscular young men, then proceeded to denounce those who opposed him by name.

When he ruled them out of office audible murmurings of outrage swelled as the anxious bodyguards drew closer to their charge. Ashen faced, Rutherford raised his hands and showed his palms to the seething assembly to gain a moment of relative calm. 'Those who love God and his truth know in their hearts that the way to eternal life is not going to be easy. It's going to be hard – very hard.' His desperate rhetoric fell on a stony-ground silence as he paused for a calculated court-room moment of anticipation before shouting, 'Let the lame ducks get out!' He could not have anticipated the reaction. Almost five hundred men and women – a good half of those assembled – stood up and quietly and purposefully streamed out of the building.[109] Rutherford was stunned into silence.

News of the mass walkout spread quickly as shadows of doubt and suspicion lengthened among rebellious British Bible Students. Soon afterwards their rankled visitor judiciously stepped out of the ruins of his crumbling credentials in Britain and returned to New York. Thereafter he began actively discouraging elders everywhere from pursuing an independent course as a localised Board of Directors. Jesse Hemery attempted to effect numerous reconciliations in Rutherford's favour, but many Bible Students in Britain, young Albert Hudson among them, defiantly refused to accept the aggressive Judge as a worthy successor to Pastor Russell.

Eventually, in 1924, young Albert parted company with Jessie Hemery at the London Tabernacle and joined forces with the dissident Bible Students in publishing Bible Students Monthly, a substitute Watchtower-style publication which served the interests of some 4,500 breakaway followers of Pastor Russell in the UK. When he was made Secretary of the Bible Students Committee in 1936, Albert Hudson effectively stepped into Pastor Russell's shoes as their spiritual leader and would remain so throughout the 20th century.

---

[109] Bible Students in Britain – Albert O. Hudson, Bible Fellowship Union, 1989.

However, in 1945 he finally left his Watchtower Bible Student days behind when he launched his own Bible Fellowship Union movement along with a re-named Bible Study Monthly magazine. He also wrote several booklets, all of which echoed the doomsday expectations of Pastor Russell. Indeed, Albert Hudson's life mirrored that of his exemplar to such an extent that he too founded his own Bible House, a retirement complex having its own meeting hall and extensive library.

Gainsborough House,[110] in the Somerset village of Milborne Port, was registered with the Charity Commission in 1979 and in 1981 welcomed its first residents – 'aged Christians of small means and especially those whose sympathies lie with the objective of the Bible Fellowship Union.' This Armageddon-driven stopgap enterprise would be funded by former Bible Students and Jehovah's Witnesses who had stepped aside from the totalitarian control of the Watchtower Society. However, the world would not meet its 20th century apocalyptic end as expected.

In 1995, when he was preparing to step down as editor of Bible Study Monthly, Albert Hudson wrote to a fellow believer in America: 'Within a few more months I shall have more time on my hands than I've had for many years. Our own head count makes for gloomy reading so far as the UK is concerned. We are down to seven organized classes with a total attendance of seventy-five. Compared with our 246 classes and 4,500 brethren in 1931, there seems to have been a slide. Between 1903 and 1925 so many came in; most of these came to the end of the way between 1950 and 1970. There has been a marked diminution since 1970. There is not much doubt that the entire Bible Student movement is petering out . . .'[111]

In the closing years of the 20th century Albert Hudson reluctantly came to realise that his retirement home for Watchtower Society defectors, which had continually failed to attract enough residents to maintain viability, was now facing bankruptcy. He died there, in February 2000, his centenary year.

---

[110] Eventually, Gainsborough House went into liquidation and was subsequently acquired by L.W.P. Homes, the Methodist Local Preachers Mutual Aid Society.

[111] Today (2021) the Bible Fellowship Union continues to promote Pastor Russell's Photo Drama of Creation online and publishes bi-monthly reprint editions of Albert Hudson's Bible Study Monthly articles plus reprints of some of his books and booklets. Surviving members of various associated breakaway movements meet annually 'for fellowship' at the High Leigh Conference Centre, Hoddesdon, Berkshire. Attendance in 2019 was 30.

Chapter Fourteen

JEHOVAH'S SACRIFICIAL SHEEP

Rutherford's Bible Students convened on Friday September 8th, 1922 in Cedar Point, Ohio to listen to their leader. The Judge's confrontational manner and steel-eyed glint somehow lent a measure of credence to his delusional oratory. Events had been unfolding as had been expected all along, he assured his followers: 'Let us look together at Matthew Chapter 24, verse 14 and then Acts Chapter 20, verse 20,' he confided. After listening intently to Rutherford's exhortation to 'preach the gospel of the kingdom from house to house', a motion to that effect was passed.

The 7,500-strong crowd obediently accepted their assignment thereby setting a doorstep-selling precedent for Bible Students and future generations of Jehovah's Witnesses the world over. It soon became mandatory for all Bible Students to turn in a written report of their preaching activities detailing the time spent promoting the doomsday philosophy by which they lived.

Conference delegates were delighted when the Golden Age, a companion magazine to the Watchtower, was launched. Featuring tabloid-styled articles on everyday non-biblical subjects, the zippy new publication was designed to attract the attention of non-religious people. Rutherford had conjured up the alluring title for his new publication when he recalled his earlier fascination with the notorious Order of the Golden Dawn, an organisation founded in 1887 by Freemason William Wynn Westcott. A cabalistic mix of Freemasonry, Rosicrucianism and Witchcraft, the movement sought to resurrect the elements of 17th century mysticism that gave birth to Freemasonry in the first place. Before its demise in the 1920's – when circulation of Judge Rutherford's Golden Age (renamed Consolation in 1937 and subsequently published as *Awake!*) was increasing, the organisation attracted notorious Satanist, Aleister Crowley.

Clayton J. Woodworth, co-author of The Finished Mystery, was appointed editor of the new journal and, with Rutherford's approval, went on to influence countless readers with his eccentric opposition to the 'demon-worshipping shamans' of the American Medical Association: 'Medicine originated in demonology . . . and during the past half century, it has tried to exorcise germs.' He campaigned against the 'barbarous practice' of vaccination as 'a direct violation of the everlasting covenant that God made with Noah after the flood' and urged readers of the Golden Age to 'use your rights as American citizens to forever abolish the devilish practice of vaccinations'.[112] Consequently, children of Bible Students were sometimes barred from schools for refusing the treatment while others would turn up with fake scratch marks on their arms as proof of vaccination.

In the 1920's the Watchtower Society promoted the idea that disease was 'wrong vibration . . . an out of tune condition of some part of the organism which vibrates higher or lower than normal'. Individuals who became ill for no apparent reason could fine-tune themselves back to good health with a device called the Electronic Radio Biola created by a Bible Student boffin who claimed it could automatically diagnose and treat many ailments 'using electronic vibrations'.

Treatment involved the patient writing his or her name in ink on a piece of paper, a tiny fragment of which would be placed in the machine. A reading of the 'electronic oscillations' of a spot of the ink on the fragment of paper was then taken. 'The diagnosis is 100 percent correct, rendering better service in this respect than the most experienced diagnostician.' Golden Age readers were urged: 'Send for a Biola today. Price $35. Cash with order.'[113]

In the 1930's the Watchtower Society claimed that cancer originated outside of the body and that aluminium cooking utensils were harbingers of carcinogens. Eating food which had been cooked in aluminium pans could also bring on 'food poisoning and insanity'. Aluminium pots and pans were 'a curse to humanity and their manufacture and use should be forbidden by law'.[114] Eating out posed a risk and further alienated Rutherford's followers from mainstream society: 'Jesus ate roast lamb and broiled fish. The lamb was roasted, and certainly was not fried in an aluminium frying pan, nor was the fish thus cooked.'[115]

'My mother died of cancer. We are quite sure it was aluminium that caused it,' said reader Harry E. Childs, of Michigan. 'I nearly died from eating cabbage cooked in an aluminium kettle. Having discarded all aluminium ware, also alum baking powders, I am no longer on a diet and am getting much better,' wrote Mrs. Mary E. Lovette. 'I was blind and couldn't work,' said Ellen Williams, of Georgia. 'Two years ago, I

---

[112] Golden Age – October 1921; Golden Age – August 1931.
[113] The Electronic Radio Biola – as advertised in the Golden Age, April 22, 1925.
[114] Golden Age – October 26, 1932; September 1937.
[115] Golden Age – January 1936.

discarded my aluminium ware, and my eyesight has come back.' The Watchtower Society subsequently trumpeted: 'Following the publication of wholesome truth on the subject, there are fewer people now purchasing aluminium cooking utensils than heretofore. There is a pronounced drop in the cancer death rate. Much aluminium used: many cancers. Less aluminium used: fewer cancers.'[116]

By the end of the 1930's the Watchtower Society's culinary scares on the use of aluminium cookware in the kitchen had run out of steam. However, the ban on vaccinations continued throughout the 1930's and on into the 1940's; up until 1952 in fact, when legal pressure forced a corporate re-think on the subject. Nonetheless guilt-inducing guidance on the subject continued to be published: 'While God did not intend for man to contaminate his blood stream by vaccines, serums, or blood fractions, doing so does not seem to be included in God's expressed will forbidding blood as food. It would therefore be a matter of individual judgement whether one accepted such types of medication or not.'[117]

Vaccination remained a matter of 'individual judgement' for Jehovah's Witnesses until 1965 when the Watchtower Society, under the presidency of Nathan H. Knorr, somewhat grudgingly conceded: 'Vaccinations appear to have caused a marked decrease in diseases.'[118] A generation earlier the same organisation had claimed, 'thinking people would rather have smallpox than vaccination, because the latter sows the seeds of syphilis, cancers, eczema, erysipelas, scrofula, consumption, even leprosy and many other loathsome affections. Hence the practice of vaccination is a crime, an outrage and a delusion.'[119]

Indeed, it was the constant promotion of such religiously inspired quackery throughout the 1920's, 30's and 40's that put lives at risk and prepared the shaky ground upon which the Watchtower Society would build its case against blood transfusions and organ transplants in the latter half of the 20th century. Today, Jehovah's Witnesses who find themselves in need of such treatment to survive a life-threatening situation immediately become the centre of attention within the local Witness community as ranks close and martyrdom beckons.

Under such dramatic circumstances religious fervour takes precedence over the enlightened opinions of doctors and surgeons as

---

[116] Golden Age – May 1930; October 1933.
[117] Watchtower – September 1958.
[118] *Awake!* – August 22, 1965.
[119] Golden Age – May 1929.

vulnerable lives are placed at risk, often to the point of death. This begs the question, why? Why, in the name of their God, do Jehovah's Witnesses choose to risk their lives and even the lives of their own children by ignoring life-saving medical advice in favour of the corporate opinion of the Watchtower Society? Tragically the all too simple answer is because the Governing Body, none of whom have any medical qualifications, says they must if they want to survive Armageddon and live for ever on a paradise earth.[120]

For those in thrall to the Watchtower Society, to disobey the pronouncements of the Governing Body, Jehovah's earthly channel of communication, is to disobey God. Those who do so risk being shunned and cut off from all association with their friends and family *by* their friends and family. That is why, even today in the 21st century, countless Jehovah's Witnesses readily sacrifice their lives and those of their children to please their God through unquestioning obedience to the directives of the Governing Body.

Meanwhile those who mourn the countless victims of this suicidal anti-social ordinance are encouraged by their spiritual mentors to comfort themselves with thoughts of 'the glorious hope ahead'. While that may be consoling for those whose minds' eyes are hypnotically fixed on the future, as portrayed by Watchtower propaganda, it will be of little comfort to those who retrospectively choose to reconsider its kaleidoscopic past on the subject.

For example, in Pastor Russell's day, blood transfusion was simply not an issue for the Bible Students of the Watchtower Society. Furthermore, during Judge Rutherford's presidency such treatment was even considered praiseworthy: 'In New York city a housewife accidentally shot herself . . . she was rushed to hospital [where] one of the attending physicians . . . gave a quart of his blood for transfusion, and today the woman lives.'[121]

It was not until 1927 that the Watchtower Society began to suggest that the dietary restrictions God had set before the ancient Israelites must now be observed by Jehovah's Witnesses, his latter day anti-typical Israelites: 'God told Noah that every living creature should be meat to him; but that he must not eat the blood, because the life is in the

[120] According to Watchtower's interpretation of Genesis 9:4; Leviticus 17: 11,12; Acts 15: 28,29.

[121] Consolation (now *Awake!*) – December 25, 1940.

blood.'[122] From then on blood sausage, for example, was off the menu for Rutherford's Bible Students.

However, the correlation between blood transfusion and the consumption of blood products was not formulated until 1945 when the Watchtower Society linked the 'pagan and God-dishonouring practice' of eating blood products to the medical practice of infusing blood into the body: 'The sanctity of blood applies to all Christians. That means not just refusing to eat animal blood, as in blood sausage, but also abstaining from human blood, as in the case of blood transfusions.'[123]

In the 1950's the Governing Body of Jehovah's Witnesses introduced their understanding of blood as a type of 'nutritious' food: 'A hospital patient may be fed through the mouth, through the nose, or through the veins. When sugar solutions are given intravenously, it is called intravenous feeding. So, the hospital's own terminology recognises as feeding the process of putting nutrition into one's system via the veins hence the attendant administering the transfusion is feeding the patient blood through the veins, and the patient receiving it is eating it through the veins.'[124]

Some three years later, in 1954, the Watchtower Society ruled that the injection of blood serums was also unacceptable to Jehovah's Witnesses: 'Blood protein or 'fraction' known as gamma globulin . . . being made of whole blood places it in the same category as blood transfusions.'[125] Some months later the organisation appeared to soften its stance when it announced that certain blood serums – diphtheria antitoxin and gamma globulin – may be resorted to as a 'matter of conscience'. Shortly afterwards, in the autumn of that year the Watchtower Society banned autologous (own blood) transfusion: 'Blood must be poured out . . . the removal of one's blood, storing it and later putting it back into the same person would be a violation of the Scriptural principles that govern the handling of blood.'[126]

Throughout the 1940's and 50's the sanctions on blood transfusions and vaccinations were never rigorously enforced and doubtless there were those who privately ignored them. Indeed, as late as 1958, Witnesses who were known to have weakened and submitted to a blood transfusion were simply looked upon as 'immature', but this unofficial

---

[122] Watchtower – April 15, 1927.
[123] Watchtower – July 1, 1945: May 15, 1995.
[124] Watchtower – July 1, 1951.
[125] *Awake!* – August 1, 1954.
[126] Watchtower – October 15, 1954.

indulgence was not to last. Three years later Jehovah's Witnesses were warned that patients undergoing blood transfusions risked involuntarily assuming the personality traits of blood donors: 'The blood in a person is the person himself . . . poisons due to personal living, eating, and drinking habits, produce the impulse to commit suicide, murder, or steal. Moral insanity, sexual perversions, repression, inferiority complexes and petty crimes – these often follow in the wake of a blood transfusion.'[127]

A few weeks later, the Watchtower Society ruled that Witnesses who voluntarily accepted such treatment would be excommunicated and consequently shunned by everyone including their own family members.[128] Thereafter, lifelong friends suddenly became enemies overnight while Witness business associates ceased trading with one another. For married couples who found themselves on opposing sides of the Watchtower divide the situation became intolerable, often to the point of separation or divorce and the inevitable extended family breakdown.

Witnesses who continued to associate with individuals who had received a blood transfusion compromised their own standing in the congregation and risked being put out of the fold as well. In no uncertain terms the Watchtower Society spelled out its divisive edict thus: 'We should not see how close we can get to relatives who are disfellowshipped from Jehovah's organisation, but we should quit mixing in company with them . . . none in the congregation should greet such persons when meeting them in public nor should they welcome them into their homes.'[129]

In 1963 a specific Watchtower ruling on blood serums, which had been in force since 1958, was clarified in a flash of 'new light' of understanding when all blood fractions were once again considered nutritious and therefore forbidden. In 1964 the lives of sick or injured domestic animals belonging to Jehovah's Witnesses were put at risk when 'new light' on the subject was focused on the animal kingdom: 'A pet should not be given a blood transfusion'.[130]

Any 'new light' of understanding is destined to be outshone and rendered meaningless sooner or later by the Watchtower Society's transient 'new light' policy on the subject – any subject – no matter how

---

[127] Watchtower – September 15, 1961.
[128] Watchtower – October 15, 1961.
[129] Watchtower – July 15, 1963.
[130] Watchtower – February 15, 1964.

confusing or contradictory its latest biblical interpretation may be. Such vacillation is explained away as [spiritual] 'tacking' through the chopping and changing maelstrom of doomed humanity in this time of the end as Jehovah guides his people – with 'new light' here and 'new light' there – to their longed-for destiny.

In 1982 medically sound traditionally proven methods of healing difficult wounds with leeches were forbidden: 'Though leeches parasitically feed on blood in their natural state . . . it would not be proper for a Christian to permit leeches to draw his blood . . . [Such treatment] would involve deliberately feeding blood to these creatures. That would conflict with the Bible's indication that blood, being sacred and representing life, should be disposed of if it is removed from a body.'[131]

It was in 1966 that the Watchtower Society first described blood transfusion as a form of 'cannibalism', a directive which, some two years later, was applied to human tissue: 'Jehovah's Witnesses consider *all* organ transplants to be cannibalism, hence unacceptable.'[132] Even more repelling were the later suggestions that unsuspecting recipients of organ transplants may unwittingly experience a parallel psychological transplant of the donor's personality.[133]

The ban on organ transplants remained in force for some thirteen years and was eventually lifted in 1980 when the Watchtower Society introduced a global network of locally organised Hospital Liaison Committees. These are small groups of specially trained elders whose sole aim is to circumvent the efforts of doctors and surgeons involved in the care of a Witness who may need a blood transfusion to survive. In such circumstances mature adults usually sign a hospital Legal Release thereby rendering themselves fully responsible for their own, usually premature, and sometimes entirely unnecessary, death.

However, impressionable teenagers, dramatically obedient children and vulnerable babes-in-arms are afforded no such freedom of choice when their fundamental human right to live is denied them by earnest Witness parents. The Watchtower Society explains: 'They know that if they violate God's law on blood and the child dies in the process, they have endangered that child's opportunity for everlasting life in God's new world.'[134]

---

[131] Watchtower – June 15, 1982.
[132] *Awake!* – June 6, 1968.
[133] Watchtower – July 7, 1966; November 15, 1967; September 1, 1975.
[134] Blood, Medicine, and the Law of God – WTBTS, 1961.

Jehovah's Witnesses are encouraged to train their offspring to 'resist a blood transfusion that has been ordered or authorised by a court' and to follow the example set by a twelve-year old girl who had been taught to 'fight any court-authorised transfusion with all the strength she could muster'. This child was so determined that 'she would scream and struggle, that she would pull the injecting device out of her arm and would attempt to destroy the blood in the bag over her head'.[135]

At the local Kingdom Hall specially formulated programmes of role-playing situations are sometimes featured in the weekly Service Meeting with a parent playing the part of a judge and a child (usually their own) arguing the case for refusing a blood transfusion. Parents are advised to continue training their children at home on a regular basis 'by having discussions and practise sessions . . . equipping them to express their beliefs with conviction'.[136]

With just six years of the 20th century remaining, the Watchtower Society issued a commemorative edition of *Awake!* featuring harrowing accounts of how some of the twenty-six children smiling out from the front cover had recently met their premature deaths – 'with power beyond what is normal' – for want of a blood transfusion. Some 21 million copies, in ninety languages of this special edition were circulated around the world by Jehovah's Witnesses as the Watchtower Society trumpeted: 'In former times thousands of youths died for putting God first. They are still doing it, only today the drama is played out in hospitals and courtrooms, with blood transfusions the issue.'[137]

Young lives are sometimes saved when custody is gained by court order. However, in many cases the Watchtower Society does triumph, as in the case of Adrian, for example. Too ill to appear in court, the 15-year-old had signed an affidavit he had prepared with the help of the local Hospital Liaison Committee at his bedside: 'You think a lot about things when you are ill, and when you are ill from cancer, you know you could die, and you think about that. I will not agree to blood or let it be used. No way. I know I could die if no blood is used. But that is my decision. No one talked me into that. The way I feel is that if I am given blood that will be like raping me, molesting my body. I do not want my body if that happens. I cannot live with that. I do not want any treatment if blood is going to be used, even a possibility of it. I will resist use of

---

135 Watchtower – June 15, 1991.

136 Kingdom Ministry – December 2005.

137 *Awake!* – May 22, 1994.

blood. To disobey God and extend my life for a few years now and then because of my disobedience to God lose out on a resurrection and living forever in his paradise earth – that's just not smart!'

Adrian was viewed as a 'mature minor' and no court order was sought. Some weeks later he was baptised in the hospital's physiotherapy tank and died the following day. Another 'mature minor' was a young girl named Lenae: 'I have served Jehovah all my life, 12 years. He has promised me everlasting life in paradise if I obey him. I want to be faithful until I die. Then I know in his due time he will resurrect me from death, then I will have plenty of time for everything I want to do.' A few days later she 'fell asleep in death in the arms of her mother'.

Commenting on similar cases of child mortality during an appearance on Séptimo Déa, an investigative TV programme (broadcast on November 29, 1998), Dr Vladimiro Naranjo, President of the Constitutional Court of Colombia, where there are said to be upwards of 100,000 Jehovah's Witnesses, condemned such religiously contrived suicidal deaths as 'a form of murder, moreover, First Degree Murder'.

However, such heartfelt opinion is rendered meaningless in the cold light of the Watchtower Society's incendiary rationale: 'Realistically viewed, resorting to blood transfusions even under the most extreme circumstances is not truly lifesaving. It may result in the immediate and very temporary prolongation of life, but that at the cost of eternal life for a dedicated Christian. Then again, it may bring sudden death, and that forever.'[138]

For decades, an editorial banner in *Awake!* boldly stated: '. . . this magazine builds confidence in the Creator's promise of a peaceful and secure new world before the generation that saw the events of 1914, passes-away.' Consequently in 1994 these martyred children, Adrian, Lenae and countless others who had gone before them, fully expected to be physically reunited on earth with their Armageddon-surviving families 'soon' – most certainly within the life expectancy of the generation which had first seen the light of day in 1914. Countless Witnesses had staked their lives on such hopes.

In the final years of the 20th century apocalyptic expectations were palpable, especially among those Witness families having to make such life-threatening decisions. The end was so close, they reasoned, that it would be foolhardy to risk the chance of everlasting life by failing to measure up to the demands of Jehovah's organisation at the very last

[138] Blood, Medicine, and the Law of God – WTBTS, 1961.

minute. A short sleep, in death, would be an insignificant price to pay, they reassured themselves. As the dubious benchmark of 1914 receded ever more into the past the credibility of this former set-in-stone interpretation of Bible prophecy became untenable.

In 1987, when corporate hopes for a 20th century fulfilment of Watchtower doomsday prophecies first began to fade, the familiar banner declaration concerning the 'generation that saw the events of 1914' ceased to be published in *Awake!* Then, to the great relief of anxious Jehovah's Witnesses the world over, it reappeared in the magazine in 1988. However, in 1995, it disappeared again, this time for good.

The Watchtower Society explained: 'Eager to see the end of this evil system, Jehovah's people have at times speculated about the time when the 'great tribulation' would break out, even tying this to calculations of what is the lifetime of a generation since 1914. However, we bring a heart of wisdom in, not by speculating about how many years or days make up a generation, but by thinking about how we count our days in bringing joyful praise to Jehovah. Rather than provide a rule for measuring time, the term 'generation' as used by Jesus refers principally to contemporary people of a certain historical period, with their identifying characteristics. Does our more precise viewpoint on 'this generation' mean that Armageddon is further away than we had thought? Not at all! The world is sinking further toward terminal ruination. The need to keep awake is more critical than it has ever been. Jehovah has revealed to us 'the things that must shortly take place,' and we should respond with an absorbing sense of urgency.'[139]

***

When, toward the end of the 20th century, the Watchtower Society sought legal recognition in Bulgaria to expand its influence in Eastern Europe, the Sofia government cited the movement's blood policy as grounds for refusal. Watchtower lawyers then secretly prepared a different presentation of the Society's controversial teachings on blood transfusions in which an element of choice would be introduced; a more accommodating interpretation which, in effect, would make the Bulgarian Witnesses themselves personally responsible for their actions.

This selective doctrinal compromise was submitted to the European Court of Human Rights to facilitate governmental recognition of the Watchtower faith in Bulgaria. The court was swayed by the presentation and assured the Sofia government accordingly: 'The applicant

[139] Watchtower – November 1, 1995.

undertook, regarding its stance on blood transfusions, to draft a statement, for inclusion in its statute, providing those members should have free choice in the matter for themselves and their children, without any control or sanction on the part of the association.'

When news of this geographically selective compromise began to leak out Watchtower spokesmen in many countries around the world, including Britain, denied the Society had changed its stance on blood transfusions. Those believers who violated the traditional Watchtower ban on blood in such territories still faced being excommunicated, they maintained. Nonetheless, Jehovah's Witnesses in Bulgaria now had something of a conditional measure of control over their medical care, something the Brooklyn leadership seemed reluctant to publicly acknowledge.

By the summer of 1998, Jehovah's Witnesses in Scandinavia were unofficially following the Bulgarian lead. Olle Hjarpe, the Watchtower spokesman in Sweden, told the Helsingborgs Dagblad: 'To receive blood is a question of personal conscience. Earlier, members were disfellowshipped if they accepted a blood transfusion. This is not the case now.' In the autumn of 1999 worrying reports from Watchtower branch offices in other parts of America and Canada sounded the alarm at the Brooklyn headquarters.

Many former Witnesses now angrily regretted encouraging their loved ones to spurn life-saving treatment in accordance with the Watchtower Society's then uncompromising policy on blood transfusion. In the spring of the new millennium, with the organisation still dragging its heels over global reform on the issue, news of a proposed doctrinal change was leaked to the British press.

In July 2000, a front-page story in *The Times* announced a 'U-turn on Blood Transfusion by Witnesses'. Apparently, not only was it now perfectly acceptable for Jehovah's Witnesses to accept certain blood components without running the risk of being condemned to everlasting death, but it would be temporarily acceptable to have a regular blood transfusion providing the recipient 'expressed remorse afterwards' and then sought the 'spiritual help and support' of the elders and others in the Witness community. This was unexpected news to Paul Gillies, the Society's press officer in London, who could neither confirm nor deny the proposed doctrinal shift. It was only after an exchange of priority telephone calls between London and New York that he was given permission to inconveniently verify the whistle-blowing press report.

A small group of Jehovah's Witnesses, who were among the first to read the early morning edition of *The Times,* immediately made their way to the newspaper's editorial offices to confront the journalist responsible for the story. This was wickedly mischievous journalism, surely the work of Satan, the recently bereaved Witnesses assured each other.

Ruth Gledhill, religion correspondent for *The Times* recalls: 'I was at my desk when, soon after 9.00 a.m., I received a call from Security downstairs. Apparently, several Jehovah's Witnesses had entered the building but had been stopped at the Security Desk. I cannot say how many there were, but I understand there were at least two men among them – described by security staff as 'angry and upset' – who were demanding to see me. They were ejected from the building.'

The breaking news of the Watchtower Society's somewhat disingenuous U-turn on its controversial blood transfusion ruling was immediately caught up in a world-wide web of exposure and spin-off media coverage. However, the unresolved blood transfusion furore soon became yesterday's news once again as the world moved on leaving behind Jehovah's Witnesses stranded on their blood-stained road to paradise.

Chapter Fifteen

THE HOUSE OF THE PRINCES

During the early years of his ministry Judge Rutherford acquired the habit of jotting down random thoughts and ideas in shorthand which he would later incorporate into the texts of his sermons and books. Sometimes there were occasions when the Brooklyn seer could hardly keep pace with the dictates of his restless inventiveness. What he really needed was a confidential personal stenographer, someone he could trust. Then one day, in the autumn of 1923, along came sixteen-year-old Bonnie Boyd.

Having recently qualified as a stenographer the young Bible Student joined the Brooklyn Bethel family at the invitation of Watchtower secretary-treasurer W. E. Van Amburgh. Having made something of a name for himself reciting Rutherford's famous Millions Now Living Will Never Die lecture across America, he had been invited to write a book of his own on the subject, one that would appeal to 'intermediate' students of the Bible.

Bonnie shared a room, on the seventh floor of the new extension to 124 Columbia Heights, with her widowed mother who was employed as one of the resident housekeepers. By the end of the year work on Van Amburgh's book was completed and Bonnie, now an attractive seventeen-year-old, was transferred, highly recommended, to the president's office. Throughout the following spring and summer, a certain rapport developed between Bonnie and the Judge, who never went anywhere without her.

Board meetings now seemed to focus more on the secular business of the Society with the Judge formulating Scriptural interpretation in private with his personal secretary at his side. Directors soon found themselves reading the president's latest pronouncements after they had appeared in print. Rutherford's lieutenants began to feel marginalised; they sensed a diminution of their boardroom status and resented the privileged young girl who appeared to have eclipsed their prominence in the holy scheme of things.

In the autumn of 1924 Van Amburgh's contribution to the Watchtower Society's canon – The Way to Paradise – was published. His observations on the Great Pyramid of Giza were even more revealing than those of Pastor Russell: 'It is quite probable that Shem, the son of Noah, oversaw its construction . . . It gives the date of the exodus of the

Children of Israel from Egypt, and the date of the birth and the death of Jesus, the French revolution as 1789, and the great World War as 1914, besides many more.'

The new book also contained encouraging advice for those who may have been wondering how on earth they would cope in the aftermath of Armageddon: 'Of course, it will take some time to get things in smoothly running order after the great stress between now and 1926. It may be ten years or more before you get your home all fixed up, and the gardens bringing forth the luscious fruits and appetizing vegetables in abundance. Even if it takes a while longer you will be that much better prepared. You will have secured the services of the best decorators you can find. Some of them used to be undertakers; but since there are no more people dying, they have had to seek some new occupation. Their experience as undertakers prepared them to become decorators with little difficulty.'[140]

As the winter of 1924 set in Judge Rutherford felt the need to distance himself from the anxious glances at the Brooklyn Bethel. Taking with him his 'personal secretary' Bonnie Boyd and her mother as 'housekeeper' he left the chill of New York and headed west for sunny California where he rented a large house in San Diego for the rest of the season. A streetwise minority at the Brooklyn Bethel chastised themselves for their idle thoughts.

Hopes were raised when the promising year of 1925 presented itself on the calendar. Just like Russell before him, Rutherford hedged: 'Many have confidently expected heavenly glory this year. This may be accomplished. It may not be.' Some Bible Students had already sold their homes in anticipation of a place in paradise while others had resigned from their jobs or dispensed with their businesses. Certain Bible Student farmers across the United States and Canada would neglect to seed their land as usual that springtime because the Bible, the sure and certain 'word of God', committed the Almighty to bring about a 'full restoration' of fallen mankind that very year. How could it not happen? Judge Rutherford would spend the rest of that doomsday year, indeed, the rest of his life, asking himself the same question.

It was during his 1924/25 winter stay in the Californian sunshine that he started drinking to excess in pursuit of his apocalyptic dreams. Sometimes, when he found himself staring into the void between his own rhetoric and reality, a forbidden snifter or two would smooth things out

---

[140] The Way To Paradise – W.E. Van Amburgh, WTBTS, 1924.

on the bumpy road to paradise. As numerous former colleagues would later observe, 'he was never the same afterwards'. Back on January 29, 1919, when Prohibition became law, Rutherford immediately arranged to thwart what he – and millions of other Americans, it must be said – saw as a devilish imposition before it came into effect the following year.

Throughout that sobering period of American history the Judge, who had always enjoyed a drink and made no bones about it, secretly imported his own personal supplies of liquor from over the border in Canada. This was achieved with the co-operation of the Society's Canadian branch office manager, Walter Salter, who later confessed to systematically 'misappropriating' the Society's funds throughout the Prohibition years to purchase 'cases of whiskey at $60.00 a case, and cases of brandy and other liquors, as well as untold cases of beer'. The contraband would then be smuggled across the border disguised as crates of 'Christian Literature' destined for the Brooklyn Bethel.

While in San Diego Rutherford consulted a chiropractor, Doctor A. G. Eckols, who put the Judge's rheumatic aches and pains down to his dampening imprisonment. Albert Eckols could sympathise with Rutherford for he too had been jailed for a month in 1921 after having been tried and convicted of 'practising Chiropractic without obtaining a licence' from the Californian Medical Board. Such mutual experiences at the hands of the State and tenuous half-forgotten loyalties to the Craft forged an unlikely affinity between the two men.

Judge Rutherford returned to Brooklyn in the spring of 1925 determined to 'bluff his way through' the rest of the year – something he had done all his life, he once confessed. When summer turned to autumn anticipation among the Bible Students peaked as an uneventful October was followed by creeping disappointment when November slipped into December as Rutherford's doomsday year of 1925 passed unremarkably into history. For many Bible Students it was the most hopeful and the most hopeless year of their squandered lives.

Rutherford was always careful to appear unmoved by the debacle of 1925 and whenever he spoke at conventions, he brazenly explained it all away as 'merely an expressed opinion . . . Some anticipated that the work would end in 1925, but the Lord did not say so. The difficulty was that the friends inflated their imaginations beyond reason', he would insist. As for brother Salter, he was often rewarded for his liquor-smuggling efforts with invitations to dine at Rutherford's Manhattan apartment or his palatial New York country residence. One such occasion was Memorial Day (Nisan 14 in the Jewish calendar) in 1926. Falling round about Easter it is the most sacred of all days in the Watchtower Society calendar.

As soon as the solemn bread and wine ceremony was over, Rutherford, accompanied by Bonnie Boyd and Walter Salter and his assistant, crossed the Brooklyn Bridge, and made their way to the Winter Gardens Theatre on Broadway for the evening performance of Al Jolson's show, 'Artists and Models – Paris Edition'. Subsequent rumours that the president of the Watchtower Society had 'attended a burlesque theatre on the most holy of days' were publicly dismissed in the Golden Age magazine as 'grossly false and libellous . . . Judge Rutherford never saw Al Jolson in his life and does not know what he looks like'.[141]

After a long summer wait news broke of a fourth assassination attempt on the life of fascist Benito Mussolini. His survival caused Pope Pius to remark, 'This is a new sign that Mussolini has God's full protection'. By the spring of 1928 Bible Student meeting attendance worldwide had plummeted from a peak of some 90,000 in 1924 to less than 20,000. In America there were now less than 10,000 Bible Students. The Judge rose above it all and re-assured the faithful that the 'ancient worthies' would indeed 'be back on earth as perfect men within a comparatively short time'. He then set about building a house fit for a king as evidence of the imminence of their resurrection. Its construction would be financed by two of his followers who had agreed to anonymously bankroll the project.

Charles Nagle, a Watchtower pilgrim, was a wealthy bachelor while Robert J. Martin, also unmarried and financially independent, was the Watchtower printing plant manager. Their generosity would not only provide for a fine witness to their own faith, Judge Rutherford had assured his financiers, it would also serve to reinvigorate the jaded beliefs of others. Renowned architect Richard S. Requa, who had designed some of the most elegant homes in and around San Diego, was consulted and following a site visit he recommended the purchase of not one but two of the largest building plots available in Kensington Heights, an upmarket rural area on the outskirts of San Diego. Together they would provide enough land area to comfortably accommodate the type of mansion house the Judge had in mind. But there was a snag.

With more than a quarter of a million winter residents coming and going each year, demand for local utilities and services sometimes

[141] Golden Age – May 4, 1927.

fluctuated to such an extent as to pose a threat to the stability of the local economy. For this reason, sales of building plots on some developments were restricted, by certain corporate vendors, to those who intended to reside permanently in the area. Private sellers were free, of course, to sell to anybody. Rutherford soon came up with a plan that would enable him to gain title to the land by proxy and at the same time camouflage his personal involvement in a back-door property deal.

The first step was to find a local resident who would be willing to buy the land on his behalf. The property would then be conveyed to the Judge by a third party. There would be nothing illegal about the procedure, more a red-taped inconvenience, he confided to his chiropractor whose 25-year-old son, Albert Eckols Jnr., was planning to get married that year and looking to earn a little extra cash.

The Judge, an expert in the tactical world of legal intent and delay, conjured up a paperchase of real-estate transactions to conceal the fact that he was both the originator and beneficiary of his carefully planned strategy. Building the house of his resurrection dreams would remain secret until ready for presentation – in much the same way as he published his theological pronouncements – thus suggesting divine providence had played a part in its construction, concrete proof of God's hand in the matter. Deeds, on file at the San Diego County Assessor's Office, record a more factual account.

Acting behind a smokescreen of third-party legal agencies, Rutherford arranged for the two building plots (property of the Union Trust Company of San Diego) to be deeded to local resident Albert E. Eckols in two separate transactions (September 15 and 27, 1929) which were subsequently officially recorded on October 5, 1929. Just three days later, on October 8, title to these properties – now theoretically on the open market – was transferred from 'Albert E. Eckols and Meriel Eckols' (his new wife) to a low-profile Watchtower official, one Robert J. Martin 'subject however to a mortgage thereon dated October 7, 1929, to Charles Nagle to secure a note of Twelve Thousand Dollars'. At the stroke of a pen Rutherford's mortgage arrangements on that day effectively fulfilled the legal requirements of all three associated transactions.

Soon afterwards Robert Martin, having acquired the title to the land, travelled west and personally contracted architect Richard S. Requa to go ahead and build the house and landscape the grounds according to Rutherford's detailed instructions. As work was nearing completion the entire property was secretly handed over to the Judge on Christmas-eve,

1929 in the New York offices of a public notary 'in consideration of the sum of ten dollars'.

The deed, which had been drawn up by Judge Rutherford, stipulated that he would have 'exclusive possession, use and benefit for and during his life on earth' of the mansion house, holding it in trust on behalf of the Watchtower Bible and Tract Society for its rightful owners: – 'David, who was once king over Israel; and Gideon, and Barak, and Samson, and Jephthah, and Joseph, formerly the ruler of Egypt, and Samuel the prophet and other faithful men who were named with approval in the Bible at Hebrews the eleventh chapter.'

The curious document further stated: 'Any persons appearing to take possession of said premises shall first prove and identify themselves to the proper officers of said Society as the person or persons described in Hebrews chapter eleven and in this deed'. Once the legalities were over the Judge made his way to the Brooklyn Bethel to attend a board meeting. It was only then that the other directors of the Society were told about the president's latest property acquisition.

Three weeks later (January 13, 1930) Joseph Franklin Rutherford moved into 4440 Braeburn Road, Kensington Heights, San Diego, California. He called his new abode Beth-Sarim – ancient Hebrew for House of Princes. It would be a lasting monument to his beliefs, and, like Russell's graveside pyramid, it still stands today. For journalists, who were invited to view the property some weeks later, it was a dream of a story.

Having commanding views over Mission Valley toward Mount Helix, the red-tiled Spanish-style house of more than five thousand square feet of living space was built and fitted out with 'the most modern appliances that science had devised'. Parked in the double garage were two new cars: a luxurious16-cylinder Cadillac sedan in sparkling yellow and a Ford saloon 'for general utility purposes and short errands'. To the rear of the property a secluded patio area with an ornamental pond encircled by tall, elegant palms and gnarled aged olive trees provided an oasis of shaded calm and serenity.

'I purposely landscaped the place with palm and olive trees, so these princes of the universe would be at home when they come to offer man the chance to become perfect . . . the climates in San Diego and Palestine are said to be almost identical,' explained the Judge. 'Down toward the canyon, paths have been landscaped to allow David and his friends to walk in meditation. Many of the fruits and trees, native to their Palestine, will greet the rulers when they arrive,' he told reporters.

The scribes were then taken on a tour of the house with its 'red leather chairs and rich drapes'. At the top of a circling staircase, they were shown into a large office 'where the very latest inverted lighting and French telephones await the touch of the princes'. Also, on display was a large Bible 'on which he is said to be an authority'. The principal bathroom was 'resplendent in shiny black tile and decorated with marble fittings specially imported from Italy'. Adding to the opulence, a gold-plated safety razor and strop complimented a range of 'Koniach Wasser from Germany to freshen the princely faces'.[142]

One day a bearded tramp, who claimed to be King David of Israel, turned up on the doorstep to lay claim to the $75,000 Southern Californian mansion. 'One morning as I was going from the house to the garage a queer-looking creature approached me, tipped his dirty hat and cried, Howdy, judge, I'm David. Go tell that to the winds, I told him, and he left without arguing the matter. I could see at once he was not David. He didn't look like I knew David would look like,' Rutherford told reporters.

When he was asked how he would identify King David or any of the other biblical characters, should they turn up on the doorstep, he replied: 'I thought all that out before I wrote the deed . . . men whom I have designated to test the identity of these men are officers of my society and, having consecrated themselves to the Lord, they will be divinely authorised to know impostors from the real princes.'

When Rutherford was asked to describe how he expected King David and the other distinguished 'ancient worthies' to look he replied: 'As perfect men, sent here to wrench the world from Satan's grip, clothed in modern garb as we are, perhaps in frock coats, high hats, canes, and spats and able, with little effort, to speak our tongue. I am not a publicity seeker, but I feel the world should know about their arrival – it will be a great news story. Everything will be theirs – the house, the land, the furnishings and even the clothes if they need them. What will I do? Oh, don't worry about me, I'll manage somehow.'[143] And manage, he did. Joseph Franklin Rutherford, who saw himself as a deserving radical and a credible visionary, lived at Beth-Sarim in sunny splendour every winter for the rest of his life.

***

---

[142] San Diego Sun – March 15, 1930; Time magazine – March 31, 1930.

[143] San Diego Sun – January 9, 1931.

There were several wooden outbuildings in the grounds of Beth-Sarim, one of which was home to a married couple – 'brother and sister Balco' – the resident caretakers of the property. When Judge Rutherford was photographed with a little girl called Bonnie during a three-day summer convention in 1931 it was sometimes whispered that the child was his. Such rumours were soon officially quashed:

'Here are the facts: brother and sister Balko are carers of Beth-Sarim. They spend all their spare time in the 'service work' in and about San Diego, both being fully devoted to the Lord . . . They have two children, a little girl now nearly two years old, and a little boy about six months. Beth-Sarim being "the house of the princes" and, as we confidently expect, to be occupied and used by some of the princes in the earth, it seemed quite appropriate that these children who are growing up there should be named in harmony with these scriptures. Hence the little girl is named Princess Bonnie Balko, and the little boy Prince Joseph Barak Balko.'

'It is hoped that these two little ones may grow up at Beth-Sarim to be with the rulers of the earth and live forever to the glory of Jehovah's name. They have been told, insofar as they can understand, that they may expect these noble men and, when they do appear, to meet them and put themselves completely under their direction. It might be that the little prince and princess would be stenographers or office children or clerks about the place or perform some other duty that will be necessary in the Kingdom.'[144]

However, brother Balko and his wife never stayed the course and in 1935 a William Clayton Short and his wife Belle became caretaker and housekeeper at Beth Sarim where they remained until the house was sold in1947. During this period, they acted as third-party agents on behalf of the Watchtower Society in numerous San Diego property deals. As for 'Princess Bonnie and Prince Joseph' – like two little frogs in a fairy tale, they simply vanished and were never seen or heard of again.

[144] The Messenger (a convention broadsheet newspaper) – July 30, 1931.

Chapter Sixteen

A PEOPLE FOR HIS NAME

In the late 1920's there was a growing resistance to Rutherford's dictatorial style of leadership and thousands of disillusioned believers left the movement. For the next three years there would be more of Russell's original Bible Students outside the Watchtower Society than there were in it. Those who defected from the organisation during Rutherford's presidency were described as 'evil servants' – a Judas-class of Bible Student. This was confusing for believers on both sides of the divide and irritating for the Judge who had yet to make the organisation his own. A spiritual demarcation line needed to be drawn between the old school of Russell's Bible Students and Rutherford's followers.

At a convention of the International Bible Students Association in Columbus, Ohio in July 1931, the Judge quoted the Old Testament prophet Isaiah[145] before proposing a resolution that would settle the matter once and for all: 'As a body of Christians forming an Association, [we] decline to assume or to be called by the name Bible Students or similar names as a means of identification of our proper position before the Lord; we refuse to bear or to be called by the name of any man . . . therefore we joyfully embrace and take the name which the mouth of the Lord God has named, and we desire to be known as and called by the name, to wit, Jehovah's Witnesses.'

A crowd of some 15,000 Bible Students demonstrated their approval with sustained and enthusiastic applause. From that moment on, they were to consider themselves the modern-day Israel of God – his chosen people, 'Jehovah's Witnesses'. The umbilical discord between Rutherford's followers and Russell's schismatic disciples had been severed. A second resolution indicting Christendom for 'her apostasy and for treating Jehovah's counsel with contempt' was then proposed and unanimously adopted by those present. Having been selected by God as 'a people for his name'[146] the newly christened Jehovah's Witnesses were now even more convinced that they were the only true Christians on earth. Five million copies of a booklet – The Kingdom Hope of the World – containing a transcript of the convention address were subsequently distributed world-wide with more than 132,000 copies of

[145] Isaiah 43; 8-12; 62: 2

[146] Acts 15:14.

Rutherford's diatribe, targeting clergymen, politicians, and businessmen alike, being delivered in the United States and Canada alone.

No longer the frustrated back-seat driver on Russell's bandwagon to paradise, Rutherford was at last behind the wheel himself and in full control. Now rid of the Pastor's excess baggage of breakaway Bible Students he would drive the Watchtower Society to the limits of Christian credibility and beyond. In his own eyes he was now a man of world-class importance and, having arrived at the convention in chauffeur-driven style, he looked the part too. Thanks to another of his wealthy patrons – a grateful Bible Student in Iowa – a second Cadillac sedan had recently been delivered to the Brooklyn Bethel. The power-driven Judge was now the proud owner of not one, but two $9,000 apiece matching luxury limousines, outshining the multimillionaire movie-star entertainer Al Jolson who only had one.

***

In 1935 Judge Rutherford identified the 'great crowd' mentioned in the book of Revelation as Jehovah's 'other sheep' – the majority who hope to live forever on a paradise earth. This gave rise to the belief that the quota of individuals with heavenly hopes – the 'little flock' of 144,000 (12,000 for each of the twelve tribes of Israel) – had now been reached and that their numbers would decline as they aged and passed 'beyond the veil'. Those who profess to be of the 'remnant' of the little flock demonstrate their self-assumed spiritual status once a year when they partake of the bread and wine during the annual Memorial ceremony.

Today this exclusive annual 'holy communion' of the 'anointed remnant' is witnessed world-wide by a 'great crowd' of some 20,000,000 'other sheep' and 'interested persons' who attend simply as observers. This ritual underpins the movement's two-tier system of guaranteed heavenly immortality for Jehovah's chosen few and conditional everlasting life on a paradise earth for 'a great crowd' of 'other sheep'. In most congregations where there are no 'anointed' members the bread and wine are solemnly passed around without being consumed.

Newly converted Witnesses who feel emotionally bound to sip the wine and swallow a morsel of the specially baked unleavened bread on that holiest of occasions are treated with great suspicion and privately lectured afterwards. Periodically, when reviewing this annual ritual, the Watchtower Society explains: 'Some have recognised that they partook [of the bread and wine] as an emotional response to perhaps physical or mental strain.'[147] Nonetheless the latest figures published by the Watchtower Society indicate that the number of Witnesses who distinguish themselves by signalling they are of the 'little flock' continues to increase.

During the 1930's Jehovah's Witnesses in America were persecuted and subjected to mob violence for refusing to salute the flag or perform military service. The Judge was now busier than ever as case after case involving his disciples demanded his attention. In one lawsuit after another Rutherford was obliged to justify the allegedly 'anti-American behaviour' of his followers. To further complicate the issue Jehovah's Witnesses were often accused of 'inciting social agitation and unrest selling [Watchtower] literature door-to-door on Sundays'.

The legal work was piling up and Rutherford was glad when lawyer Olin R. Moyle, a sincere and dedicated believer since 1918, left his home in Wisconsin and, along with his wife and teenage son Peter, moved into the Brooklyn Bethel to take up the post of Legal Counsellor for the Watchtower Society. Moyle was to win some favourable decisions from the United States Supreme Court on such issues but closer to home he soon found himself at odds with Rutherford's administration.

Moyle and his wife had been drawn into the movement as an idealistic couple with a young child. The Great War was over, and they too had wanted to be among the 'millions who would never die'. Brother Moyle took his beliefs very seriously, but in the late 1930's, when he was actually living his dream alongside the president of the Watchtower Society, he was often troubled with unsettling doubts. He noticed that unlike the rest of the headquarters staff, the president and his personal attendants worked in air-conditioned rooms and, apart from sporadic appearances in the communal dining rooms, lived in isolated luxury.

He was also 'shocked to witness the spectacle of brethren receiving a trimming – a tongue-lashing' from the Judge who was apparently in the habit of publicly humiliating and lambasting anyone he suspected of stepping out of line. Rutherford's adversarial manner and intimidating demeanour was 'one of the things you have to get used to,' it was whispered. Moyle, a teetotaller, soon realised that 'there appeared to be a definite policy of breaking in newcomers' into the liquor drinking culture. 'You can't be a real Bethelite without drinking beer,' he was told. The disillusioned lawyer found it 'shocking and nauseating to hear vulgar speaking and smut at Bethel'. Then there were the 'filthy jokes

[147] Watchtower – August 15, 1996.

exchanged in the dining room, often with the loudest raucous laughter coming from the president's table'. One evening he overheard Rutherford say to one of his cronies: 'We can't do much with Moyle, but we'll make a man out of [his son] Peter.'

As the Society's lawyer, having oversight of all its legal transactions, Olin Moyle was the only person outside Rutherford's inner circle who knew of the Watchtower Society's growing portfolio of property holdings in California. Some four years later he was jolted back into reality when a copy of a whistle-blowing letter of resignation fell into his hands. It had been written by Watchtower Canadian branch office manager W F Salter, the president's former bootleg runner. Against a background of murmuring gossip about the private life of the president, and with brother Salter's revelations in mind, he felt that the time had come to think again.

***

William P. Heath Snr. was a pioneering chemical engineer who founded the Crystal Carbonic Company, manufacturers of carbonic gas essential in the early development of Coca-Cola. He was married with two young children when, in 1914, his wife became interested in Pastor Russell's Bible Students movement. Following a takeover of his own company in 1919, Dr Heath was subsequently made Vice-president of Coca Cola. His son William P. Heath Jr later became an executive in the sales department of Coca-Cola soon after graduating from the University of Georgia. Much influenced by his Bible Student mother, William Jr was eventually baptised into the movement in 1932. Some three years later, to the great consternation of his father, he resigned from Coca-Cola, proceeded to divorce his wife, and moved into the Brooklyn Bethel. He was immediately welcomed into the Judge's inner circle as a member of Rutherford's personal staff and in no time at all was given a seat on the board of directors as Presidential Secretary. Within weeks Heath found himself dining at the top table in the Brooklyn Bethel and being privately entertained by the Judge and Bonnie Boyd.

Rutherford, who was then in his late sixties and now being cared for by sister Verna Peal, his 'personal dietician and nurse', bowed to the attraction between his unsung former mistress and her wealthy young suitor, brother Heath. This did not go down too well with Vice-president N. H. Knorr and his friend and fellow director Frederick W. Franz who sometimes despaired at the president's drinking habits and erratic behaviour.

Some two years later Judge Rutherford and Verna Peale were joined by William Heath and Bonnie Boyd for a winter stay at Beth-Sarim. It was there that Heath received word that his divorce had been finalised. Seven days later 'Bonnie and Bill' took a trip to Nevada and after a brief visit to a Las Vegas wedding chapel on January 25, 1938, the couple returned to California as Mr and Mrs William P. Heath. Soon afterwards the newly-weds purchased a seven-acre plateau of farmland surrounded by seventy-five acres of mainly rough terrain adjoining the Beth-Sarim residence for a second house which would provide additional accommodation for the 'soon to be resurrected princes' when they appear on earth. Construction began in the spring of 1939.

The spacious house was specifically designed to provide safety, shelter, and self-sufficiency during the coming 'great tribulation'. Among the various outbuildings was a barn which concealed an underground reinforced concrete air-raid shelter of substantial proportions while in the main house a secret entrance led to an underground place of refuge which was stocked with provisions. It also had its own diesel-powered generator and water supply.

Appropriately enough Bill and Bonnie called their new house 'Beth-Shan' (House of Security). The property was signed over to the Watchtower Bible & Tract Society on May 20, 1940 in a deed which had evidently been drafted by Judge Rutherford: 'Whereas the grantor W. P. Heath, Jr. and other parties who have contributed toward said premises, thoroughly believe and expect the return of faithful men to earth who are hereafter named, and who according to the Scriptures (Psalm 45:16 and Isaiah 32:1) shall be made visible rulers on earth, and desire to prepare the property for Abel, Enoch, Noah, Abraham, Isaac, Jacob, Sara, Joseph, Moses, Rahab, Gideon, Barak, Samson, Jephthah, David, Samuel.'

The entire project was financed by Coca-Cola Vice-president William P. Heath Sr. The wealthy industrialist is also on record as having secured the release from custody of his son, William, Jr, who had been arrested earlier in the day during a disturbance at nearby Madison Square Garden where Judge Rutherford had been speaking. Bail had been set at $3,000. Following a worrying call from Rutherford's office, William P. Heath Sr. turned up shortly before midnight at the Police Station on 54th Street in New York one June evening in 1940 with the cash.[148]

---

[148] New York Supreme Court (Index 15845) – Moyle V Watchtower, 1944.

When news leaked out that the Judge and his cronies had built themselves a House of Security in the event of war, Pastor Russell's loyalists accused him of compromising not only his faith in God but also his much-trumpeted condemnation of big business. Although Rutherford had his suspicions about Moyle, he chose to quell the rumours with a public announcement: 'Some unreliable person is responsible for the circulation of a report that Beth-Sarim is being enlarged as a place of security and that this is being built by the Society. There is absolutely, not one word of truth in the report.'[149]

Deeds registered at the San Diego County Assessor's Office reveal that Rutherford's Beth-Sarim and Heath's Beth-Shan were not the only Watchtower Society properties to be held in trust for the 'soon-to-be-resurrected princes'. In a deed dated February 15, 1940, William and Bonnie Heath signed over a huge tract of their land 'situated in the valley containing eleven acres' to the Beth-Sarim caretaker. The document granted 'life estate to William Clayton Short and remainder over to Abraham, Isaac and Jacob named at Hebrews 11'.

Other legal documents show that the Watchtower Society had been profitably involved with secret real-estate deals in San Diego for some fifty years. Eventually two hundred acres of land – 'All that portion of Lot 23 of Rancho Ex-Mission' – were sold to a private investor by Vice-president W. I. Barry and Assistant Secretary-Treasurer L. A. Swingle on behalf of the Watchtower Society. Today that land is part of the Kensington Hillside Open Space Project having been acquired by the City of San Diego in 1985 for 'an amount not to exceed $275,000'.

***

Early in the morning of July 21, 1939, Olin Moyle, along with his wife and son, quietly vacated their living quarters and casually strolled out of the Brooklyn Bethel unnoticed. On a side table in the lobby, he left behind a copy of his open letter of resignation to Judge Rutherford in which he condemned the president's 'scolding, petulant outbursts of temper, and discrimination against the Bethel brethren' and lamented the fact that Watchtower studies had degenerated into mere 'reading lessons'. Graphic descriptions of Rutherford's culture of drinking at the Bethel home concluded: '. . . therefore you must assume your share of the Bacchus-like attitude exhibited by members of the [Bethel] family'. Moyle ended his letter with the plaintive admission: 'We sold our home

[149] Watchtower – June 15, 1940.

and business when we came to Bethel and fully intended to spend the rest of our lives at this place in the Lord's service.'

In a ponderously wordy public response, Rutherford described Moyle's letter as 'being filled with false, slanderous, and libellous statements, not only against the president but against the entire [Bethel] family, and for that reason the letter has not been published by the Society. The members of the board of directors hereby recommend that the president of the Society immediately terminate the relationship of O. R. Moyle to the Society as legal counsel and as a member of the Bethel family'.[150] Soon afterwards Judge Rutherford invited Hayden C. Covington, a tall hard-drinking Texan, to the Brooklyn Bethel to help argue a backlog of cases involving the American Bill of Rights. Covington had been admitted to the Texas bar in 1933, a year before he was baptised as one of Jehovah's Witnesses.[151]

Olyn Moyle returned to private practice in his hometown of Milwaukee in Wisconsin and took legal action against the Watchtower Society, suing the president and his entire board of directors for libel. Rutherford was unrepentant; he had other things on his mind. Earlier in the year he had been diagnosed as suffering from bowel cancer and the prognosis was not good.

[150] Watchtower – October 15, 1939.

[151] After riding high arguing the civil rights of the Watchtower faithful Covington was disfellowshipped as an alcoholic. Years later, following several 'drying-out' treatments at Speers Hospital in Drayton, Kentucky, he was eventually reinstated as a member of the Watchtower Society and continued to associate with Jehovah's Witnesses until his death on November 19, 1978.

Chapter Seventeen

THE RESTLESS CORPSE

At 2.22 pm New York time on Sunday December 7, 1941, 360 Japanese warplanes swooped down on the U.S. Pacific Fleet in its home base at Pearl Harbour in Hawaii. It was a massive surprise attack in which five battleships were sunk or seriously damaged. Fourteen other ships and two hundred aircraft were also destroyed in the assault which took the lives of more than 2,400 people. Jehovah's Witnesses saw this unexpected outrage as another sign that Armageddon was imminent and that their deliverance was at hand. As the author of their fantasies lapsed into stupor and melancholy, they read and re-read his doomsday literature with a renewed and life-giving interest as America was propelled into war.

Meanwhile, on hidden knoll some three hundred feet to the rear of Beth-Sarim, and a further one hundred feet down the canyon, excavations for a hillside crypt were going ahead. Set ten feet into the rocky slope, a concrete superstructure, 25 feet in length and ten feet in height began to take shape. When finished it would be faced with decorative granite and Spanish-style wrought-iron work.

In accord with Rutherford's dying wish to be buried – 'at dawn facing the rising sun . . . in honour of the King of the East, Christ Jesus' – in a favourite spot in the grounds, William Heath had taken it upon himself to establish The Beth-Sarim Rest Corporation (a non-profit cemetery association) to legally administer the secluded (150 x 75 feet) plot. According to the Health & Safety Code, a private cemetery so proportioned would provide for the burial of an additional six or more human bodies.

As he lay dying, Rutherford summoned three Watchtower officials to his bedside where, on December 12th, 1941, in the quiet opulence of Beth-Sarim, he relinquished his presidency in favour of Vice president Nathan H. Knorr. The deathbed transfer of power – officially likened to the biblical account of the passing on of Elijah's prophetic mantle[152] – was witnessed by two senior directors, Frederick Franz, and Watchtower lawyer Haydon Covington. All three then returned to New York.

Just after one-thirty in the afternoon of January 8, 1942, Joseph Franklin Rutherford was pronounced dead; he had been in a coma for

---

[152] 2 Kings 2; 8, 11-14.

several days. Within the hour William Heath, accompanied by the local undertaker, applied for a temporary burial permit for internment in the hillside tomb. That same evening, after the Judge's body had been transferred to the Lewis Mortuary for embalming, a special permit to delay the burial was issued. Some one hundred days later his corpse was still there.

During that time William Heath made numerous legal representations to the local authority but all efforts to secure permission for the backyard burial of the late president of the Watchtower Society were thwarted by delegations of protesting local residents, who argued that property values would be undermined by the proposal: 'We feel that to have a cemetery in or near our beautiful district would impair the restricted qualities now enjoyed by the residents,' said Mrs. W.E. Sweet, president of the Kensington Women's Guild.[153]

Eventually Heath abandoned his crypt project, modified the original application, and sought planning permission for the burial to take place in his own backyard in a 'one grave cemetery on an isolated promontory extending into the upper reaches of Mission Valley' on his 200-acre Beth-Shan estate. 'It would be absolutely inaccessible by road; impossible for anyone to get there except by cutting the brush away,' he pleaded.

'Soon we probably will see San Diego featured in Ripley's well-known column as The City of the Unburied Dead,' a protester wrote to the county Board of Supervisors. To add to the furore, the San Diego Veterans of Foreign Wars reminded the County Council: 'Mr. Rutherford, during his lifetime, practised and taught religious intolerance, and his followers do not believe in saluting the flag and are considered unpatriotic.' The Watchtower Society responded with a series of petitions and letters of support which were sent to the county supervisors asking for a favourable decision.

An appeal was heard in the San Diego Superior Court on April 20, 1942: 'The closest house now is half a mile away,' Heath contended; 'I feel that prejudice dictated the planning commission's decision. One grave in the centre of 100 acres of private land wouldn't hurt anybody.' The San Diego-Tribune subsequently reported: 'Despite an eloquent final plea by W. P. Heath Jr, secretary to the late Judge Joseph F. Rutherford, world leader of Jehovah's Witnesses, the County Board of Supervisors today voted unanimously to approve the planning commission's

---

[153] San Diego Union – January 27, 1942.

recommendation denying a permit to bury Rutherford in an isolated private plot adjoining the Kensington-Talmadge district.' Although the writ of mandate was subsequently denied, the ruling failed to quell Heath's obsessive determination to honour the deathbed promise he had made to his beloved mentor. He prayed for guidance.

A few days later a crated casket containing the Judge's remains, accompanied by Bill and Bonnie Heath, was transferred to the freight car of a train heading east. Ostensibly, interment would take place on Saturday, April 25, 1942, near Rutherford's Staten Island country residence which also housed the Society's Radio Station WBBR. It was here that Judge Rutherford lay in repose as arrangements were made for his internment.

Rutherford's widow Mary and his son Malcolm were neither contacted by the Watchtower Society following his death nor were they consulted regarding Heath's 'private' funeral arrangements for the Judge. The lonely dawn ceremony, which was attended by William and Bonnie Heath in the presence of San Diego mortician Mr Lewis and his assistant, was briefly acknowledged in the Watchtower magazine some weeks later.

Over the years ghoulish stories have emerged of the Judge's remains being transferred to a wooden packing crate prior to the dawn burial of an empty casket. Macabre Watchtower legend has it that Bill and Bonnie Heath then made the long journey back to San Diego with the Judge's cadaver in the back of a truck. Years later, a former gardener at Beth-Sarim claimed he had been seconded into burying 'a large wooden crate' deep under the floor of an outbuilding in the garden.

***

Joseph Franklin Rutherford was an austere and somewhat overbearing man. During his presidency of the Watchtower Society, he banned a whole range of popular customs, both religious and secular, as 'worldly'. The crucifix – which had adorned the Society's literature throughout the entire ministry of Pastor Russell and beyond – was eventually consigned to the 'spiritual darkness' of the past: 'Christ died on a stake, not a two-beamed cross,' he asserted.

Birthday celebrations were branded unchristian and were to be avoided. The birthday of Jesus had become of greater interest to people than the ransom provided by his death, he claimed. Furthermore, the three wise men who presented their individual gifts to the baby Jesus on that unspecified day of his birth were demon-inspired astrologers – magi whose gift-giving was not something true Christians should emulate. Indeed, parents who told their children stories about Santa Claus were lying to them; St. Nicholas – Santa Claus – was just another name for the Devil himself.

Older Bible Students who sported beards after the style of Pastor Russell were accused of creature worship and frowned upon at the Brooklyn headquarters. Such expressions of personal vanity were discouraged in branch offices and printing plants throughout the world. Consequently, Watchtower literature featuring illustrations of Jesus always depicted him as being handsomely white and clean shaven, the implication being that the unblemished face of a perfect man such as Christ would not have had whiskery facial hair. However, this teaching was reversed when the Society later announced: 'Biblical evidence is the most reliable testimony to be found on [the question of beards] and a recent careful review of what it says indicates that Jesus did indeed have a beard.'[154] Nonetheless, today – except for a tiny minority of mainly blacks and Hispanics – Rutherford's denigration of Russell's bearded image continues to be reflected in the clean-shaven majority of Bethelites the world over.

Rutherford declared that Mother's Day – first observed in America in 1914 – was a feminist plot and suggested that it would be morally wrong for men to demonstrate any deference to women by adopting the 'sinful custom' of standing when a lady entered the room. Even the gentlemanly tradition of tipping of a hat to a lady was viewed as demeaning to Christian men.

As an advocate Judge Rutherford favoured the spoken word. Back in 1922, he had been quick to recognise the potential of the new medium of radio when he made his broadcasting debut in front of a live audience at the Metropolitan Opera House, Philadelphia. Soon afterwards he purchased land on Staten Island and built his own broadcasting station. Few Bible Students ever knew it was principally yet another luxurious private residence for the Judge.

Licensed by the U.S. government, Radio WBBR was the first non-commercial radio station in New York. Inaugurated on February 24, 1924, when Rutherford boomed out a lecture – Radio and Divine Prophecy – over the airwaves, it was to be the first of many. The station operated on an initial broadcasting power of just 500 watts (later increased

[154]Watchtower – May 12, 1968

to 1,000 watts) throughout the New York metropolitan area and the neighbouring States of Connecticut and New Jersey.

The prospect of being heard by such a huge cosmopolitan audience fascinated the Judge. He reasoned that his newly discovered radio voice would be heard by 'as many Italians as there were in Rome, more people of Irish origin than there were in Dublin and more Jews than there were in the entire country of Palestine'. When he broadcast his talk Freedom for the People in 1926, Rutherford claimed to have 'addressed a global audience over 107 radio stations, the world's largest hook-up, costing about $50,000'. In 1930 he broadcast an attack on the government – Prohibition – of God or the Devil? – and at one point he even persuaded New York's Gimmbel Brothers department store to promote his 'Christian broadcasts'. However, the retailer eventually withdrew its controversial sponsorship in the shadow of a threatened Catholic-inspired boycott campaign.

In dreary contrast to Rutherford's crackling radio performances his rather more long-winded British counterparts were somewhat less enthusiastic about the new-fangled 'wireless service'. In 1928 the British Broadcasting Company invited London elder Henry Shearn to give a presentation of the Bible Student faith 'on the air' but he declined because he felt he could not say what he wanted to say in the fifteen minutes he was allotted. The invitation was never repeated.[155]

Joseph Rutherford was an intolerant and deeply prejudiced man whose mouth sometimes ran away with him, usually when he had downed a tongue-loosening drink or two. Former Jehovah's Witness James Penton shares a memory of his parents who were present when Judge Rutherford was giving a talk on the return of the Jews to Palestine. They were attending a Bible Student convention in Winnipeg, Manitoba in the early 1920's, when the Judge let slip: 'I'm speaking of the Palestine Jew, not the hooked-nosed, stoop-shouldered little individual who stands on the street corner trying to gyp you out of every nickel you've got.'[156]

Later, he went even further when he announced that natural Jews no longer played a significant part in the apocalyptic end game: 'Be it known once and for all that those profiteering conscienceless, selfish men who call themselves Jews, and who control the greater portion of the finances of the world and the businesses of the world, will never be

---

[155] Bible Students in Britain – Albert O Hudson, Bible Fellowship Union, 1993.

[156] Apocalypse Delayed – M. James Penton, University of Toronto Press 1985

the rulers in this new earth. God would not risk such selfish men with such an important position.'[157]

In 1933 he abandoned his Zionist beliefs altogether when he instructed Jehovah's Witnesses in Germany to appease the Nazis by holding a convention in a hall festooned with Swastikas and singing one of their own sacred songs to the tune of the German national anthem. Hitler was not impressed and vowed, 'This brood will be exterminated in Germany'. Eventually almost all of Rutherford's German followers, like many other minority groups, ended up in Nazi concentration camps where most of them were to die before the end of the war.

In America during the Depression years Rutherford sometimes attracted the attention of labour leaders and socialists who privately welcomed his vehement attacks on big business and commerce. Certain politicians admired the Judge's vitriolic public denunciations of Hitler's Nazis and Mussolini's Fascists while significant numbers of Protestants of all persuasions discreetly warmed to his devastating condemnations of the Roman Catholic Church.

However, Rutherford had little time for Protestantism claiming it existed 'only in name, not in fact'. He accused the Roman Catholic hierarchy, the Fascists, and the Nazis of conspiring together to gain control of the world. He reminded both Catholic and Protestant clergy that Adolph Hitler had joined the Nazi party in Munich, Germany in 1919 – the same year the Fascist movement under Mussolini had taken root in Italy – and that both leaders and the ideologies they foisted onto a war-torn world initially enjoyed the blessing of the Vatican. He condemned the Pope's 'involvement in politics' as unworthy of true Christianity and further proof that God had removed his blessing from the Church of Rome.

By the end of the 1930's congregations were organized as 'companies' supervised by 'company servants' who were appointed by the Watchtower Society. The faithful 'colporteurs' of old were now called 'pioneers' – those at the sharp end of things – spreading the word 'placing' books and literature where no-one had ventured before. Early in his presidency Judge Rutherford introduced a thought-controlling system of Bible study which remains in force today as the Watchtower Society's principal method of indoctrination.

Every week millions of Jehovah's Witnesses the world over assemble in Kingdom Halls or other meeting places to listen and follow along

---

[157] Golden Age – February 23, 1927.

with their own copy of the Watchtower magazine as an appointed reader takes them through the material one or two paragraphs at a time. The Witnesses prepare for the Watchtower study by digesting the material beforehand and underlining the answers to the footnote questions exactly as they appear in each paragraph. Questions pertinent to each paragraph are then read out by one of the local elders (usually the presiding overseer). Members of the congregation who respond by raising a hand are then invited to answer the question by paraphrasing the key thought expressed in the paragraph or simply by reading aloud the required answer as it appears in the text. Spontaneous debate is out of the question.

In this way the Witnesses are systematically conditioned and indoctrinated to believe that Jehovah is somehow involved in the preparation and understanding of the editorial content of the Watchtower magazine and to readily accept, without question, the scriptural interpretations and lifestyle guidance to be found within its pages. Everyone, including the youngest of children, is encouraged to passively conform to this method of Bible study. 'Heavy research is not necessary,' the faithful are assured, 'the Watchtower has done it for you . . . Jehovah caused the Bible to be written in such a way that you need his human channel to understand it.'[158]

These 'study editions' of the Watchtower magazine, which feature lengthy propaganda articles dealing with various aspects of the Society's ever-changing scriptural interpretations are no longer circulated in the door-to-door ministry as before. This selective censorship, which effectively masks the existence of the mind-controlling question and answer editions of the Watchtower magazine, was first introduced in 2008 when a simplified 16-page introductory Watchtower magazine, minus the study article was first offered to the public.

During his ministry Judge Rutherford produced twenty full-length books – an average of one a year during his presidency – which eventually sold more than 76 million copies world-wide. These works were published as brightly coloured hardbacks which collectively came to be known as 'Rutherford's Rainbow'. He also produced more than seventy booklets containing transcripts of his radio talks and convention addresses claiming that any one of these publications 'could be read in just fifteen minutes [giving the reader] more genuine satisfaction and more profitable pleasure . . . than can be gotten from studying the Bible by yourself for a whole year'.

---

[158] Watchtower – June 1, 1967

Rutherford's first hardback book – The Harp of God – was published in 1923. It soon became a best-seller which was translated into twenty-two languages with a grand total of more than 5,819,000 copies being sold world-wide. Early editions were subtitled Proof Conclusive that Millions Now Living Will Never Die. Essentially it was a condensed reiteration of Russell's eschatology in which the Judge attempted to mollify his detractors by appearing to agree with their tortured sentiments that the late Pastor was God's 'wise and faithful servant'.

However, when Rutherford realised, he had unwittingly portrayed himself as a mere presidential head of a corporation, as opposed to a spiritually appointed spokesman for God on a par with his predecessor, he revised the text. Subsequent editions bore no mention of Charles Russell as 'God's special messenger'. Toward the end of his life Rutherford announced that the 'strange work of the Lord' was ending and stressed the importance of remaining unencumbered by domestic responsibilities: 'Should men and women, both of whom are 'other sheep' of the Lord [those hoping to live forever on earth], now marry before Armageddon and bring forth children? They may choose to do so, but the admonition of the Scriptures appears to be against it.' To many believers at that time the very idea of marrying and having children seemed inconceivable.

In a tribute to the late president the Watchtower Society noted: 'Brother Rutherford had the unspeakable privilege of putting nearly 400,000,000 books and booklets in the hands of the people, feeding them on the Lord's Word.' However, in the changing climate at the Brooklyn headquarters 'Rutherford's Rainbow' soon began to fade away.

His successor, Nathan Homer Knorr, was born in the small town of Bethlehem in Pennsylvania in 1905 and raised in the faith of his parents who were members of the Dutch Reform Church. When he was fifteen years old the family was living in Allentown, Pennsylvania where he attended a dramatic public lecture, Million's Now Living Will Never Die, which was delivered by colporteur Frederick W. Franz.

Two years later young Nathan took the plunge and was baptised as a Bible Student in 1922. Public speaker Frederick Franz, who had been a full-time travelling preacher for the Watchtower Society since the heady days of 1914, gave the ceremonial talk at the baptism and the two struck up a lifelong friendship. A year after his baptism, the eighteen-year-old became a full-time colporteur and four years later, much to the dismay of his parents, he moved into the Brooklyn headquarters to live and work as a member of the Bethel family.

In 1932 Rutherford offered his eager young protégé, then still in his twenties, the post of General Manager of the New York printing plant and administrational offices. Then in 1940, after years of unquestioning loyalty to the organisation and grim obedience to the domineering Judge, Nathan Homer Knorr was appointed Vice-president of the Watchtower Society. However, in 1944, some two years into his eventual presidency he found himself once again in the shadow of his predecessor.

Olin Moyle, who was judged to have been telling the truth about the late president of the Watchtower Society, was subsequently awarded $15,000 damages plus costs by the New York Supreme Court. The Watchtower Society chose not to appeal and quietly paid up. News of the damning libel verdict, along with copies of the open resignation letters of lawyer Olin Moyle and Walter Salter, Rutherford's former Prohibition bootleg runner, eventually reached the Society's London headquarters and the office of Pastor Russell's former ally, Jessie Hemery.

For many years it had been Hemery's practice to submit material to be considered for publication by invitation from Pastor Russell; it was an arrangement that continued throughout the presidency of Judge Rutherford. However, the former friend and collaborator of both Russell and Rutherford was now beginning to feel that some of their prophecies were not entirely in accord with the Scriptures and the facts of history – a belief that surfaced in his writing. Consequently, his submissions for publication were now continually rejected by the Watchtower Society throughout the 1940's.

Eventually, Jessie Hemery decided to independently publish his own Biblical interpretations. Spurred on by the revelations of Olin Moyle and Walter Salter, along with the financial assistance of two friends within the organisation, he launched his own Goshen Society in 1951 with the publication of Revelation Unfolded. It was the first of several books which, as Albert Hudson would later recall, 'led to some very lively exchanges' among Britain's fragmenting Watchtower Society defectors in the 1950's.

For his pains Jessie Hemery was eventually disfellowshipped by President Knorr but defiantly continued to exercise his 'unconditional legal right' to remain in his 'bed and board' private quarters in the Mansion House 'in perpetuity', as originally granted by Pastor Russell. However, the leasehold on the property was coming up for renewal in

1960 and the Watchtower Society planned to move into a custom-built printing and residential complex (The Ridgeway, London NW7 1RN), which they did, in 1959. Subsequently, having agreed an out-of-court financial settlement, and relinquishing his Mansion House residential rights into the bargain, Jessie Hemery moved into a modest 'rent-free' private house[159] in north London which had been willed to the Watchtower Society. He died there in 1963, his centenary-year, his Goshen Society having come to nothing.

***

Back in 1942, President Knorr, feeling vulnerable and exposed in the glare of the New York Supreme Court ruling against the Watchtower Society, sought the advice of his colleague and friend Fred Franz, appointing him Vice-president of the Watchtower Society in the process. Rather more a mystic than an academic, life-long bachelor Franz was a university drop-out and self-taught linguist with a basic working knowledge of written Latin and Greek. Among the rest of the largely high-school grade Watchtower directors on the board scholarly Franz stood tall; he would be the principal source of Watchtower doctrine for the next fifty years.

In comparison with his larger-than-life predecessor president Knorr was a dull, colourless, and thoroughly institutionalised yes-man, having spent more than twenty years in Rutherford's shadow, striving to please God to the satisfaction of the cloistered organisational demands of the Watchtower Society. He was not particularly well educated and possessed neither the persuasive old-world charm of Pastor Russell nor even a hint of the charisma of Judge Rutherford. However, he certainly made up for his lacklustre personality with his acquired organisational skills.

During his presidency, membership of the movement snowballed in the immediate post-war years and throughout the 1950's as the Witnesses became less confrontational in their evangelising work. The distribution of leaflets or the offering of Watchtower magazines at the entrances to churches and other places of worship was stopped. Gone were days of 'information marches' when long lines of men and women would tramp silently through towns and cities with placards bearing slogans such as 'Religion is a Snare and a Racket'. Jehovah's Witnesses would be more tactful in future.

---

[159] 137, Bathurst Gardens, Willesden, London.

Rutherford's 'companies' of Jehovah's Witnesses became Knorr's 'congregations' who gathered in Kingdom Halls to be watchfully presided over and marshalled into obedience by a pecking order of elders and servants. Under the new president the Watchtower Society's board of directors would evolve into a secretive Governing Body – a corporate 'faithful and discreet slave' – as the world approached its end.

The Watchtower Society was now obliged to maintain the collective mind-set of Jehovah's Witnesses to focus on the doomsday timetable which had been firmly anchored to the year 1914 by both Russell and Rutherford. Throughout the remaining years of the 20th century this would be achieved principally by the third president of the organisation Nathan H. Knorr and his close friend and Vice president Frederick W. Franz. Between them these two men held the fate of millions in their hands as they schemed to mould the thinking and expectations of Jehovah's Witnesses in a war-ravaged world.

Conscious of his inability to formulate biblical commentary or interpretation of his own, Knorr cleverly saved face and veiled his inadequacy by decreeing that in future all Watchtower Society literature would be published anonymously, thus enhancing the belief that the organisation was truly theocratic into the bargain. He established the Gilead Missionary Training School at South Lansing, New York, and organised local Theocratic Ministry Schools in congregations throughout the world providing training in preaching methods and slick doorstep presentation techniques. He also produced a modern American New World translation of the Holy Scriptures.

This mammoth task was undertaken in great secrecy by Vice-president F. Franz and two other Watchtower directors, Albert Schroeder, and George Gangas, neither of whom had any knowledge of Hebrew or Greek and chaired by Knorr himself. The New World Translation of the Holy Scriptures was initially released in six volumes over a ten-year period from 1950 to 1960. Even though no transliteration of the original ancient Hebrew Tetragrammaton (YHWH) is anywhere to be found in the original Greek Scriptures from which the New Testament was translated, the Watchtower Society 'restored' the name Jehovah more than 230 times in their version of the text.

Everyone, from the youngest to the oldest in the congregation, was encouraged to take part in the door-to-door ministry, sharing the good news of the coming kingdom by 'placing' as much literature as possible. All 'publishers' were now obliged to fill out a monthly Field Service Report detailing the number of hours spent 'on the work' and the number of books and magazines placed. Every member of the organisation now had to earn their place in paradise by working for the Watchtower Society, even children: 'Parents who love their children and who want to see them alive in God's new world will encourage and guide them toward goals of increased service and responsibility.'[160] Adult slackers were coerced into greater service with cloying stories of the fearless doorstep evangelising efforts of tiny-tots who were singled out as infant models of Watchtower conformity: '. . . by the time she was five, on her own she would go from house to house and offer the Watchtower and *Awake!*'[161]

During the war one of Jehovah's Witnesses rose to newsworthy prominence through the activities of her son who had assumed command of allied forces mustered for an amphibious attack on French North Africa. His success in that operation led to him being selected as supreme commander for the 1944 Anglo-American invasion of occupied France. Few at the time knew that General Dwight D. Eisenhower had been raised as one of Pastor Russell's Bible Students.

---

[160] Watchtower – March 15, 1962.
[161] Watchtower – October 15, 1979.

Chapter Eighteen

THE WATCHTOWER AND THE WHITE HOUSE

When Nathan Homer Knorr became the Watchtower Society's third president in 1942, Jehovah's Witnesses throughout the world numbered just 106,000. Among the 30,000 or so American believers at that time were David Jacob Eisenhower and his wife, Ida. They met as students at a small United Brethren college in the town of Lecompton, Kansas and married on September 23, 1885, setting up home in a modest white framed house on South 4th Street in Abilene, Kansas.

David soon introduced his young bride to The Brethren in Christ Church, a Calvinistic sect which had been formed during the Civil War. Most of David Eisenhower's relatives belonged to this community. Indeed, his father, the Reverend Jacob Eisenhower, was a River Brethren minister. They were popularly known as River Brethren because their first churches were located near rivers. They had much in common with another Christian sect known as the Mennonites.

Charles Russell's early teachings reflected much of the theology of both movements and although there were differences in doctrine between all three sects, there were persuasive similarities – Protestant, conservative, opposed to war, end-time beliefs and condemnatory of 'worldly ways'. However, young David, who had never really felt comfortable with the hell-fire teachings of his Puritanical upbringing, occasionally attended the Lutheran and Methodist churches.

It was in 1895, when disaster struck, that David and Ida rejected their former beliefs and readily embraced the teachings of Pastor Russell. At the time, the young couple were proud parents of five boys when suddenly, life itself lost all meaning. Their fifth son, baby Paul, had succumbed to Scarlet Fever at just eight months old. They found little or no comfort in their own inherited faith as word of their hopeless desolation spread in the local community. In her grief Ida was comforted and consoled by three women who lived close by.

Mary Thayer and two other Bible Student neighbours persuaded David and Ida to consider reading just one volume of Pastor Russell's Divine Plan of the Ages. There was, they said, no other way to understand the hope that the Bible held out for those who mourned. Some weeks later David and Ida obtained the other two volumes in the series available at that time and soon afterwards took out a subscription to Zion's Watchtower magazine.

It was about a year later, when their third-born son Dwight was coming up to his sixth birthday, that the sad but hopeful couple opened their home as a meeting place for a neighbourhood Bible class using Russell's books and his journal as a basis for their weekly study. In April 1899 Zion's Watch Tower reported that on the evening of Nisan 14 (March 26th that year) 'ten persons celebrated the annual Memorial Supper in Abilene, Kansas. We are glad of this: it generally indicates good spiritual condition'. These meetings would continue for the next twenty years with David Jacob Eisenhower officiating as elder and Bible-study conductor.

Dwight D. Eisenhower's schoolboy friend at that time, R.G. Tonkin, later recalled attending some of those home Bible-studies: 'Whatever the religious convictions of the [Eisenhower] boys may have been, they did not talk about them. I never knew any of the family to attend the River Brethren Church. They seemed to have organised a schismatic branch of their own. Every Sunday afternoon about fifteen people would gather at the Eisenhower home. There was a small organ, and the group would sing and pray for hours – at least it seemed that long to me.'

More than sixty year later, Edgar Eisenhower recollected: 'Our parents' religious interests switched to a sect known as the Bible Students. The meetings were held at our house, and everyone made his own interpretation of the Scripture lessons. Mother played the piano, and they sang hymns before and after each meeting. It was a real old-time prayer meeting . . . I have never forgotten those Scripture lessons . . . mother impressed those creeds deep in our memories. Even after I had grown up, every letter I received from her, until the day she died, ended with a passage from the Bible.'

By the year 1915, when Armageddon hopes were high, the Abilene Bible class had outgrown the Eisenhower home and Sunday meetings continued in a local hired hall. It was also the year in which 24-year-old Dwight D. Eisenhower graduated from West Point Military Academy.

To mark the occasion his mother presented him with a copy of the American Standard Version of the Bible which at that time was favoured by Pastor Russell because of its numerous references to God as Jehovah.

David Eisenhower first became disillusioned with Russell's Armageddon prophecies when nothing happened in 1914, even more so after 1915. By 1919 his interest in the Bible Students was very much on the wane He lost interest altogether in 1928 when Judge Rutherford dismissed Pastor Russell's 'pyramidology' as 'unscriptural and demonic'. However, his abiding interest in the allegedly built-in secrets of the Pyramid of Giza stayed with him. For years David Eisenhower would fascinate his five sons with explanations of how the inner and outer dimensions of the Great Pyramid of Giza, with its many and varied triangular aspects, added up to a mathematical and logical understanding of Bible prophecy. Unlike most other Bible Students at the time David Eisenhower encouraged self-determination in his sons. Consequently, for all five boys, there was a slow drift away from the social confinement of the religious convictions of their parents toward a more expressive secular freedom.

Son, Edgar, reflected: 'Father was a really free thinker . . . he read all the religious literature available. All his life he was searching for an answer. He even left [Judge Rutherford's] organisation because he couldn't go along with the sheer dogma that was so much a part of their thinking.' His brother Arthur added, 'He tried to prove prophecies for the future as well as prophecies in the Bible that had been fulfilled. By extending the lines of the pyramids . . . he proved to his own satisfaction that the Bible was right in its prophecies. I want to point out, though, that when you reach a conclusion, you can always find evidence to prove your point, and I think that is what dad did, he was very much satisfied with [Pastor Russell's] chart.

David Eisenhower died, in March 1942, at the age of 78. Naomi Engle, a Witness friend of the family who was helping to nurse Ida at home, arranged a Jehovah's Witness funeral for her late husband on her behalf. The service was conducted by James L. Thayer who was assisted by Fred K. Southworth, a friend of the family since 1901. Afterwards, despite its alleged satanic origins, an impressive wall-chart (five feet high and ten feet in length), a replica of the original platform back-drop used by Pastor Russell in the British port of Liverpool at the start of his first world tour, remained on permanent display in the Eisenhower home.

The following spring Ida Eisenhower's attendance at a convention of Jehovah's Witnesses made front page news: 'The 82-year-old mother of America's famous military leader . . . was the centre of attraction at the meeting Sunday, and her name was heard in just about every conversation, speech and discussion. The programmes' subject was How to become a good Jehovah's Witness.'[162]

Writing to his brother Arthur (May 18, 1943), General Eisenhower commented: 'Not long ago I saw a clipping in which some reporter made a point of the fact that our dear old mother liked to go to conventions of her beloved Jehovah's Witnesses. As far as I am concerned, her happiness in her religion means more to me than any damned wisecrack that a newspaper man can get publicised – I know full well that the government is not going to measure my services as a soldier by the religious beliefs of my mother.'

In 1944 Edgar Eisenhower wrote to Naomi Engle expressing his suspicions that his mother – then aged 82 – was being used by the Watchtower Society 'for distributing religious literature'. He did not want her to be 'exhibited as the mother of General Eisenhower . . . solely for attempting to influence anyone'. Subsequently Naomi Engle was eventually removed and was replaced by a Mrs. Robinson who became Ida's nurse.

Commenting on Bela Kornitze's 1955 Story of the Five Eisenhower Brothers, Jack Anderson alleged that both Dwight and his brother Milton checked the manuscript before publication. A few days later Milton privately asked the publishing company (Farrar, Strauss & Cudoy) to delete a direct reference to their parents' involvement with Jehovah's Witnesses, but to no avail.[163] Thus, Pastor Russell's skeleton in the Eisenhower cupboard, like a friendly ghost, would haunt them all for the rest of their lives.

***

In the summer of 1944 Richard Boeckel, a serving soldier in the United States armed forces, became a 'person of goodwill' after reading some Watchtower Society literature. While he was on leave, he attended a Jehovah's Witness convention which was being held in Denver, Colorado. He later recalled his experiences following that 'important furlough'. 'I sat next to Lotta Thayer, a Witness from Abilene, Kansas. I [talked] about the problems I was having trying to serve God in a

[162] The Witchita-Beacon – April 1943.

[163] Detroit Free Press – September 23, 1956.

military environment, in view of what I had learned from Isaiah 2:4 and related scriptures. 'Do you know who my neighbour is?' she asked. 'It's General Eisenhower's mother. She is one of Jehovah's Witnesses. Would you like her to write to you?' I sure would! I exclaimed'.

Toward the end of August, while on manoeuvres in Colorado, soldier Boeckel made his decision to become one of Jehovah's Witnesses and took his first stand for pacifism by refusing to take part in guard duty. He was ordered to go to the headquarters tent and while he was waiting outside there was a mail call. Someone handed him a letter. It was dated August 20, 1944, and it was signed by 82-year-old Ida E. Eisenhower:

'A friend returning from the United Announcers Convention of Jehovah's Witnesses, informs me of meeting you there . . . and of your desire to have a word from General Eisenhower's mother whom you have been told is one of the witnesses of Jehovah. I am indeed such and what a glorious privilege it has been . . . Generally, I have refused such requests because of my desire to avoid all publicity. However, because you are a person of goodwill towards Jehovah, God I am happy to write to you. I have been blessed with seven sons of which five are living . . . I feel that Dwight my third son will always strive to do his duty with integrity as he sees such duty. I mention him in particular because of your expressed interest in him. And so, as the mother of General Eisenhower and as a witness of and for the Great Jehovah of Hosts (I have been such the past 49 years) I am pleased to write to you and urge you to faithfulness.'

Just as he had finished reading the letter Boeckel was ordered into the tent to explain himself. He later recalled: 'As I entered, where all the 'top brass' had gathered, I did not salute. One of the officers said, 'Don't you salute your superiors?'

'No sir.'

'Why not?'

'Respectfully, I gave my reasons, based on my understanding of the Bible. At that the officer said, General Eisenhower ought to line you Jehovah's Witnesses up and shoot you all!'

'Do you think he would shoot his own mother, Sir?'

'What do you mean by that?'

I just received this letter from the general's mother while waiting for you to call me.

Reaching in my pocket and taking out sister Eisenhower's letter, I handed it to him. As he read the letter, the other officers also gathered around to look at it. Thoughtfully, and with a greatly changed attitude, he handed it back to me.'

'Get back to the ranks,' he said, 'I do not want to get mixed up with the General's mother.'

'The timing of her letter could not have been better! Her encouragement was just what I needed.'[164]

The letter, allegedly signed by Ida Eisenhower, which was later published in full in the Watchtower magazine[165] was somewhat disingenuous, having been written by Naomi Engle – more than likely with the help of an elder in the local congregation of Jehovah's Witnesses who would have checked it for doctrinal accuracy before it was sanctioned by the Watchtower Society. Indeed, the mode of English used in the letter and the phraseology employed reads like a piece from the pages of the Watchtower magazine. The letter was, as J. Earl Endacott, a former Eisenhower Library curator, alleges, 'not in the words of Ida, who at the time could hardly write her own name. Her memory had started to fail following the death of her husband and she was not always mentally alert. Sometimes she could not even remember the names of her own sons'.

Edgar had written his letter of complaint to his mother's carer when the Eisenhower sons read a press report about the letter incident. When there was no response from Naomi Engle it fell to Milton Eisenhower to dismiss her. He then hired non-Witness Mrs Robinson to take care of his mother. It later transpired that Naomi Engle and another JW 'sister' had persuaded Ida to write her name several times on a sheet of paper – to keep herself mentally alert, they told her. According to Mrs. Robinson, the most legible signature was then cut from the sheet and pasted on the bottom of the letter which Engle had written. Endacott later revealed: 'In one of her lucid moments Ida told Mrs. Robinson what had happened and gave the sheet with the cut-out name to her. When the Eisenhower Foundation took over the home, Mrs. Robinson told me the story and gave me the sheet which I still have.'

On September 11, 1946, Ida Stover Eisenhower died in Abilene, Kansas. At the time of her death, she left behind a fifty-year collection of Watchtower magazines in her home on Southeast Fourth Street.

---

[164] *Awake!* – December 22, 1993.

[165] Watchtower – October 15, 1980.

Almost to the end of her life she was often seen in downtown Abilene hawking the Watchtower Society's literature on street corners, or on her favourite pitches outside certain business premises.

Notwithstanding such singular devotion and ignoring the intentions of the local congregation of Jehovah's Witnesses, a private conventional Christian service was conducted at her home followed by a public service at the graveside. Both services were taken by an army chaplain from Fort Riley and the pallbearers were three American Legionnaires and three Veterans of Foreign Wars. In an obituary which appeared in Time magazine General Eisenhower's mother was described as having been 'a member of the River Brethren, a Mennonite sect'.

A few weeks later the Watchtower Society countered: 'Mrs. I. S. Eisenhower, like all Jehovah's Witnesses, believed religion a racket and the clergy in general, including army chaplains, to be hypocrites. She harboured no special pride for 'General Ike'; she was opposed to his West Point appointment. It was a gross disrespect to the deceased for an army chaplain to officiate at the funeral. As for the pallbearers, the American Legion particularly, and the Veterans of Foreign Wars, are repeatedly ringleaders in mob violence against Jehovah's Witnesses. Only death could keep the body of Mrs. Eisenhower from walking away from a funeral so disrespectful of all that she stood for.'[166]

Following the establishment of NATO in 1950 General Eisenhower was made Supreme Commander of its combined land forces and two years later his popularity, both at home and in Europe, won him nomination in the presidential elections. He once explained that his parents 'had been deeply religious people, though somewhat rebellious, not easily satisfied with any church'. He also said of his parents, in a speech in 1952: 'Their Bibles were a live and lusty influence in their lives, and they tried their best to instil it, its beliefs, its convictions, in their sons.' When a Republican friend urged him to join a church, Ike replied that while he had no real objections he had always 'sort of treasured' his independence in that regard. He and his brothers had always been 'a little bit nonconformist in the business of actual membership of a particular sect or denomination,' he claimed. 'We were all very earnestly and seriously religious, we could not help being so considering our upbringing.'

After he was sworn in before Chief Justice Vinson, on 20th January 1953, mutterings of resistance and surprise among the press could be

---

[166] *Awake!* – October 26, 1946.

heard when he spoke: 'My friends, before I begin the expression of those thoughts that I deem appropriate, I ask you to bow your heads. Almighty God, my future associates in the executive branch of the Government join me in beseeching that thou wilt make full and complete our dedication to the service of the people . . . regardless of station, race, or calling. May co-operation be permitted and be the mutual aim of those who, under the concept of our constitution, hold to differing political beliefs, so that all may work for the good of our beloved country and for thy glory, Amen.'

Dwight D. Eisenhower became known as 'the most religious President in our history'. He helped sponsor a nationwide moral crusade and religious revival, and in general he sought to encourage the cause of American religious interests. During his administration, the much publicised 'Prayer breakfasts' were introduced and the phrase 'Under God' was placed in the pledge of allegiance to the flag. He proclaimed Days of Prayer for the nation, backed the Foundation for Religious Action and invited Billy Graham and other prominent religious leaders to the White House. His presidency was described by one commentator as 'a crusade for moral and religious goals'.

There were those who attacked Eisenhower with accusations that he 'never joined a church until after he became President', the implication being that his Sunday worship as the presidential leader of the American people somehow smacked of hypocrisy. However, Paul Hutchinson noted: 'President Eisenhower seldom wrote a speech without some reference to the nation's need for spiritual strength. He attends church more frequently than most of his predecessors. He goes to prayer meeting breakfasts. His cabinet sessions begin with a prayer. He is never too busy to receive church delegations and several of his most important speeches have been delivered at church gatherings. . . again and again, as he wrestles with the requirements of the presidency, Abilene shows through. Its mark is plain on him. Occasionally, it betrays him into a belief that some problems are simpler than they are, and their solutions are quickly to be found.'[167]

Some years later an independent journalist commented: 'President Eisenhower, whose mother once sold Bible tracts for the Jehovah's Witnesses, is looking for a delicate way to clear the family name of this affiliation. He is sensitive about the fact that Jehovah's Witnesses do not believe in saluting the flag or serving under arms. Now the

---

[167] Life magazine – March 22, 1954.

Eisenhower brothers would like to find a graceful way to announce that their mother was not, at heart, a Jehovah's Witness.'[168]

When Eisenhower was sworn in as president for a second term in office, he used the American Standard Version of the Bible. However, a British journalist pointed out that other press reports had failed to quote accurately the words the President had read from his ASV version of the Bible – 'Blessed is the nation whose God is Jehovah' – and substituted the word Lord for Jehovah to 'distance President Eisenhower from the faith of his parents' by not using a term that was intimately connected with the Watchtower Society.[169]

***

In Britain during the war years Prime Minister Winston Churchill established a remarkable ascendancy over parliament and public alike, but in peacetime the British bulldog was reported as being shaken at his July 5, 1945, election defeat. This led his stoic wife, Clementine, into suggesting that they would now have more time to renovate and reinvigorate the large somewhat neglected country house in Kent which had been theirs since 1922. Surrounded by 300 acres of farmland Chartwell was only twenty-four miles from London and it was here that Churchill was able to satisfy his curiosity about General Eisenhower's whispered 'family connections' with Jehovah's Witnesses during the war years.

In the summer of 1948, during one of his stays at Chartwell, Churchill called at one of the farm cottages on his land where he found himself interrupting a doorstep conversation between his tenant and 'pioneer' Jehovah's Witness, seventeen-year-old Michael Davey, who later recalled his chance encounter with the illustrious statesman:

'Mister Churchill took note of the Watchtower [magazine] and commended me for my work. Several days later I was out preaching again when I rang the doorbell of a large house. A butler opened the door, and when I requested to speak to the man of the house, he asked if I knew who that was. I had no idea. 'This is Chartwell,' he said, 'the home of Winston Churchill.' At that moment, Mr. Churchill appeared. He remembered our previous meeting and invited me in. We spoke a little, and he accepted three books and invited me to return. Later, on a warm afternoon, I returned and was again invited in. Mr. Churchill offered me some lemonade and, after a brief greeting, said: 'I will give you half an hour to tell me what you think God's Kingdom is, but then you must let

---

168 Detroit Free Press – December 1956.

169 The London Daily News – February 2, 1957.

me tell you what I believe it to be.' That is what we did. Mr. Churchill felt that God's Kingdom would be established through God-fearing statesmen and that until men learned to live at peace, it would never come. . . [he] was very cordial and indicated he respected our work. Unfortunately, I was never again able to contact him.'[170]

[170] *Awake!* – December 22, 1993.

Chapter Nineteen

STAYING ALIVE TILL SEVENTY-FIVE

The immediate post-war years proved to be a time of unprecedented growth for Jehovah's Witnesses. In 1958 the vibrant city of New York played host to more than a quarter of a million believers when the largest convention ever organised by the Watchtower Society was staged at the Yankee Stadium and the Polo Grounds simultaneously. The Divine Will International Assembly attracted Jehovah's Witnesses from around the world. A local press report noted: 'Eight special trains, 500 chartered buses and 18,000 auto pools are bringing the members, besides the two chartered ships and 65 chartered planes.'[171] The Watchtower magazine later observed: 'Further evidence of Jehovah's blessing on the ministry of his servants was seen when 7,136 at this convention symbolised their dedication by water immersion – well over twice the number that were baptised on the historic occasion of Pentecost 33 C.E., as reported in the Bible!'

On Thursday afternoon, July 31, the Watchtower Society's president, Nathan H Knorr, announced the release of its latest publication, From Paradise Lost to Paradise Regained. Everyone was urged to offer the book in the field ministry. Parents were told they would find it helpful in teaching Watchtower truths to their children because it employed a simple and straightforward writing style and was abundantly illustrated. Some years later Grace A. Estep, a schoolteacher who was raised in a small town near Pittsburgh, Pennsylvania, recalled: 'A whole generation of children have grown up fingering the Paradise book, carrying it to meetings with them, sharing it with their playmates, being able to relate, long before they were old enough to read, a whole series of Bible stories just from the pictures.'

Former Jehovah's Witness Presiding Overseer David A. Reed has some quite different recollections about the Paradise book: 'In the concluding chapter it states plainly that only the preachers of God's kingdom can expect to be protected during the end of this world and live through Armageddon into the new world. A whole generation of Jehovah's Witness children were frightened by the illustrations of Armageddon . . . youngsters are shown fleeing in panic as buildings topple and burn, falling into huge crevasses as the earth opens beneath their feet,

---

[171] New York Daily News – July 26, 1958.

swallowing up screaming children together with their toy dolls, bicycles, and pet dogs.'[172]

The caption to the illustration paraphrases the words of an Old Testament prophet to remind young readers of the fate awaiting those who choose to ignore Jehovah's warning: Their flesh shall rot while they are still on their feet, their eyes shall rot in their sockets, and their tongues shall rot in their mouths. Eaten up will be the tongues of those who scoffed and laughed at the warning of Armageddon! Eaten up will be the eyes of those who refused to see the sign of 'the time of the end'! Eaten up will be the flesh of those who would not learn that the living God is named Jehovah!! '[173] Some Witnesses privately confess to recalling such distressing imagery when dealing with the ridicule, insults and abuse they sometimes endure during their door-to-door ministry.

On the eighth and final day of the assembly, a record-breaking crowd of 253,922 delegates from 123 lands learned that further educational programmes had been put in place that would benefit the worldwide organisation. Watchtower president Nathan Knorr explained, 'The educational work is not on the decline, but rather it is on the move forward.' He then outlined plans for providing a ten-month training course in Brooklyn for travelling overseers from the Society's branches all over the world in addition to one-month training courses for those having oversight in local congregations: 'We want to move to higher levels of understanding so that we can get deeper into the thoughts of Jehovah as he has expressed them in his Word.' The eager crowd then listened intently as Judge Rutherford's successor delivered his compelling public address: God's Kingdom Rules – Is the World's End Near?

***

During the late 1950's and early 1960's the world was in the grip of the Cold War and the fate of mankind seemed to be in the hands of two superpowers. Where would it all end? The Watchtower Society's latest hardback publication – Your Will be Done on Earth – explained how the Bible had long ago foretold just how this global situation would signal the imminence of Armageddon. The struggle between the 'king of the south' and the 'king of the north' described in the eleventh chapter of the book of Daniel foreshadowed the uneasy co-existence of two world powers prior to the breakdown of world order and its inevitable apocalyptic end. Daniel's 'king of the north' was identified as the Soviet

---

[172] Jehovah's Witness Literature – David A Reed, Baker Book House Co. 1993.

[173] Zechariah 14: 12 – 19.

Union, the Communist bloc which 'since it seized power in Russia in 1917, has held world domination as its aim to this day,' while the 'king of the south' was believed to represent the 'British-American alliance'.[174]

This was stirring stuff for Jehovah's Witnesses. You can read it for yourself, they would say to those they called upon: 'And ye shall hear of wars and rumours of wars: see that ye be not troubled: for all these things must come to pass, but the end is not yet. For nation shall rise against nation and kingdom against kingdom; and there shall be famines, and pestilences, and earthquakes, in diverse places. All these things are the beginning of sorrows . . . And this gospel of the kingdom shall be preached in all the world for a witness unto all nations; and then shall come the end.'[175]

For the indomitable Witnesses there was simply no doubt about it. As far as they were concerned the stark reality of the Cold War simply could not be denied and therefore neither could the Watchtower Society's 'new light' on the Scriptures. Given the biblical life expectancy of seventy years, the famous generation of 1914 that would witness the onset of Armageddon was now middle-aged and time was marching on.

The Watchtower leadership was now faced with the colossal task of sounding the alarm and spreading the 'good news of the kingdom' world-wide in the 'short time remaining'. However, the impressive growth in the number of converts pouring into the New World Society of Jehovah's Witnesses during the post-war years had levelled off by the early 1960's suggesting to the leadership that Jehovah had temporarily withdrawn his blessing from his people.

It was at this point that interest in the mysterious cabalistic potential of the number forty was revived at the Brooklyn Bethel. Watchtower Vice-president Fred Franz, now well and truly installed as the Society's self-appointed oracle, cast his mind back to 1935 when, he believed, Jehovah had revealed he had selected the very last of the 'anointed remnant' of a heavenly government of 144,000 individuals from earth's population. A forty-year testing period for the remainder of humanity from that momentous year seemed to confirm when the 'last days' of the 1914 generation would come to an end. Convinced he was on-track for personally regaining God's blessing and further guidance, Franz set

---

[174] Your Will be Done on Earth – WTBTS, 1958.

[175] Matt 24: 6,7, 14. KJV.

to work, plotting a more detailed and mathematically convincing route to paradise.

In spring 1966 a new songbook – Singing and Accompanying Yourselves with Music in Your Hearts – was released. Melodies and sentiments which had previously been borrowed from traditional Christian hymns in earlier songbooks had been rooted out and replaced with compositions which more accurately reflected the organisation's prophetic teachings. The Watchtower Society sang its praises: 'with the ever-increasing light there are new truths, new themes, clearer understanding and a change of emphasis.'[176]

In addition to this promising overture the Watchtower Society's most tantalizing assurances were published in a book which spelled out, in no uncertain detail, how the year 1975 would herald the beginning of Christ's millennium reign and the end of the world. The new publication was released at large assemblies of Jehovah's Witnesses where excited delegates queued up in their hundreds and thousands to get their hands on a copy of In Freedom of the Sons of God. Within weeks Jehovah's Witnesses all over the world were peeling through the Society's latest offering with the keenest of interest:

'Since the time of Usher intensive study of Bible chronology has been carried on. In this twentieth century an independent study has been carried on that does not blindly follow some traditional chronological calculations of Christendom, and the published timetable resulting from this independent study gives the date of man's creation as 4026 B.C.E. According to this trustworthy Bible chronology six thousand years from man's creation will end in 1975 . . . So, six thousand years of man's existence on earth will soon be up, yes, within this generation . . . How appropriate it would be for Jehovah God to make of this coming seventh period of a thousand years a Sabbath period of rest and release . . . It would also be most fitting on God's part, for, remember, mankind has yet ahead of it what the last book of the Holy Bible speaks of as the reign of Jesus Christ over earth for a thousand years, the millennium reign of Christ.'[177]

In the autumn of that year smouldering expectations once again flickered into life when the Watchtower Society posed the question, 'How much longer will it be? Does God's rest day parallel the time man had been on earth since his creation? From the most reliable investigations

[176] Watchtower – May 15, 1966.
[177] In Freedom of the Sons of God – WTBTS, 1966.

of Bible chronology, harmonizing with many accepted dates of secular history . . . we can expect the immediate future to be filled with thrilling events for those who rest their faith in God and his promises. It means that within relatively few short years we will witness the fulfilment of the remaining prophecies that have to do with the 'time of the end'.[178]

As sales figures for Watchtower Society literature surged there was a noticeable influx of converts throughout the world. Soon there were more than two million active Witnesses with sometimes up to five million hopefuls attending the annual Memorial Supper. In 1968 the Watchtower Society fuelled further growth in membership and increased its literature sales with the following announcement: 'There are only about ninety months left before 6,000 years of man's existence on earth is completed. Most people living today will probably be alive when Armageddon breaks out.'[179]

This riveting message was initially restricted to baptised believers – via Kingdom Ministry (an in-house publication) – who relished this conspiratorial foretaste of what was to come as a clear sign that Jehovah was preparing the faithful in advance for the joy (and the horror) of Armageddon. It concentrated minds and gripped the imagination of Jehovah's Witnesses everywhere. From then onwards they would spend as much time as possible 'on the [preaching] work' announcing the coming of God's kingdom. Consequently, millions of magazines and books were enthusiastically sold – and there was more to come.

Anticipation was further heightened when the Watchtower Society confidently stated: 'The immediate future is certain to be filled with climactic events, for this old system is nearing its complete end. Within a few years at most the final parts of Bible prophecy relative to the last days will undergo fulfilment, resulting in the liberation of surviving mankind into Christ's glorious 1,000-year reign. What difficult days, but at the same time what grand days are just ahead!'[180]

Some three months later the Watchtower Society announced: 'One thing is certain, Bible chronology reinforced with fulfilled Bible prophecy shows that six thousand years of man's existence will soon be up, yes, within this generation! This is, therefore, no time to be indifferent and complacent. This is not the time to be toying with the words of Jesus that "concerning that day and hour nobody knows, neither the angels of

---

[178] *Awake!* – October 1966.

[179] Kingdom Ministry – March 1968.

[180] Watchtower – May 1, 1968.

the heavens nor the Son, but only the Father." To the contrary, it is a time when one should be keenly aware that the end of this system of things is rapidly coming to its violent end. Make no mistake; it is sufficient that the Father himself knows both the "day and hour".'

Millennial hopes were further stimulated when the Watchtower Society assured readers: 'From the most reliable investigations of Bible chronology, harmonising with many accepted dates of secular history, we find that Adam was created in the Autumn of the year 4026 B.C.E. Sometime in that same year Eve could well have been created . . . In what year, then, would the first 6,000 years of man's existence and the first 6,000 years of God's rest day come to an end? The year 1975.'[181]

In the spring of the following year attention was focused on the youth of the movement: 'If you are a young person, you also need to face the fact that you will never grow old in this present system of things . . . you will never fulfil any career that this system offers. If you are in high school and thinking about a college education, it means at least four, perhaps six or eight more years to graduate into a specialized career. But where will this system of things be by that time? It will be well on its way toward its finish, if not actually gone! Do not pursue higher education. There is little time left! Make pioneer service, the full-time ministry with the possibility of Bethel or missionary service your goal.'[182]

During the summer of 1969, a new pocket-size publication – The Truth That Leads to Eternal life – was released as a new study-aid in a last-chance quest for converts. It became known as the Truth book. So concise and to the point was the new publication that Witnesses who were currently conducting Bible studies with 'interested persons' were advised: 'Since there is such a short time left, study no longer than six months with a prospective convert'.[183] It was this directive, more than any other, which added impetus and urgency to their door-to-door ministry.

Outsiders who remained unconvinced following a guided study of the Truth book in their own homes would no longer be courted or cajoled into continuing with their study in the hope that one day they too might embrace the Watchtower creed. From now on such procrastinators would be decisively abandoned in favour of others who might respond more positively, more readily. Jehovah was now believed to be

---

[181] *Awake!* – October 8, 1968

[182] Watchtower – March 15, 1969.

[183] Watchtower May 15, 1969.

urging his Witnesses to search out deserving ones with purpose and resolve. 'Angelic guidance' in this 'life-saving' ministry was often alluded to during meetings.

The Truth book did not rely solely on the Society's interpretation of the Bible to promote its doomsday pronouncements. Prominent personalities and certain experts in the secular world were quoted as unwitting advocates of Watchtower wisdom: 'Back in 1960 former U.S. Secretary of State Dean Acheson declared that our time is 'a period of unequalled instability, unequalled violence'. And he warned: 'I know enough of what is going on to assure you that, in fifteen years from today, this world is going to be too dangerous to live in'.[184]

A secular book – Famine -1975, written by nutritionists William and Paul Paddock (who were not Jehovah's Witnesses) – was seized upon as independent academic confirmation of the Watchtower Society's doomsday predictions and regularly cited by Watchtower officials all over the world. Among the favourite quotations were: 'By 1975 a disaster of unprecedented magnitude will face the world. Famines, greater than any in history, will ravage the undeveloped nations . . . when the new crisis will be upon us in all its awesome importance . . . By 1975 civil disorder, anarchy, military dictatorships, runaway inflation, transportation breakdowns and chaotic unrest will be the order of the day in many of the hungry nations.'[185]

During the late 1960's and early 70's the growth in the number of converts was spectacular. Witness conventions and assemblies around the globe were awash with throngs of bright-eyed hopeful candidates, young and old, queuing up to take their turn in mass public baptisms. The Watchtower leadership was swept along on an unstoppable tide of religious euphoria: 'We have proof more than ever before that God enthroned his Son in 1914, and that we are now in the time of the end.'[186]

A sprinkling of celebrities – musicians, entertainers, and athletes – from the alien worlds of sport and show business were drawn into the movement. Such individuals are usually, and somewhat uneasily, indulged regarding their worldly distinction for they appear to broaden the appeal of the movement. However, few, if any, such trendy believers ever fully commit themselves to the organisation.

---

[184] In later editions of the 'Truth book' (those printed after 1975) Dean Acheson's substantive phrase, 'fifteen years from today' was deleted and misquoted as the indefinite adverb 'soon'.

[185] Famine-1975 – William and Paul Paddock, Little-Brown, 1969.

[186] Watchtower – December 15, 1971.

David Reed, a former Witness, recalls being present at the summer 1973 Divine Victory International Assembly of Jehovah's Witnesses when a packet of tracts – Is Time Running Out for Mankind? – was provided for everyone in the audience: 'They were to be distributed door-to-door world-wide during a ten-day period, from September 21 through 30. I remember President Knorr telling us that breaking a leg would be about the only thing that might excuse us from participation in this vital work. The world's end was close, and it was essential that every household receive a copy as their official notification of this fact.'[187] The 1975 Yearbook subsequently reported that 512,738 people had taken part in a blitz distribution of 43,320,048 copies of that tract in the United States alone.

Not since the 1950's had Jehovah's Witnesses been able to claim that theirs was 'the fastest growing religion in the world'. Witnesses were urged to join the Society's pioneer service, and thousands of them answered the call, selling prospering businesses or giving up their jobs in the process. Having been persuaded 'to finish out the rest of their days in this old system in the pioneer service', some families even sold their homes and property to do so. Others were reminded that 'the world is passing-away, and so is its desire'[188] and encouraged to follow suit: 'Certainly this is a fine way to spend the short time remaining before the wicked world's end.'[189]

In the early 1970's many older Witnesses cashed in their investments and withdrew pension funds; they cancelled insurance policies and, in some cases, delayed seeking medical attention or postponed scheduled surgical operations altogether. Many were less than prudent in their financial planning in general and saw little point in renewing their household 'building and contents' insurance policies in the run-up to Armageddon.

For many couples, the imminence of Armageddon was 'a major factor in their decision not to have children'.[190] Thousands of young men and women, many of whom would qualify for higher education in the normal course of events, were persuaded to 'pioneer' for the Watchtower Society. Getting by on part-time menial employment to spend more time 'on the [preaching] work', they happily encouraged one

---

[187] Jehovah's Witness Literature – David A Reed, Baker Book House, 1993.
[188] 1 John 2:17. NWT.
[189] Kingdom Ministry – May 1974.
[190] *Awake!* – November 8, 1974.

another with the mantra, 'muddling through, making do, staying alive 'till seventy-five'.

In the spring of 1975 Watchtower Society President Nathan H. Knorr and Vice-president Frederick Franz set out on a world tour. The talks they delivered to expectant conventioneers were primarily focused on the significance of 'a year of great possibilities – tremendous possibilities'. Addressing an enraptured audience of expectant Witnesses in Toronto, Ontario, Canada, Vice-president F. W. Franz, stated that he and his associates at Watchtower headquarters were 'looking forward confidently' to what the autumn of that year would bring.

Much excitement was generated when hushed and attentive congregations of Jehovah's Witnesses the world over were advised not to slacken in their door-to-door work by assuming that the coming apocalypse may yet be some years away. Those thinking of starting up time-consuming business ventures were cautioned to think again. Younger ones – those who were perhaps contemplating getting married and starting up a family or spending years in pursuit of a higher education – were strongly advised to focus their attention on staying on the road to paradise. And many of them did just that. However, there was a diversion ahead.

Expectations were dampened somewhat during the doomsday year of 1975 as the Watchtower Society applied brakes of caution to the racing hearts of more than two million active Jehovah's Witnesses when it reluctantly admitted; 'although 6,000 years of human history will end in September, there is a short time interval between Adam's creation and that of Eve. Whether that period amounted to weeks or months or years, we do not know. So, we do not know exactly when Jehovah's great 'rest day' began, nor do we know exactly when it will end. The same applies to the beginning of Christ's millennial reign.'[191]

The following year disappointed Witnesses everywhere were chided for their selfishness and spiritual immaturity: 'It is not advisable for us to set our sights on a certain date. If anyone has been disappointed through not following this line of thought, he should now concentrate on adjusting his viewpoint, seeing that it was not the word of God that failed or deceived him and brought disappointment, but that his own understanding was based on wrong premises.'[192] Many Witnesses found that hard to swallow.

---

[191] Watchtower – May 1, 1975; October 1, 1975.

[192] Watchtower – July 15, 1976.

Among those who were beginning to entertain doubts in the wake of the 1975 debacle were special pioneers Mark and Jean Lett who eventually freed themselves from the constrictions of the Watchtower Society in 1978 to go into business with their youngest son Timothy. Ironically, their eldest son Mark Stephen Lett distanced himself from his 'spiritually weakened' family and remained stubbornly faithful to the Watchtower Society. Having entered the pioneering service immediately upon graduation from high school at the age of sixteen, he resolutely demonstrated he was of the 'anointed class' while serving at the Brooklyn Bethel when he was just 20 years old. His broken-hearted parents were devastated. Today brother Lett is a member of the Governing Body, having been appointed in 1999.

Back in 1975, Nathan Homer Knorr was never aware of any looming prophetic failure. As he watched and waited through the doomsday winter and into the spring of 1976, terminal brain cancer began to take its toll. Upon his death, on June 7, 1977, he was succeeded by Frederick William Franz who, at the age of 83, became the Watchtower Society's fourth president. *Time* magazine (July 11, 1977) commented: 'Though few people know his name, he has acquired more-than-papal power over 2.2 million souls around the world.'.

Two weeks into his presidency, when he was delivering a talk in Toronto, Ontario, Canada, Franz confidingly asked: 'Do you know why nothing happened in 1975?' There was an anticipatory moment of heightened expectancy as the speaker drew himself up and made a sweeping finger-pointing gesture to the assembly as he shouted: 'It was because YOU expected something to happen!' Referring to that incident former Canadian Witness, James Penton, recalls: 'Incredibly, Franz placed the blame for the entire fiasco on the Witness community and acted virtually as though he had no responsibility in the matter at all.'[193]

Leaving a great swathe of broken hearts, fractured lives and shattered dreams in its wake, the Watchtower Society continued printing endless copies of the 'Truth book' for quite some time afterwards; so much so that it was listed in *The Guinness Book of World Records*. The first mention was in 1982 in the Highest Printings category. A later edition, published in 1990, noted that by May 1987 Jehovah's Witnesses had sold 106,486,735 copies of The Truth that leads to Eternal Life in 116 languages.

[193] Apocalypse Delayed – M James Penton, University of Toronto Press, 1985.

Chapter Twenty

A VOICE IN THE WILDERNESS

Toward the end of the 19th century Watchtower Society founder Charles Russell observed: 'The endeavour to compel all men to think alike on all subjects, culminated in the great apostasy and the development of the great papal system, and thereby the gospel, the one faith that Paul and the other apostles set forth, was lost – buried under the mass of uninspired decrees of popes and councils.'[194] In commenting on the Inquisition, which was established by the Church of Rome in the 13th century and lasted for more than six hundred years, the Watchtower noted: 'No one was free to worship as he pleased or to express opinions conflicting with those of the clergy. This clerical intolerance created a climate of fear throughout Europe. The church established the Inquisition to root out individuals who dared to hold different views.'[195]

Reading through the above, we might conclude that the Watchtower Society today acts with tolerance and understanding toward their own Jehovah's Witnesses who might sometimes question certain teachings of the organisation. Nothing could be further from the truth. Individuals within the movement who venture to express an opinion contrary to the Society's transient interpretations of alleged Bible prophecy, even in private, are dealt with ruthlessly.

One such free-thinking individual was Carl Olof Jonsson, a Swedish elder, who, back in 1968, embarked on a programme of independent Bible-study, researching the Watchtower Society's chronological timetable. He continued his private investigation during the run-up to 1975 and by the turn of that 'Armageddon year' he was having serious doubts about the doomsday creed to which he and his friends and family had devoted their entire lives.

Two years later, now convinced the Watchtower Society's eschatology was flawed and therefore unreliable, he posted a copy of his meticulously researched treatise to the New York Bethel. Some months later Lloyd Barry, a member of the Governing Body, replied to Jonsson regarding his thesis: 'No matter how strong the argumentation may be in support of those views, they must, for the present, be regarded as your

---

[194] Watchtower – September 1893.
[195] Watchtower – September1989.

personal viewpoint. It is not something that you should talk about or try to advance among other members of the congregation . . . We are sure you appreciate that it would not be appropriate for you to begin to state your views and conclusions on chronology that are different than those published by the Society.'[196]

In August 1978, Albert D. Schroeder, another member of the Governing Body, held a meeting in Europe with senior representatives from European Watchtower branch offices who were informed that there was a campaign, within the movement, to discredit the Society's chronology. Soon afterwards Jonsson was summoned to a hearing before two representatives of the Watchtower Society in Sweden. They told him that the Society did not need or want individual Jehovah's Witnesses to become involved in research of this kind and cautioned him not to share the knowledge and understanding he had gained through his research at the British Library in London.

For his honest investigative and well-intentioned approach to the Watchtower leadership the Swedish elder was vilified for his 'independent thinking' and shunned by all his Witness friends and associates and, even worse, his own immediate family. Jonsson and his sympathisers were subsequently condemned from the platforms of Kingdom Halls and at Witness assemblies as 'rebellious and presumptuous apostates, demon-possessed blasphemers who, having flooded the Society with criticism, should have been disfellowshipped long ago'. However, Jonsson's stinging arrow of truth had already found its mark and pierced the very heart of the Watchtower Society's secretive administration.

In the spring of 1979 three prominent members of the Brooklyn Bethel family, who had originated the most recent books and study material published by the Watchtower Society, came under suspicion. Having read through Jonsson's revealing exposition these long-serving elders were now beginning to question the casuistry of the organisation's creed, something to which all three of them had personally contributed, hugely. Among the three was Ray Franz, a somewhat reluctant member of the Governing Body who was a nephew of Frederick W Franz, the president of the Watchtower Society.

Ray Franz was a third generation Jehovah's Witness who, having faithfully served the Watchtower Society at every level of its infrastructure for more than forty years was made a member of its Governing

---

196 The Gentile Times Reconsidered – Carl Olof Jonsson, Commentary Press, 1986.

Body on October 20, 1971. Initially he fought against his nagging conscience but eventually, after nine years in high office, he concluded that the Society's depiction of its executive council – the collective 'faithful and discreet slave whom his master appointed over his domestics, to give their food at the proper time'[197] – elevated an elite body of men (himself included) to near Godly status. It was a situation he felt increasingly uncomfortable with during the latter years of his involvement in the movement.

Soon after his elevation Ray Franz was not entirely surprised to learn that organisational policies and religious dogma were not mysteriously formulated by angelic divine guidance, as Jehovah's Witnesses are led to believe, but merely by a show of hands at a board meeting. A two-thirds majority vote on current scriptural interpretation was all it took to invoke Jehovah's blessing and transform the vacillating Watchtower theology into the collectively imagined 'revealed truth' of the moment.

It soon became evident to Ray that those who favoured and fawned over his uncle Fred contributed little more than an agreeable raising of a hand, invariably preceded by a sideways glance, to reassure themselves that they were in the majority. Reluctantly he came to realise that his entire life course had been based on the persistent doomsday dreams of a succession of well-meaning, but nonetheless, gratuitously deluded men, and one chimerical character in particular – his uncle, the president of the Watchtower Society.

Sometimes in the privacy of his troubled mind he would recall the unnecessary suffering, deprivation and deaths of countless Witnesses who had acted in good faith upon directives from the Watchtower Society – the make-believe administration in which he was now playing a leading role. Torn between loyalty to the Governing Body and concern for the millions of Witnesses who looked to the organisation as a life-saving beacon of light and truth, he began, perhaps for the first time in his life, to learn how to independently think for himself.

Prior to the next executive meeting Ray Franz made copies of the first twenty pages of the material sent in by the Swedish elder for consideration by the other members of the Governing Body. As soon as the meeting was under way Lyman Swingle, head of the Writing Department, who was already familiar with Jonnson's thesis, reminded those assembled of certain insistent statements regarding Armageddon which had been published by the Watchtower Society in the past. Then, as the

---

[197] Matt 24:45 NWT.

entire Governing Body sat in glum-faced silence, he read a short extract from elder Jonsson's paper.

'The Watchtower Society claims to be God's sole channel and mouthpiece on earth. Summing up its most distinctive teachings: it asserts that the kingdom of God was established in heaven in 1914, that the last days began that year, that Christ returned invisibly at that time to inspect the Christian denominations, and that he finally rejected all of them except for the Watchtower Society and its associates, which he appointed in 1919 as his sole instrument on earth . . . to teach clearly and adamantly that the generation of 1914 would positively not pass away until the final end came at the battle of Armageddon when every human alive except active members of the Watchtower organisation would be destroyed forever. Jehovah's Witnesses of the 1914 generation fully expected to live to see and to survive that doomsday and then to live forever in paradise on earth.'[198]

This unwelcome recitation was followed by a navel-gazing silence. The reader then revealed that he was only about four years old in 1914 and too young to remember anything about it all, but he did remember the discussions that took place in his home regarding the 1925 expectations. He then referred to what had not happened, as the Society had predicted, in 1975 and pointedly said that, speaking for himself, he would not want 'to be misled regarding another date'.

Encouraged by such candour, Ray Franz pointed out that there was absolutely no historical evidence whatsoever to support the Society's 607 B.C.E. starting date for its countdown to Armageddon: 'If the organisation's traditional teaching is valid, how can we possibly apply Jesus' accompanying words to the people living in 1914? He said: "When you see all these things, know that he is near at the doors," and "as these things start to occur, raise yourselves erect and lift your heads up, because your deliverance is getting near." The publications regularly stressed, that those words began applying from 1914 onward, to those Christians living in 1914 – but if so, then to whom among them could this apply?' Once again, an eyes-down silence followed.

To the great discomfort of those assembled, Ray Franz then continued with his argument reasoning that a middle-aged believer in 1914 would now have to have survived well past his centenary year to 'see these things' and live through Armageddon. 'Why, even a thirty-year

---

[198] The Gentile Times Reconsidered – Carl Olof Jonnson, Commentary Press, 1986.

old would now be 95 [in 1979, the time of the discussion]. How meaningful could the application of Jesus' words have been in 1914 if the only ones who could hope to see them fulfilled were children just in their teens or younger?'[199] The shuffling silence that followed was not one of contemplation, but of creaking unease in the rare presence of such common-sense critical thinking in that cloistered echo-chamber at the heart of the Watchtower Society.

It was then suggested that if there was an explanation to be had that harmonised with Scripture the whole thing would have to be very carefully researched at the highest possible level in the organisation. Would the Governing Body be interested in having this done? Again, this was met with a protracted silence. Toward the end of the session a majority show of hands indicated that the pivotal year of 1914 and its 'generation' would continue to be stressed.

There were two abstainers; Ray Franz, who remained silent, and Lyman Swingle, who then said, somewhat abruptly, 'All right, if that's what you want to do. But at least you know that as far as 1914 is concerned, Jehovah's Witnesses got the whole thing – lock, stock and barrel – from the Second Adventists.' There was no response to this unexpected candour and the meeting was awkwardly concluded in prayer. The stony-faced president of the Watchtower Society glowered at his outspoken nephew as nepotism instantly morphed into ostracism. As for Ray Franz, it was time for reflection and reappraisal, and there was much to think about.

***

The Watchtower Society in Mexico was originally registered as a 'Cultural Organisation' because, under Mexican law, religious organisations were not allowed to own land. And yet, world-wide property ownership and the Society's vast and impressive global network of real-estate holdings is constantly emphasised and presented as solid proof of Jehovah's blessing on the organisation. Over the years such commercially driven corporate deception began to gnaw away at the troubled conscience of Ray Franz as he reviewed the situation.

During the 1960's and 70's the problem of compulsory military service for Jehovah's Witnesses in Mexico was solved by the simple expediency of bribery (with the blessing of the Watchtower Society). Men of draft age were required to register for military training every week during a one-year period. Attendance was recorded on a certificate. To

---

[199] Crisis of Conscience – Raymond Franz, Commentary Press 1983.

have your cartilla [marching card] signed and stamped without taking part in the regular training sessions was an illegal punishable offence. However, officials could be bribed to fraudulently fill in the attendance record and young male Mexican Witnesses took advantage of such corruption as advised by the Watchtower Society's counsel on the matter in a letter, dated June 2, 1960, to the Mexican Branch Office:

'If members of the military establishment are willing to accept such an arrangement upon the payment of a fee, then that is the responsibility of these representatives of the national organisation. In such cases the money paid does not go to the military establishment but is appropriated by the individual who undertakes the arrangement. If the consciences of certain brothers allow them to enter such an arrangement for their continued freedom, we have no objection.'

At the same time the above letter was written there were scores of young Witness men in the Dominican Republic spending precious years of their life in prison for refusing to take part in a similar programme of 'marching card' military training with an identical bribery get-out option. Unaware of the Watchtower Society's dispensation extended to their Mexican brothers, some of these conscripts were sentenced two or three times over for their continuing refusal to attend military training and spent as much as a total of nine years of their young manhood in prison.

President Knorr and Vice-president Franz had travelled to the Dominican Republic during those years and visited the prison where many of these men were detained. However, the dichotomous eye of the Watchtower Society could see no further than Mexico. Ray Franz later recalled: 'How the situation of these Dominican prisoners could be known and, yet such double standards be applied is incomprehensible to me.' He was a missionary at the time and powerless to do anything about it: 'I could not personally comprehend how grown men could fail to see the inconsistency in all of this, could fail to be repelled by it, could not be deeply moved by its effect on people's lives. It simply convinced me that organizational loyalty can lead people to incredible conclusions, allowing them to rationalize away the grossest of iniquities.'[200]

Similarly, Jehovah's Witnesses in Malawi – equally determined to obey the Society's directive not to buy a compulsory political party card – were being beaten, tortured, and raped while their homes were destroyed as terrified families fled to neighbouring countries. By 1972

---

[200] Crisis of Conscience – Raymond Franz, Commentary Press, Atlanta, 1992.

authoritative estimates indicated that there were 8,975 Witness refugees in Zambia and 11,600 in Mozambique.

Malawi (formerly Nyasaland) was a one-party state, ruled by Dr H. Kamuzu Banda, head of the Malawi Congress Party, who styled himself 'President for life' of the country. Those Witnesses who had inquired were categorically told, by the Society's branch office that to obtain such a card with bribery would be a 'violation' of their Christian neutrality. Malawian Witnesses who followed this official guidance suffered enormously. Many of them lost their lives, needlessly.

Ironically, in Pastor Russell's day military service was considered a personal and private matter: 'There could be nothing against our consciences in going into the army. Wherever we would go we could take the Lord with us.'[201] The ban on military service and alternative non-combatant public service was first written into the Watchtower creed by Judge Rutherford in 1933. Failure to uphold his ruling would result in excommunication from the movement and being shunned by friends and family alike. There was no middle ground. As a result, in some countries, young male Witnesses who refused to take part in military training were executed.

In 1983 the Watchtower magazine boasted: 'An examination of the historical facts shows that not only have Jehovah's Witnesses refused to put on military uniforms and take up arms but, during the past half-century, they have also declined to do non-combatant service or to accept other work assignments as a substitute for military service.' However, this long-standing ruling on alternative public service was inexplicably reversed in 1996 when 'new light' on the subject was revealed. Young conscripts were instructed to now 'make their own decisions based on an informed conscience . . . national civilian service is a "good work" that can be performed in obedience to the authorities'.[202]

Two years later, responsibility for the unnecessary suffering and deaths of countless young male Witnesses during the previous 63-year period, was laid at the feet of the victims themselves: 'In modern times, there have been some Witnesses who were very strict in their view of what they would do or not do. For that reason, they suffered more than others. Later, increased knowledge helped them to expand their view of matters. But they have no reason to regret having earlier acted in harmony with their conscience even when this possibly brought extra

---

[201] Zion's Watch Tower – April 1903.

[202] Watchtower – May 1996.

suffering. It is truly commendable that they demonstrated their willingness to suffer in faithfulness to Jehovah.'[203]

Ray Franz had privately entertained doubts and reservations about certain aspects of his Watchtower faith since 1965 when he was given the opportunity to leave the missionary work in the Caribbean to join the Bethel family in New York where he would serve in the writing department. It would prove to be a profound life-changing experience. However, it was in 1966, when the doomsday year of 1975 came to the fore, that he was jolted into seriously thinking about the corporate deception that lay at the heart of the Watchtower Society. From then on, with each passing year, the fanciful notion of an Armageddon panacea seemed to be more and more unlikely and untruthful.

After years of unease Franz, now a prominent writer for the Society, attempted to introduce a reforming measure of honest scholarship and fresh-air candour into his research and independent Bible study. However, he soon became aware of a marked reluctance, on the part of the Governing Body, to face up to the fact that it was not the world that was doomed but, rather, the time-warped theology of the Watchtower Society itself.

Things came to a head on Wednesday March 5, 1980, when he took his place at the large oval table in the private conference room where the Governing Body assembles every week. Meetings are held in total secrecy, except for just one trusted secretary, who is usually called in, after deliberations have concluded, to record any appropriate directives or decisions which may have been rubber-stamped as 'spiritual food' for the flock. Rank and file Jehovah's Witnesses all over the world routinely assume heavenly guidance is somehow mysteriously dispensed on these occasions.

As Ray Franz bowed his head in prayer at the start of that crucial meeting he resolved to speak up. Driven by his troubled conscience and his determination to shed the organisational pretence and self-righteous posturing into which he had been unwittingly drawn, he calmed himself and waited for his moment of truth. A Chairman's Committee of three members of the Governing Body had apparently taken it upon themselves to 'prayerfully consider' the 1914 problem and claimed to have come up with a solution. Apparently, a reconsideration of certain biblical texts in conjunction with a touch of imaginative rocket science appeared to throw 'new light' on the subject. Each member was then

---

[203] Watchtower – August 15, 1998.

solemnly handed a curious document equating various scriptural quotations and references with numerous press reports and commentaries from the 1950's.

The idea was then put forward that the generation which, according to the words of Jesus,[204] was destined to experience the end of the world, was not the 'generation of 1914' after all; it was the generation that witnessed the launching of the first Russian satellite, in 1957. The suggestion was that Russia's outer-space global spectacular had taken place in fulfilment of the words of Jesus who prophesied: 'Immediately after the tribulation of those days shall the sun be darkened, and the moon shall not give her light, and the stars shall fall from heaven . . .'[205] This new understanding would advance the beginning of the 'last days' by some forty-three years, it was suggested.

This contrived attempt to re-set the doomsday clock was subsequently rejected by a majority when it was suggested that there was still time for Jehovah to act within the schedule which had been so painstakingly written up for him by the Watchtower Society since 1879. 'People were living longer and longer nowadays,' someone else volunteered. Apparently, some hardy individuals in a certain part of the Soviet Union were said to have reached their 130th birthday, while in many other parts of the world it was commonplace for people to live for an entire century and beyond.

As the meeting wore on it seemed to Ray Franz that his wavering colleagues were morally incapable of honest and meaningful debate. It was as if the entire leadership had been caught up in a spiritual mind-game of pass-the-parcel – a parcel that none of those taking part in their deadly game of make-believe wanted to open. However, when the Watchtower Society's elaborate package of baseless doom-laden pronouncements and empty promises fell into his lap on that unbelievable day, the heavenly music stopped for brother Franz. After fifteen years of dark foreboding and troubling flashes of doubt, he finally woke up and realised it was time to get off the organisation's mindless treadmill of corporate obedience and fanciful expectation and step into the beckoning world of reality.

With just $600 between them, Ray Franz and his wife, Cynthia, took advantage of a long overdue leave-of-absence to consider their options. They had not had any real time off together for years and, with no home

---

204 Matthew 24: 34. KJV

205 Matthew 24:29. KJV.

of their own, no work to go to, and certainly no income, they needed some time and space away from the now oppressive atmosphere of the Brooklyn Bethel in which to re-evaluate their lives.

Randall Waters, a member of the Bethel family at the time, later described what happened while Ray Franz and his wife were away: 'A special committee was established to extract confessions from all of his close friends and acquaintances, to determine every word, he had uttered in private; anything that could be used against him. For two weeks these committees intimidated members of the Bethel family in this way and tape-recorded their confessions.'

Upon being summoned to return to Brooklyn to attend a 'special meeting', Ray Franz found himself listening to these recordings in the presence of his grim-faced uncle and the entire Governing Body who then voted unanimously to have him disfellowshipped. Other members of the Bethel family who were suspected of gossiping about the affair were subjected to long hours of intense interrogation by a special Watchtower Committee – in effect, a 20th century Inquisition.

Many faithful Witnesses were disfellowshipped, as 'mentally diseased spiritual fornicators' who had fallen prey to 'the teaching of demons'. One member of the Governing Body called them 'suckers' and 'liars'. In one committee meeting a married couple were disfellowshipped having faithfully served for decades. Within hours they were cast out of the mighty Watchtower only to find themselves back outside, homeless, jobless, and practically penniless on the streets of New York. Spies were everywhere, and many members of the Bethel family, anxious to demonstrate their own faith in the Watchtower Society, turned in their own friends on suspicion of apostasy.

As for Ray Franz, he was subsequently excommunicated from the organisation on a technical point – he had once 'lunched with a disfellowshipped person'. It was only after he managed to break free that he publicly spoke out on the subject: 'From lifelong experience among Jehovah's Witnesses in many countries, I know that for a large percentage the organisation has a certain aura, as though a luminous radiation surrounds it, giving its pronouncements an importance above and beyond that normally accorded the words of imperfect men . . . I am ashamed of what I took part in'.[206]

On the morning of April 30, 1980, Governing Body member Karl Kline delivered a breakfast table pep-talk to the entire Bethel family: 'If

---

[206] Crisis of Conscience – Raymond Franz, Commentary Press, Atlanta, 1992.

you have a tendency toward apostasy, get a hobby and keep yourself busy to keep your mind off it. Stay away from deep Bible study to determine the meaning of the scriptures,' he warned. Thereafter some of the more defiant members of the Bethel family began holding their own independent Bible studies in secret.

A month later Lloyd Barry, another member of the Governing Body, addressed all the elders of the Bethel family on one of the Society's key doctrines: 'Jehovah doesn't give individuals interpretation . . . We need a guide, and that is the faithful and discreet slave. We should not be getting together in a clique to discuss views to contrary. We must recognise the source of our instruction. We must be like an ass, be humble, and stay in the manger; and we won't get any poison.'

He then brandished a copy of the Society's organisational Guide for Elders, a book which is not available to the rank-and-file publisher. 'We serve not only Jehovah God, but we are under our mother, the organisation. Our mother has the right to make rules and regulations for us . . . If there are some who feel that they cannot subject themselves to the rules and regulations now in operation, such ones ought to be leaving and not be involved here . . .'

When some previously faithful and hardworking members of the Bethel family admitted to not being able to conscientiously believe in and teach certain doctrines – notably, those connected with the '1914 generation' – they too were declared 'spiritually dead' and ruthlessly dispensed with. By the end of the summer some fifty key members of the headquarters staff had walked out of the Brooklyn Bethel for good. For being true to themselves they were now branded as worthless in the eyes of God. Worse still, they would be forever shunned by their own families and friends who had been systematically pressured by years of Watchtower propaganda to believe that this was Jehovah's way of 'sifting and refining' his people in readiness for the end.

Those who remained were advised to keep in mind the apostle Paul's letter to the Romans: 'I exhort you, brothers, to keep your eye on those who cause divisions and occasions for stumbling contrary to the teaching you have learned, and avoid them . . . By smooth talk and complimentary speech, they seduce the hearts of guileless ones.'[207] Soon afterwards the Watchtower Society defiantly announced: 'If the wicked system of this world survived until the turn of the [20th] century, which is highly improbable in view of the world trends and the fulfilment of

---

[207] Romans 16: 17, 18. NWT.

Bible prophecy, there would still be survivors of the World War 1 generation.'[208]

The end of that tumultuous year marked the end of a decade of remarkable growth in the numbers of Jehovah's Witnesses worldwide. It also witnessed the salutary exit of more than eight hundred thousand members of the organisation during one of the most glossed over periods in its history.

---

[208] Watchtower – October 15, 1980.

Chapter Twenty-One

FAITH, HOPE AND DEBATABLE CHARITY

As the 20th century inched toward its end more than three million active Jehovah's Witnesses were urged to sacrifice yet more of their time in the 'life-saving' house-to-house ministry. Singled out for special attention were those who might be planning to raise a family: 'It is, therefore, appropriate for Christians to ask themselves how getting married or, if married, having children will affect their share in that vital work . . . since the time left is reduced, married couples would do well to weigh carefully the pros and cons of childbearing in these times.'[209] This hint was further strengthened some months later with the promising suggestion that the apostle Paul, in his preaching and teaching work, had been 'laying a foundation for a work that would be completed in our 20th century'.[210] However, a year later this emotive scriptural comment was reappraised in the annual bound-volume edition of the Watchtower as: 'laying a foundation for a work that would be completed in our day.'

Time was moving on apace and it was about to catch up with the president of the Watchtower Society himself – referred to as King Saul by those at the Brooklyn headquarters who prayed to see the back of him. Frederick W. Franz ended his days lost in a thickening haze of demented end-time conviction and confusion, fussed over (according to an insider) by 'a possessive limp-wristed personal attendant'. He died on December 22, 1992, at the age of ninety-nine. Nonetheless, he had the last word from beyond the grave when, some months later, in the summer of 1993, the Watchtower Society published the late president's final thoughts on the countdown to Armageddon:

'Truly we have been [living] in the last days since 1914 and are nearing the culmination of Bible prophecies involving our time . . . Jesus said regarding the era that would experience the "beginning of pangs of distress" from 1914 onward: "This generation will by no means pass away until all these things occur." Thus, all the features of the last days must take place within the lifetime of one generation, the generation of 1914. So, some people who were alive in 1914 will still be alive when this system comes to its end.[211]

---

[209] Watchtower – March 1, 1988.
[210] Watchtower – January 1, 1989.
[211] What is the Purpose of Life? – WTBTS 1993.

Frederick W. Franz was succeeded by Milton Henschel, an eighty-two-year-old former personal secretary to N. H. Knorr. Entirely without charisma or command, his presidential power was to be largely figurative, with the day-to-day running of the Watchtower Society's business falling mainly into the hands of financial controllers and corporate attorneys along with their attendant teams of compliant bureaucrats.

In September 1998, an unspoken calendar-induced sense of an impending fin-de-siècle raised the temporal hopes and expectations of Jehovah's Witnesses everywhere. However, the Watchtower Society, sensing this awareness, re-set its doomsday clock with a timely quotation from newspaper columnist Charlie Reese whose reflections on the fast-approaching millennium had recently been published in The Orlando Sentinel: 'The 1914-18 war that destroyed the 19th century is not over. History does not pay attention to calendars. The 19th century – defined as a set of beliefs, assumptions, attitudes, and morals – did not end on January 1, 1901. It ended in 1914. That is also when the 20th century, defined the same way, began.

What were the Witnesses to think now? What did the Watchtower Society have to say? 'Jehovah is the great timekeeper. His timing of events will prove to be perfect. Things may not always appear to be shaping up the way we personally expected . . . He may be allowing things to go on longer than many had expected.' Had they had been wrong-footed by their own zeal and enthusiasm, perhaps? Undoubtedly, many Witnesses were now asking themselves why had they 'got it wrong' for 120 years? 'I'll tell you why,' volunteered Watchtower Circuit Overseer, Mike Spurr, 'Because we never ever, ever, would have gotten his preaching work done. Nobody would have been missionaries, nobody would have gone abroad, nobody would have pioneered – they would have all raised children and gone to university.'[212]

In the last two years of the 20th century, many countries in the western world, including Britain, Canada, Germany, Poland, Finland, Italy, Japan, New Zealand, Spain, Australia, France, Sweden, Switzerland, Belgium, Netherlands, Norway, Denmark, and Austria registered negative or zero growth in the numbers of Jehovah's Witnesses, not to mention a significant 4% decrease in the United States of America. Despite these arresting figures, the ranks of Jehovah's Witnesses in general inexplicably continued to increase. So much so that toward the end of the

---

[212] From a recorded 'public talk' in a Kingdom Hall in Lincoln, England, August 20th, 1998.

20th century there were three times as many Witnesses as there were in the doomsday year of 1975. In the penultimate year of the 20th century more than 323,000 converts were baptised.

On the first day of the New Millennium the Watchtower Society trumpeted that there were now 5,912,492 active Jehovah's Witnesses currently 'spreading the good news' of God's kingdom and warning mankind of the 'fast approaching' Armageddon. In the year 2003 a huge propaganda assault on world opinion was launched with the global distribution of 139 million copies (in 299 languages) of a brochure – Enjoy Life on Earth Forever! As a result, a further 258,845 individuals were publicly baptised as Jehovah's Witnesses.

These apparently contradicting statistics are better understood in relation to the marketing tactics employed by certain commercial giants in the global marketplace. In the face of growing resistance to the Society's doomsday philosophy in the western world, a decision was made to take a leaf out of the tobacco manufacturers' book of survival strategy and target third-world countries and emerging eastern-European countries of the former Communist-bloc.

To facilitate their efforts in this regard the Watchtower Society secretly applied for – and, in 1991, was subsequently granted – membership of the United Nations as a 'non-governmental organisation'. An NGO affiliated with the United Nations is officially described as, 'A non-profit, voluntary citizen's group which is organised on a local, national or international level [and which is] task-oriented and driven by people with a common interest.' Over 1,500 NGOs with strong information programmes on issues of concern to the United Nations are associated with the Department of Public Information (DPI) giving the United Nations valuable links to people around the world.

Back on December 12, 1918, the executive committee of the Federal Council of Churches of Christ in America held their annual meeting during which they debated an idea which had been initially proposed by President Wilson in January 1918. They subsequently endorsed the president's plan for a League of Nations with a Declaration which in part stated: 'The war crisis of the world has passed, but a world crisis is upon us . . . The time has come to organise the world for truth and right, justice and humanity. To this end, as Christians we urge the establishment of a League of Free Nations . . . Such a League is not a mere political expedient; it is rather, the political expression of the Kingdom of God on earth . . .'

In January 1919, the Declaration of the Federal Council of Churches in America was duly conveyed to the International Peace Conference in Paris. This led to the signing of a peace treaty, including the Covenant of the League of Nations, in Versailles, France, on June 28, 1919. 'The churches of Christendom have turned away from God and were now looking to politicians to solve the problems of the world,' declared Judge Rutherford.

From its inception the League of Nations, known today as the United Nations, was branded 'a product of Satan, and an abomination in the sight of God,' by the Watchtower Society condemning it as an ungodly organisation in which 'men join to give praise to individuals . . . in setting up a great idol to which they give honour and glory [predicting] it will achieve great things for suffering humanity . . . Religious clerics lend their moral support and look upon it as God's way of ushering in peace. The U.N. has become a graven image.'[213]

When applying to the United Nations for NGO status the Watchtower Society failed to mention that Jehovah's Witnesses do not share its values and principles by any stretch of the imagination. Indeed, the Society has roundly condemned both the United Nations and its forerunner, the League of Nations, as evil organisations to be avoided by true Christians at all costs, even to the extent of lying by default, a tactic officially recommended by the Watchtower Society: 'In Jehovah's eyes a person is not obliged to divulge truthful information to people who are not entitled to it.'[214]

For decades Jehovah's Witnesses have looked upon the United Nations as the symbolic 'scarlet-coloured wild beast' of Revelation; an organisation which is regularly and routinely described in Watchtower literature as a blasphemous multinational idol. For example, in 1988, just three years before applying for their coveted NGO affiliation the Watchtower Society published Revelation – its Grand Climax at Hand! in which it said of the UN: 'Its life span will be short, for according to God's decree, it is to go off into destruction. The UN's founders and admirers do not have their names recorded in God's scroll of life. The UN is actually a blasphemous counterfeit of God's messianic kingdom.'

Officially, NGOs associated with the United Nations 'should have statutes/bylaws providing for a transparent process of taking decisions, elections of officers and members of the Board of Directors'. The

---

[213] Watchtower – December 15, 1929; March 1, 1950.

[214] Watchtower – December 1993.

Watchtower Society does not – and never will – fulfil any of these requirements. Notwithstanding this anomaly, Milton Henschel, the organisation's president at the time and other top executives, flew round the world (business class) on the back of a UN diplomat's pass for some nine years whenever the need arose to curry favour or ease things along with agencies in foreign lands such as Bulgaria, for example, where the preaching activities of Jehovah's Witnesses might be scrutinised by the tax authorities or curtailed or even suppressed in some way because of its anti-blood transfusion doctrine.

As millions of Jehovah's Witnesses in more than two hundred lands across the globe continued to look upon the United Nations organisation as 'a loathsome and disgusting thing', certain members of the Watchtower Society's hierarchy regularly posed as representatives of a regular mainstream Christian Association that was, in effect, sanctioned by the United Nations. This grand deception and corporate duplicity only came to light when a Watchtower defector, idly trawling the United Nations website, came across the NGO listings. Subsequent reports in a London newspaper[215] appeared on the internet resulting in Watchtower headquarters in New York and branch offices in many countries around the world being swamped with calls from puzzled and angry Jehovah's Witnesses. Two days later the UN issued an official statement, which appeared in principal newspapers on both sides of the Atlantic:

PUBLIC NOTICE

11 OCTOBER 2001

To Whom It May Concern

Recently the NGO Section had been receiving numerous inquiries regarding the association of the Watchtower Bible and Tract Society of New York with the Department of Public Information (DPI). This organisation applied for association with the DPI in 1991 and was granted association in 1992. By accepting association with the DPI, the organisation agreed to meet the criteria for association, including respect of the principles of the Charter of the United Nations and commitment and means to conduct effective information programmes with its constituents and to a broader audience about UN activities. In October 2001, the Watchtower Bible and Tract Society of New York requested termination of its association with the DPI. Following this request, the DPI has [chosen] to disassociate the Watchtower Bible and Tract Society of New York as of 9 October 2001.

Watchtower officials in New York subsequently instructed Paul Gillies, the Society's press officer in London, to forward their explanatory

[215] The Guardian – August 15; October 15, 2001.

letter for publication, to *The Guardian* complaining that the articles (written by journalist Stephen Bates) contained several 'factual errors' and misrepresented the background to the registration of Jehovah's Witnesses with the United Nations. The letter emphasized that the Watchtower Society had innocently registered with the United Nations as a non-governmental organisation (NGO) 'for the sole purpose of gaining access to [its] extensive library for research purposes' and stressed 'there was nothing secret about it'. It was also claimed that 'no signature was required' at the time of the initial application. Apparently, it was 'only years later', when the Governing Body became aware that they were required to support the goals of the United Nations, that the Watchtower Society's membership as NGO was withdrawn and the ID card was returned.

What Paul Gillies referred to as a simple library pass was in fact accreditation as an NGO to obtain access to the United Nations, which is what the WTBTS secured in 1992, after applying in1991. However, although access to the UN library is granted to representatives from registered NGO's, anyone anywhere may access the UN library resources in a variety of ways, including the www online.

In accordance with resolutions 1296 and 1297 of the United Nations, passed in 1968 and published as Criteria for Association, accredited organisations are required to subscribe to the aims and ideals of the UN charter. Furthermore, the accreditation was required to be renewed annually during the WTBTS's membership. In fact, a high-ranking Watchtower official filled out and signed a form every year for ten years, and each time he had to give a signature.

Responding to the Watchtower press officer's letter on behalf of The Guardian, journalist Stephen Bates replied: 'I have just been shown your letter. I would be grateful if you would allow me to circulate it to the thousands of Jehovah's Witnesses who have contacted me since the articles appeared because, if there was nothing secret about your association with the Scarlet-Coloured Beast, I am surprised that so many followers did not know of it, given the WTBTS's frequent condemnation of the UN in its publications. This may account for the Witnesses' feelings of betrayal and sense of hypocrisy over the whole affair. If it was not secret and was only done to obtain a library ticket, why did you not tell me when I spoke to you several days before the article appeared? And why did the WTBTS decide to disaffiliate only two days after the article appeared, when the WTBTS "learned about a situation" which was anyway not a secret? *The Guardian* will not publish your letter because it appears to us to be untruthful, or part of your sect's ludicrously entitled "theocratic war strategy". Perhaps you might also like to explain the truly distasteful images of Armageddon, including the destruction of skyscrapers, in your literature, which would appear to undermine any public expressions of sympathy by the WTBTS over the events of September 11, 2001.'

There was no response from the Mill Hill press office and the U.K. branch of the Watchtower Society made no further attempts to get *The Guardian* to print their fabricated story.

***

Even though they perform no charitable works, Jehovah's Witnesses are officially registered as a non-profit 'charitable organisation' in many parts of the world. This spurious arrangement allows the Watchtower Society to function as a legitimate commercial enterprise on a global scale virtually tax-free. Nowhere in the world has this anomaly been utilised by Jehovah's Witnesses with such money-making efficiency than in the teeming cities of New York and London.

For example, in 1995 sociologist Werner Cohn, noted 'inconsistencies in Watchtower practice and beliefs' and claimed that 'Brooklyn property taxes not paid by the Witnesses cost the city of New York $10 Million a year'.[216] In 2001 Newsday magazine listed the Watchtower organisation as one of New York's richest corporations with revenues of more than $950 million. According to a recent analysis by the Downtown Brooklyn Partnership, Jehovah's Witnesses living and working in their tax-free New York City properties had additionally been exempt from paying at least $368 million in property taxes in the period 2004-2016.

Formerly, Watchtower literature had long been offered to the public free of charge, with householders being 'invited' to make a suggested charitable donation to the 'world-wide Christian work' of Jehovah's Witnesses. In the U.K., for example, value-added tax (VAT) was additionally avoided by describing magazine subscriptions and doorstep-sales of books and Bibles as 'charitable donations' in the annual accounts and returns submitted to the Charity Commission.

British law on charities is particularly lax and wide open to abuse. The legislation originally dates from 1601 and was refined in 1891 to give four classifications for charitable uses of money: 'relief of poverty, advancement of education, advancement of religion and other purposes

---

[216] Brooklyn Heights Press & Cobble Hill News – June 1, 1995.

beneficial to the community'. Despite the Watchtower Society in the UK not 'relieving poverty', actively discouraging 'advancement of education' and doing nothing at all which is remotely 'beneficial to the community', its tax-free charitable status in the 21st century remains profitably unchallenged.

In 1998 the Charity Commission launched its first-ever review of the 187, 200 registered charities on its books at that time but has yet to determine what a religion is, or what a charity is, or what it means to be religious in a charitable sense. The Commission is at odds with other European countries who think that the Watchtower Society is an anti-social destructive cult. On the contrary, the Commission continues to believe that the Witnesses are 'charitable in concept', with the untold tax advantages that brings. And yet the British do not quite agree with the Americans who approve of the charitable status of the, apparently Godless, Church of Scientology – a controversial multi-million-dollar pseudo-psychological cult – which is officially classed as conceptually 'Christian' simply because it calls itself a church and displays a huge neon-lit crucifix on its headquarters building.

The Charity Commissioners in London ruled that because there is no deity central to Scientology's beliefs, the movement no longer qualified for charitable status. In the confusion that followed, Tom Spring, an American lawyer retained by the Scientologists flew over to London to challenge the new ruling. He believed the new classification was unfair, prejudicial, and contrary to the new Human Rights Act, introduced at that time in the UK. He was also keen to find out how the apparent ambiguity and confusion surrounding the charity issue in the UK had been so successfully exploited by the Watchtower Society. However, one country within the EU had already taken steps to plug the credibility gap of bogus charitable status.

In France, a motion was adopted (June 29th, 1995) for a resolution by Mr. Jacques Guyard and members of the Socialist Group to create a Board of Inquiry – charged to study [a report on] the phenomenon of cults and to propose, if necessary, the adoption of the texts in force. The government sponsored study had been initiated by a worrying trend in religious fanaticism.

Among the cases of religious extremism cited were the tragedy in Waco, Texas, on April 19th, 1993, when 88 members of the Branch Davidian cult died, either by suicide or during a violent confrontation with police; the Solar Temple movement when 53 members of the cult lost their lives on October 4th 1994, having committed suicide or been assassinated in Switzerland and Canada; the ricin gas attack on the public by end-time fanatics in a subway in Tokyo in which eleven innocent people lost their lives and 5,000 others made sick or seriously injured. Then there was the horrific collective suicide of 923 members of the People's Temple in Guiana, back in 1978.

The report – written by Alain Vivien at the request of the French Prime Minister and published under the title 'Cults of France: Expression of Moral Freedom or Factors of Manipulation' – was based on the findings of Alain Gest who had investigated the phenomena of fringe religions and sects and cults in France in the name of the Board of Inquiry. His wide-ranging commentary concluded that the Jehovah's Witness movement was the largest of the cults scrutinised and classified the Watchtower Society as 'Apocalyptical, Evangelical, a movement resulting from the Judaeo-Christian trunk, persuading followers of the credibility [of its doomsday predictions]'. The report, which was published two days later, made the following observations:

'The approach of the year 2000 could, indeed correspond to a considerable multiplication of broken families, mental illness, and suicides. Some psychiatrists today are still unaware of the process of mental manipulation practised by Jehovah's Witnesses. Followers lost their free will and sometimes became unconditionally fanatical, ready to believe, say, and do all, no matter what . . . they often engage completely, until they lose part of their identity. The intervention of the public authorities is essential when engagement leads to a psychological dependence which the leaders exploit to their own profit. The education of the children [of Jehovah's Witnesses] should not indeed consist of just one indoctrination based on a particularly cataclysmic vision of the world in which only followers of the sect would be preserved.'[217]

Jehovah's Witnesses have in the past declared themselves to be a 'cultural association' in France, but the Council of State judged that the publishing and sale of religious books could not be regarded as cultural activities. However, it also noted that the government should not create particular legislation because of the risk of making Jehovah's Witnesses appear as martyrs: 'There exists today in France no structure equipped with sufficient means to follow with precision the whole of the cult phenomenon . . . To remain passive would be, indeed, not only irresponsible, but dangerous for the democratic principles on which our republic is founded. In France we do not feel threatened by a tragedy of the Waco

---

[217] CULTS IN FRANCE – NATIONAL ASSEMBLY (No 2468), December 1995.

type, but the germs of such dramas exist in our territory, and prevention is essential . . . the sectarian phenomenon also calls for, indeed, a global response.'

The Commission examined this report during its meeting of December 20, 1995, and adopted it unanimously. Consequently, the French government ruled that while Jehovah's Witnesses are not denied their basic human rights to practice their religion, their profitable publishing business would in future be taxed, just like any other commercial enterprise.' This shock judgement not only set a precedent that continues to be monitored and reconsidered by numerous other countries in the European Union today, but it also sent worrying ripples of unease and discomfort across the Atlantic.

American Watchtower lawyers immediately set to work. From their experience they knew just how to tap into the persuasive and emotive value of the ubiquitous non-specific reverential attitude toward 'belief in God' and instructed their French brothers to defy their government. The advice from New York was to ignore the civil disobedience aspect of the situation and play for sympathy; get public opinion on their side by fighting it out in the name of Christianity in general.

The French Witnesses refused to co-operate with the authorities and continued to file nominal 'charitable status' tax-returns as before. The Watchtower Society reported zero growth in France during 1996, and a two-percent decrease in 1997 was followed by a further drop of two percent in 1998. That same year a penalty of FF300 million was imposed on the French branch of the Watchtower Society for non-payment of backdated taxes, and a lien was declared on all French property belonging to the Watchtower Society.

The case went to appeal, but judgement was upheld on July 4, 2000. More than six million followers of the movement swamped politicians on both sides of the Atlantic with letters of protest. Full-page announcements appeared in the *New York Times* and principal newspapers across France seeking public sympathy and support. Twelve million copies of a leaflet – People of France, You Are Being Deceived – were delivered by Les Témoins de Jéhovah as thousands marched through the streets of Paris calling for an end to the 'defamatory statements spread about us'. Witness children were insulted and harassed at school and some adults lost their jobs and were threatened because of their religion.

President Clinton appealed for 'tolerance toward religious sects', while French President Jacques Chirac declared that the subject would not be on the agenda in future bilateral talks. Alain Vivian, chairman of the ministerial committee which sat in judgement on the Watchtower Society accused the American administration of compromise and deference towards religious sects in exchange for political finance. These developments in Europe, which were constantly monitored from Watchtower Headquarters in New York, resulted in certain 'legal readjustments' being made to its charitable status in Britain to utilise the UK's expansive charity laws to the international advantage of the Watchtower Society.

The Watchtower Bible & Tract Society of Britain (Registered charity 1077961) is not autonomous and remains under the overall control and command of the Watchtower Society in New York. However, the legal 'adjustments' to its registration with the Charity Commission, which were made in the summer of 2000, in effect rendered the movement 'financially autonomous' in Britain and therefore singularly responsible for the conveyance of the Society's funds between Watchtower branch offices anywhere in the world as and when directed by New York.

Today this UK-based Watchtower Society cash-conduit effectively disguises American involvement in the financing of, supposedly legitimate, tax-dodging Watchtower activities in sensitive areas of the world. It also provides a ready safe-haven for staggering amounts of money that may be at risk from a slew of class-action lawsuits threatened by increasingly vocal dissenters and victims of the widespread sexual misconduct of Jehovah's Witnesses in many countries around the world.

An immediate benefit from the charitable state of the Watchtower Society in Britain meant that opposition to the French government's crackdown could now be financed directly from London without revealing the controlling involvement of the Governing Body of Jehovah's Witnesses in America. When several public announcements regarding the Watchtower's intended adjustments to its charitable status were published in *The Times* over a period of weeks, as required in British law, the Charity Commission in London was inundated with letters of protest from former Jehovah's Witnesses in many parts of the world, particularly America: What was the Commission thinking of in facilitating the corporate endorsement of a puppet regime whose strings were being pulled in Brooklyn? Did they not know that the Witnesses in the UK perform no recognisable charitable work that benefits the public?

The Charity Commission responded: 'There are stringent tests and controls which are applied to all religious charities in the UK. Any mere disapproval of the tenets and practices of a religion does not amount to grounds for withholding registration. In the absence of clear and adverse public-interest factors, the commission cannot decline registration of a religious charity. The choice of religion is a personal one and capable of provoking strong feelings. The Watchtower Society is established for religious purposes and there is no legal requirement for it to help people in need.'[218]

When asked to comment on the lucrative tax-free status of certain religious charities which perform no charitable acts or recognisable public service, a British tax inspector commented: 'Unless it can be shown that the Exchequer is being deprived of funds, the Inland Revenue is powerless to act. What is needed is legislation to clarify in law just what 'charity' is and whether religious belief without 'charitable works' can be deemed charitable.'[219]

Watchtower Society UK accounts, published by the Charity Commission, reveal a widely fluctuating annual income/expenditure pattern for the five-year period 2013-2017. Cash income varies between some £30 million and £90 million, and notes: 'We have a formal arrangement with Jehovas Zeugen in Deutschland (JZD). We also receive at times funding from (JZD).' Charity Choice, a commercially independent advisory service provider, reports: 'The UK Watchtower Society raised an additional £60,679,000 in the year ending 31st August 2017 through their fundraising efforts.' The May 20, 2019, Charity Commission report on the Watchtower Society states: 'Total funds held – £148,966,406.'

***

The Watchtower Society's official stance on charity is clearly demonstrated by the experience of one of Jehovah's Witnesses in Scandinavia. In January 1986 Rud Persson, a Swedish elder, became a member of the Red Cross after being moved by the plight of starving millions in Ethiopia. When his wife mentioned to a JW friend that she and her husband had agreed to make modest annual payments to the Red Cross by banker's order, word of their charitable attitude eventually reached the presiding overseer of the congregation.

A secret Watchtower investigation was soon under way involving the local body of elders, the circuit overseer (equivalent to a church Bishop) and the Governing Body of Jehovah's Witnesses in New York. The Watchtower Society responded via an official letter (October 15, 1986) to the Swedish branch office:

---

[218] In correspondence with the author.

[219] The Spectator – October 28, 2000.

'Dear Brothers, We now write to you concerning the information you provided the Society that brother Rud Persson has become a member of the Red Cross. It is claimed that the purpose of the organisation is to relieve human suffering, but we must, nevertheless, remember that the organisation had its beginning on the battlefields. It performs a large part of its work directly or indirectly in conflict with the thoughts outlined at Isaiah 2:4. Too, the organisation is one of the world's biggest suppliers of blood for transfusions. It is also involved in political matters and often acts as mediator between nations at war. A person's motive for joining an organisation also comes into the picture. Why does he wish to join a certain organisation? Does he approve of what that organisation stands for? It may happen that someone becomes a passive member of such an organisation to qualify for a course in first aid. Nothing else is required of the individual. A Christian might think that his conscience allows for this. On the other hand, if someone says that he is defending everything the organisation advocates, then, of course, his privileges in the congregation would be affected. If someone should become a member and actively support, for example, the world-wide blood programme the Red Cross stands for, that could lead to disfellowshipping.

Hence, in your case we recommend that you talk to brother Rud Persson about this and examine his motive for joining the Red Cross. Is he of the opinion that what this organisation stands for is good and proper? Is he aware of its programme in support of blood transfusions? And its activities as mediator between [warring] nations? What is his attitude to food containing blood served at school? Has he informed the teachers about our position regarding this? Birthday celebrations and so forth, in connection with school activities?'

Rud Persson was baptised as one of Jehovah's Witnesses in 1959. His younger brother also served the local congregation as an elder while his mother – also one of Jehovah's Witnesses – had previously been offered help, and gratefully accepted it, from the Swedish Red Cross invalid service when she became permanently incapacitated through illness. After months of hurtful gossip and humiliating interrogation at the hands of the local elders Rud Persson and his wife disassociated themselves from the movement to which the Swedish elder had devoted more than twenty-seven years of his life.

Chapter Twenty-Two

THE LAST DAYS OF THE WATCHTOWER SOCIETY

When commenting on the words of Jesus – 'This generation shall not pass, till all these things be fulfilled'[220] – the Watchtower Society has persistently emphasised that he was referring to the entire human family that would be in existence in 1914 plus all those who were yet to be born within that defining generational timeline. Seventy years on from that pivotal date attention was focussed on the significance of Psalm 90 which describes the length of the average lifespan as 'three-score and ten' (70 years) or 'four-score' (80 years) for those of special strength.

A teasing edition of the Watchtower magazine focussed attention on living examples of that specific generation. Sixteen elderly male and female members of the New York Bethel family, in their 70's, 80's and 90's and all hoping to survive Armageddon, 'any day now', were pictured on the front cover along with the eye-catching slogan: **1914**, THE GENERATION THAT WILL NOT PASS AWAY.[221] The oldest among the aged hopefuls featured in this global PR promotion was 92-year-old Dickran Derderian who died from 'natural causes' later that year. Inevitably, within seven years, the rest of that representative '1914 generation' photo-shoot, confidently looking forward to the realisation of their Armageddon dreams, had all dropped out of the picture.

It was during those dying years of the 20th century that clouds of doubt began to drift among Jehovah's Witnesses everywhere. To refresh jaded hopes and alleviate pre-millennial tension, the Watchtower Society then declared that age was no longer considered a determining factor in identifying the 1914 generation: 'Rather than provide a rule for measuring time, the term "generation", as used by Jesus, refers principally to contemporary people of a certain historical period.'[222] However, this did little to stem the flow of disillusioned Witnesses ('faders') waking up to reality and abandoning their doomsday expectations in many countries of the western world.

During the New Year 2000 all eight Governing Body members were advised by the legal department to technically relinquish their executive

---

[220] Matthew 24: 34 KJV
[221] Watchtower – May 15, 1984.
[222] Watchtower – November 1, 1995.

control of the organisation while publicly retaining their all-important pontifical supremacy as a 'spiritually anointed advisory committee'. Theoretically, it was assumed, this administrational tinkering would render the Governing Body unimpeachable in the event of legal action, civil or otherwise, being taken against the Watchtower Society.

To illustrate: When asked to attend court in San Diego to give evidence in an historic child-abuse case being heard in 2014, Gerrit Losch, a member of the Governing Body since 1994, refused and sent a wordy 4-page-letter to the court claiming: 'I do not have, and never have had any authority as an individual to make or determine corporate policy for Watchtower or any department of Watchtower.' The former Austrian hotel waiter was found to be in contempt of court and his evasive and disingenuous retort was met with a $13.5 million judgement against the Watchtower Society.

Similarly, when questioned about his role in the administration during an investigation of the Watchtower Society by the Australian Royal Commission 2017 – which highlighted 1006 perpetrators of child sexual abuse not reported to authorities – Governing Body member Geoffrey Jackson, who had been summoned (subpoenaed) to attend the hearing while visiting his ailing father, claimed he had no executive power at all: 'Policy is not my business,' he told the court. When asked if the Watchtower Society's Governing Body were God's only channel of communication to mankind, he stuttered: 'That would be presumptuous.'

However, when New York's Child Victims Act came into effect in 2019, temporarily lifting the statute of limitations, it opened a year-long window of opportunity – later extended for an additional five months – for victims of sex crimes to seek justice no matter how long ago they took place. Inevitably, a lawsuit against the Watchtower Society, naming all eight members of the Governing Body as defendants, and demanding a trial by jury, was immediately filed in the State Supreme Court in Brooklyn, New York.

This came as big shock to a leadership unaccustomed to explaining and justifying the Society's money-making doomsday teachings – not to mention the systematic cover-up of child abuse and other serious crimes within its ranks – outside the Watchtower bubble. For example, probing reporters, attending conventions where a member of the Governing Body is scheduled to conclude with a rousing 'public talk' (invariably scripted by a committee in the Writing Department), are routinely brushed aside by security guards as the targeted speaker scuttles away.

Watchtower lawyers responded to the lawsuit on behalf of the Watchtower leadership with a wordy attempt to redefine clergy-penitent privilege, a clause in the law which was originally designed to protect the 'privacy of sins confessed' to priests. This has little to do with Watchtower's long history of not only failing to report such alleged 'sins' of child sex-abuse to the appropriate authorities, but any wrongdoing which would be considered a crime in the outside world.

'This organisation has allowed the sexual abuse of children to fester within its ranks for decades. This [lawsuit] goes all the way up the chain to the top, and that's why we're suing the top,' said lawyer Irwin Zalkin. 'The First Amendment does not exist to provide religious institutions with a free pass to operate outside of the law.' A spokesman for those accused immediately responded: 'Watchtower's stand on the subject of child abuse is clear, we abhor child abuse in any form.' The case, along with countless others in the pipeline, looks set to continue for years to come.

Congregational overseers the world over were subsequently instructed to inform their flocks: 'The Society is expecting lots of fake claims for mishandling child sex abuse due to a change in the law. It is being driven by apostates and greedy lawyers, and now it's being picked up by the media and others.' Barbara Anderson, a former confidential researcher in the Brooklyn Bethel headquarters countered: 'In the late 1990's the Watchtower Society had 23,000 cases of child abuse on file in Brooklyn.'

The Watchtower Society in the UK faced its first ever child molestation lawsuit in 2018 when it was charged with failing to protect a child who was sexually abused by one Peter Stewart, a ministerial servant, over a five-year period in the 1980's and failing to warn other parents. After appealing judgement to pay £275,000 damages to the victim, which Lord Justice Floyd rejected, the Watchtower Society was further ordered to pay additional legal costs totalling £1,000,000 in settlement. Kathleen Hallisay, a London solicitor currently pursuing similar civil law- suits in Britain commented: 'Secrecy is a tenet of the religion, [sexual predators] know they can operate with impunity, and unfortunately, the policies of the Watchtower Society allow them to continue to do that again and again.'

The Catholic church, which has steadfastly refused to acknowledge the existence of child abuse within its cloisters for centuries, has been paying the price of such deception for decades and continues to do so. Likewise, the Watchtower Society is finally being called to account for its customary failure to report such crimes – a disturbing percentage of which have proven to be of an incestuous nature – to the appropriate authorities.

In January 2019, the House of Representatives in the Netherlands commissioned a report from the University of Utrecht when Justice Minister Sander Dekker launched a wide-ranging investigation of alleged child abuse within the Jehovah's Witness community. A total of 751 individuals were invited to share their experiences of sexual abuse via an electronic contact point that was specially created for the purposes of the study. These included 292 accounts of personal involvement in sexual abuse and 459 accounts of sexual abuse made by another person on behalf of an alleged victim.

An academic programme of discreet validation and substantiation, which was meticulously researched over a twelve-month period, revealed 'the reported abuse often took place within the nuclear family (father/brother, 34%), fellow JW's (27%), relatives (uncle, grandfather 16%)'. The Dutch branch of the Watchtower Society had originally agreed to co-operate and encouraged the faithful to take part in the official inquiry, but upon reading an advance copy of the report they legally attempted to prevent its publication. However, in January 2020 the Dutch Court ruled that it should be published in the public interest.

The following month, February 13, 2020, the High Court in the UK set an important precedent when it ruled: 'The rights of children outweigh those of confidentiality when disclosures of information about allegations of abuse are made to ministers.' Back in 2016, when the mother of a girl aged 12 and a boy aged 10 had told elders that their father, who was a member of their congregation, was sexually abusing them, the elders remained silent. They had argued they were 'under a spiritual duty not to disclose confidential religious communications. Mrs Justice Lieven countered, 'The facts of this case raise very great concern about the safeguarding of children within the Jehovah's Witness community.'

On one occasion the Society admitted there were such offenders among the Bethel family: 'Shocking as it is, even some who have been prominent in Jehovah's organisation have succumbed to homosexuality, wife-swapping and child molestation.'[223] Among such prominent

[223]Watchtower November 1, 1995.

offenders in the organisation were Leo Greenlees, a member of the Governing Body (1964-1984), who was eventually removed from office as homosexual. Ewart Chitty, also on the Governing Body (1974-1979), stepped down following allegations involving a ten-year old boy. It is widely believed they were not alone in their transgressions at the slippery upper climbs of Watchtower's pyramid of power.

Broadcasting on JW.org in 2015, Governing Body member Steven Lett – who recently declared: 'there is more evidence that Jesus' kingdom began ruling in heaven in 1914 than there is for gravity, electricity and wind' – dismissed child abuse accusations against Jehovah's Witnesses as 'apostate lies and dishonesties'. He went on: 'If anybody takes [sic] action against someone who would threaten our young ones, it is Jehovah's organisation.'

However, Steven Lett was personally involved in a child-abuse case back in 2002 when a five-year-old girl was raped by the son of an elder. Having reported the matter to the police, the child's parents Tim and Lisa Manion, were subjected to the persuasive weight of the Watchtower Society to drop all charges and reluctantly decided not to 'bring reproach on Jehovah's name' by dragging his organisation through the courts. Tim then wrote to brother Lett in graphic detail and pleaded with him as a member of the Governing Body to modify the Society's notorious 'two witnesses' rule. In reply he received a sympathetic, but none-committal, corporate acknowledgement signed by Governing Body member Steven Lett, his former friend and Bible Study conductor who first led Tim to baptism in 1975. Soon afterwards the distraught couple renounced their Watchtower Society faith altogether.

The official 'two witnesses' rule which congregational elders are duty-bound to take is based on an interpretation of Deuteronomy 19:15 which the Watchtower Society spells out thus: 'If the accused denies the accusation the investigating elders should try to arrange a meeting with him and the accuser together. If the accusation involves child sexual abuse and the victim is a minor, the elders should contact the branch office before arranging a meeting with the child and the alleged abuser. If the accuser or the accused is unwilling to meet with the elders or if the accused continues to deny the accusation of a single witness and the wrongdoing is not established, the elders will leave matters in Jehovah's hands.'

In a remarkably unconscionable display of intransigence on the subject, Watchtower 'helper' Gary Breaux, broadcasting on JW.org, stressed how the Bible is 'very clear' on the subject: 'Before a judicial committee can be convened there *has* to be a confession or two witnesses. We will *never* change our scriptural position.' Such contempt of the most naturally family-oriented sensitivities of its vulnerable followers was condemned by the Australian Royal Commission of 2017 and numerous law-courts the world over as a corporate attitude which 'does not speak very well for the leadership of the Watchtower Society or indeed, its compliant adherents'.

***

In the uncertainty of the years following the theoretical realignment of power at their Brooklyn headquarters, Jehovah's Witnesses were subjected to endless rounds of vacillating Watchtower tautology which culminated in a flash of 'new light' first introduced at District Conventions in 2010: 'The generation referred to at Mathew 24:34 comprises two groups of anointed Christians. The first group was on hand in 1914 when "the sign" of Christ's presence began to be observed. The second group of those who were anointed later, are contemporaries of the older group.'

Individuals who were baptised and sufficiently cognizant of the events of 1914 were now to be considered the primary generation which has been succeeded by a subsequent secondary 'overlapping generation' of those born during the average lifetime of the primary generation. With scant regard for the exactitude of the English language, Governing Body member David Splane described this Watchtower-speak definition of the 1914 generation as 'a clarification of our understanding which connects with the urgency of our times'.

Consequently, many critics saw the Governing Body as living in a nonsensical Lewis Carrol Looking-Glass world of Watchtower semantics in which words mean whatever they want them to mean. They scoffed and raged at such a 'laughably unbelievable' attempt to re-start a failed count-down to doomsday and accused the Watchtower Society of awarding itself 'extra-time' in an audacious replay of a religiously inspired mind-game it had so resoundingly lost. Watchtower's 'doomsday generation' – its world-famous raison d'être – had simply not lived up to its fictitious promises. Game over! they cried as the road to paradise took a worrying turn for the worse.

Although recruitment appeared to be up in some east-European and southern hemisphere countries, an alarming cash-flow disparity between congregational head counters in more than 239 lands around the world and calculating bean-counters in New York flagged up the

Watchtower Society as an inherently costly labour-intensive endeavour of diminishing cash returns. In truth, the crumbling 19th century foundational beliefs of the Watchtower Society could no longer credibly support the organisation in the 21st century. The future of the movement's bricks and mortar conglomerate in the heart of New York, its very own Vatican City – the 'big apple' of Jehovah's eye – was doubtful. As Governing Body member Steven Lett would later plead, there was 'more money going out than money coming in'.

Back in 2004 the Watchtower Society had secretly initiated a worldwide programme of cost-cutting property sell-offs, staff redundancies and a relocation of the Brooklyn Bethel headquarters; an embarrassing down-sizing move that was not made public for ten years. Eventually, in 2014, a two year-long programme of redundancies was revealed to the shocked Bethel family in New York. During that period of layoffs, printing, and shipping operations, along with laundry, housekeeping, and catering services, were gradually reduced before they were withdrawn altogether prior to the final liquidation of the remaining properties in 2017.

There was no programme of support or financial resettlement aid – certainly, no charity – for those who were summarily dismissed, some of whom had sold their homes and donated the proceeds to the Society prior to serving the organisation for years, in some cases, decades. Such ones were 'lovingly counselled to lean on Jehovah' as they stumbled back into the outside world, unwanted, unemployed, and now homeless. Residential volunteer workers in Watchtower branch offices around the world were similarly dealt with as Bethel families everywhere were ruthlessly slimmed down to the bone, sometimes dispensed with entirely.

Paradoxically, during this 2014 period of ruthless cost-cutting, the Watchtower branch office in London unveiled its ambitious plans for relocation when it applied to the local authority in Chelmsford, Essex. The intention, according to a local newspaper report, was to 'construct a printing plant capable of producing 180,000 religious magazines an hour, fourteen accommodation blocks for up to 1,200 residents, a medical facility plus various utilities and recreational space' on a 33-hectare plot of land in the nearby countryside. The estimated cost would be £150 million.

The official presentation of Watchtower's Master Plan, which took place in the Civic opulence of Chelmsford Town Hall, which was photographed for the national archives, briefly appeared as a two-minute presentation on JW.org in 2018. However, it was soon taken down when www exposure of an 18th century map superimposed on Watchtower's proposed layout of the site appeared to show 'building 33' sitting on the former site of a Templars Old Order place of worship. Coincidental? Perhaps, but a nerve had been touched.

The original Temple Farm Master Plan was later modified in line with the rapidly changing, if not waning, fortunes of the organisation as the printshop along with eight accommodation units and several other facilities in Watchtower's optimistic building plans were axed altogether.

***

Back in the first year of the new millennium three new administrations – The Religious Order of Jehovah's Witnesses, Kingdom Support Services and The Christian Congregation of Jehovah's Witnesses – were quietly incorporated into the Watchtower Society's 'mother organisation' in anticipation of 'future developments'. The Religious Order of Jehovah's Witnesses could be described as a sect within a cult. Its pious function and mode of purpose appears to reflect the sentiments of the ancient Knights Templars, a Christian sect of 12th century monastic knights who built a large training and administrative complex centred around Temple Church in the city of London, England in the year 1185.

Having taken a vow of poverty their mission was to protect pilgrims journeying to and from the Holy Land during the Crusades. To do this they developed an international banking system which enabled pilgrims to deposit money with the Templars in London that could be accessed in other countries at various points on-route. As a result, they became rich and powerful until they were driven out of the Holy Land in 1312. Eventually the Templars disbanded and went underground.

A hidden strain of that somewhat self-righteous discipline – with a hint of theoretic Freemasonry, perhaps – shows signs of having survived within the ranks of Jehovah's Witnesses today. Suitably qualified believers, sworn into this elitist 'special servant' category, are trained to imperviously 'follow the money regardless' in the irreligious world of property investments, stock market dealing and international high finance. They operate anonymously within the movement as crusading bankers to their religious cause – the survival of the Watchtower Society.

The UK Charity Commission report for 2018 states: 'The Watchtower Society is often assisted by religious ministers who are members of the Worldwide Order of Special full-time Servants of Jehovah's Witnesses (the Order). These individuals are not employed and do not receive remuneration or any kind of benefit in kind for the activities or service they perform . . . Although such ones do at times help the Society, their service involves many other assignments as well, not connected to the Society.'

What are these 'other assignments not connected' to the famous doorstep preaching work of the Watchtower Society? Could the acquisition of eleven top-end private houses in the vicinity of the former London Bethel headquarters for no known charitable purpose be one of them? Maybe the building of eight luxurious apartment blocks on the quiet (without the customary JW volunteer workforce) in upmarket areas of London is another. Some of the apartments in these properties – all of which were put up for sale in a programme of 'asset consolidation' which was launched by the Order in 2014 – were maintained as occasional clandestine retreats for privileged members of the Order and other high-ups travelling incognito.

Real estate is money in the bank for property owners and the acquisition and sale of such assets is now the Society's principal source of income. However, a succession of multi-million-dollar settlements awarded to sex abuse victims (with many more to come) and flagging, if not static contributions from poorer congregations in less affluent countries in recent years have shaken the Watchtower down to its foundations. Tax-free charitable status is another financial lifeline for the Society's special Order to take into consideration.

During the latter half of the 20th century the Watchtower Society rolled out an ambitious programme of global expansion. Loans (with interest at the going rate) were made available to congregations looking to buy land or building sites and materials for the construction of Kingdom Halls all over the world. These properties would be largely voluntarily built, maintained, and eventually paid for and owned by local communities of Jehovah's Witnesses everywhere.

This all changed when the Watchtower Society's in-house mortgage system was terminated in 2014 with the boastful announcement that all such existing debts were now being generously written off – and not only that; the Society would also assume full responsibility for the maintenance and repair of all Kingdom Halls and any associated property or land owned by local Witness communities wherever they were. The deal would be sealed once the freeholds of the properties had been legally signed over to Watchtower's world-wide Real Estate department (www.ibsaproperty.com), an allegedly religious but strictly secular company masquerading as Pastor Russell's original British-based International Bible Students Association. Its American portal is Valley Farms Corporation (Real Estate dept.) 900, Red Mills Road Wallkill NY.

Congregational elders the world over were instructed to propose a resolution that 'at least the same amount as the cancelled monthly mortgage repayment' would continue to be paid as a voluntary contribution to the 'worldwide Christian work' of the Watchtower Society. Anonymously written individual pledges to that effect added up to the specific regular monthly payments that the New York headquarters could bank on receiving from each congregation.

Before the year was out an anonymous committee of special servants of the Order had craftily secured the freehold ownership of thousands of buildings and land properties around the world on behalf of the Watchtower Society. Soon afterwards, in 2015, an entirely unexpected programme of branch office closures and Kingdom Hall sales was introduced along with the ensuing mergers of displaced congregations. Anxious Jehovah's Witnesses the world over were assured: 'The Governing Body wants to make it clear that they are confident that Jehovah is currently blessing the worldwide work.' Apparently, 'Jehovah's celestial chariot' was, in effect, 'changing direction and speeding up as it moves forward'.[224]

However, official figures on Watchtower's MGMT Property Hub, which briefly appeared on screen during a 2019 JW.org broadcast clearly showed an organisation in retreat – a global property empire that was intent on folding in on itself. A breakdown of the graphic showed that 1,518 Kingdom Halls across the world had already been sold. Additionally, a further 3,695 Kingdom Halls with land plus 677 residences and 423 landsites were earmarked for sale.[225]

Hapless Jehovah's Witnesses viewing the programme were told the Society's multi-billion-dollar international real estate liquidation illustrated how 'a perceived need for several thousand more Kingdom Halls all over the world' was being resolved by 'making better use of existing

---

[224] Ezekiel 10: 1 – 22. KJV

[225] These included, for example, an initial 516 Kingdom Halls in the USA, 850 in Brazil, 299 in Finland, 406 in central America, 71 in Spain, 210 in Nigeria, 262 in the Philippines, 137 in Argentina and thousands of others throughout the world. The billion-dollar global sell-off – which during the summer of 2020 had realized $2.6 bn (including $2.3 bn worth of USA Watchtower property) – continues apace today.

properties'. Offset against those sales were '778 acquisitions' in a profiteering buying and selling programme of bare-faced asset stripping which was rolled out as 'consolidation and realignment' following the Watchtower Society's humiliating – 'get out of town and run for hills-style' – change of address in both New York and London.

Among the organisation's allegedly 'perceived needs' is a relatively lavish South American property acquisition which did not feature in the programme. Nordelta is an exclusive residential walled-in gated district of Buenos Aires, Argentina, having its own medical facilities and schools. It was created in 1999 by Edwardo Constantino as a peaceful refuge for ultra-wealthy Argentinians looking to avoid the 'incessant crime, noise, and smells' of even the most exclusive neighbourhoods in the capital city. Built on reclaimed wetlands at the expense of the poverty-stricken surrounding communities, it is currently home to some 30,000 affluent residents with plans in place for an additional 50,000.

Nordelta – 'a city within a city' – is often criticised for its social divisiveness with its security checks – 'Barrío Privado' – at exits and entrances. It is also the incongruous location of the Watchtower Society's new 'branch office' in Argentina. Commissioned in 2018 by Watchtower's Department of Real Estate on behalf of Asociación de los Testigos de Jehová, Argentia. Boulevard de la Plaza No 55 in Nordelta was exclusively designed and built by upmarket construction company CRIBA. The project was completed in 2020. Today, the 'branch office' is commercially described as a 'mid to large sized shopping mall with an office and apartment complex set in landscaped green spaces with underground parking'.

As Watchtower's global property sell-off continued, plans to 'consolidate media production' were announced in October 2019. The new facility, located on a 242-acre site in Ramopo, NY, is two miles from the Society's Warwick compound. Construction, which will start in 2022, is scheduled for completion in 2026. The project calls for 1,500 volunteers a day. Watchtower spokesman Keith Cady told reporters: 'Our printed publications are well-known all over the world, but in recent years we have greatly increased our production of audio programmes and films.'[226]

---

[226] Among Watchtower video productions appearing on JW.org are 'educational cartoons' specifically programmed for children. One features a little girl being encouraged by her mother to forgo an ice-cream treat in favour of slotting her pocket money coins into 'that little contribution box' at the back of the Kingdom Hall. Another

Watchtower acquired the building site ahead of Loterdan Properties – (looking to build a tax-paying housing estate, much favoured by the local community) – who accused Watchtower of 'a tremendous breach of trust' following a doubtful two-year period of alleged hedge-betting and double dealing in the murky world of 'screwing' the local tax assessors, on the part of the Society's Order operatives. 'The purpose of the complex is strictly religious and as such the facility is tax exempt,' stressed Watchtower spokesman Jared Lopes.

Evidently, the overriding real estate trading, wheeler dealer property management and charmless corporate survival strategy of the Watchtower Society's pseudo-religious real estate activities of recent years appears to have eclipsed the old-fashioned evangelical intentions of Pastor Russell's 19th century Bible Students and Judge Rutherford's 20th century Jehovah's Witnesses. Today's financially-bloated administration – which has in the past thrived on continuous hope of pre-millennium fulfilment – now finds itself lost in time and space in the 21st century, for it never expected to be here in the first place.

Having recalled thousands of missionaries from abroad, the Society's Gilead Missionary Training School in New York is now reduced to coaching 'special overseers' who are sent out to encourage and assist sluggish congregations in much the same way industrious Progress Chasers chivvy slackers on the factory floor. Local congregational Ministry Schools, which previously offered Jehovah's Witnesses training sessions in public speaking and doorstep presentation skills, have been terminated and replaced with token 15-minute instructional talks.

Most Witnesses avoid the hated doorstep preaching work as and when they can, preferring nowadays to validate their obligatory preaching time by standing on street corners idly manning carts of Watchtower literature and directing any inquiring members of the public to the Society's website JW.org. There are few, if any, takers. Book sales have plummeted and the flag-ship Watchtower and *Awake!* magazines – now reduced to little more than leaflets – are in terminal decline. Indeed, the organisation appears nowadays to be in asset-stripping limbo and the leadership all but admits it has nothing new to say.

For example: Broadcasting on the Watchtower JW.org channel in March 2020, Governing Body member Anthony Morris Jr. talked about how the preaching work would conclude sooner rather than later: 'We

---

cartoon shows two little boys raiding their piggy banks to help fund 'Jehovah's worldwide Christian work'.

feel that we now have enough in the toolbox with the six Watchtower magazine study articles [first published over a two-year period which ended in late 2019] followed by a further two years using the same study material.' He then hinted that there would come a time when 'no preaching work would be done at all' prior to the immediate onset of Armageddon: 'We will have to wait and see,' he teased.

The Vietnam war veteran then drew on his military experiences to describe the much-anticipated scenes of Jehovah's apocalyptic slaughtering of billions of innocent men, women and children for not being his Witnesses: 'I know what's coming at Armageddon . . . lotta dead people . . . lotta dead people. So, let's get out there and help as many as we can because when it comes it's going to be numbing for you. Their bodies are going to burst like hot-dogs . . . Stick with us, you'll be safe,' he assured the faithful.

Soon afterwards, when the pestilent Coronavirus was making its death-dealing presence felt all over the world, Anthony Morris appeared on JW.org with words of encouragement for the world-wide community of Jehovah's Witnesses: 'Cheer up! It's going to get worse. We keep a sense of humour with it. What we're experiencing right now is this global pandemic . . . it's a fact . . . I've been telling them for some time now . . . it doesn't bother me . . . we've been waiting for this.' His rambling and hesitant delivery was readily dismissed by online Watchtower critics and commentators alike as familiar intemperate waffle, and for good reason.

Twelve months earlier (31st March 1919), on a wet late Sunday morning, brother Morris, cloaked in a nondescript Lieutenant Columbo-style raincoat with a beret-cap pulled down to hide his distinctively balding head, swept through the security gates of the Watchtower Society's Warwick headquarters in his white Cadillac, and headed for a distant branch of the Bottle King liquor store. For the truant day-tripper it was a familiar round trip of some 34 miles and one which had previously afforded the lone shopper a comfortable degree of anonymity. However, on that fateful day he was caught red-handed on candid-camera by a sharp-eyed ex-Jehovah's Witness visitor to the store who chanced to recognised him from his regular appearances on the JW.org channel.

Within hours an unmistakeable Anthony Morris of JW.org fame made a surprize appearance on YouTube. As millions of Jehovah's Witnesses around the world were dutifully studying a Watchtower magazine article or attending the, not to be missed, Sunday morning public talk at the local Kingdom Hall, brother Morris was studiously reviewing the tempting range of whiskey on display at his favourite branch of the cut price liquor store. Eventually he spent $857 on a dozen bottles of top end single-malt scotch whisky following an impromptu discussion with a 'worldly' stranger on the alternative merits of a more affordable well-known Irish whiskey: 'You can't go wrong with that one,' he encouraged his fellow-shopper, 'it's a favourite of my wife.' After discarding the tell-tale presentation packaging of all twelve bottles at the checkout, he stashed his booty in a plain canvas bag for the return journey to Watchtower's high-security compound in Warwick and the privacy of his lakeside apartment.

The official Terms and Conditions all Bethel residents are required to sign up for and formally swear by state: 'Those who are accepted for special full-time service at the world headquarters of Jehovah's Witnesses all subscribe to a vow of poverty and to live the simple, nonmaterialistic lifestyle, as have all the members of the Governing Body. They are provided merely food, shelter, and a moderate amount for expenses – enough for immediate needs but no provision for the 'laying up of money'. Additionally, they are required to 'abstain from secular employment' and to turn over 'all income received from any work or personal efforts' to the Watchtower Society.[227]

Numerous property deeds and tax records on file in Baldwin County, Alabama have been tracked down and brought to light by a former second generation Jehovah's Witness.[228] These official records clearly indicate that Governing Body member Steven Lett and his wife Susan may well have been 'laying up money' since 1986 when his father died and left five condominium investment apartments to his two sons, thus making Steve, as he prefers to be known, a shareholder in the family realestate partnership on the quiet – Lett Builders & Development located in Lillian, Alabama. An online Business Directory states: 'Lett Builders, established in 1978 – primarily operating in the Single-family housing construction market in and around the towns of Lillian, Foley and Gulf Shores, Baldwin County, Alabama for 42 years. Estimated to generate revenues of $1,000,000 and employs approximately 3 people at this single address.'

The original three employees, as we learned earlier, were Stephen Lett's parents – Mark and Jean Lett and Steve's younger brother Tim,

---

227 Jehovah's Witnesses – Proclaimers of God's Kingdom (p351) – WTBTS, 1993.

228 The BLUE ENVELOPE website features well-documented evidence of Steven Lett's ongoing financial involvement in Lett Builders & Development.

who was best man at Steve's Kingdom Hall wedding in 1971. Staunch Jehovah's Witnesses at the time, their parents were unable to attend the ceremony for they were miles away urgently spreading the 'good news of God's kingdom' for the Watchtower Society as special pioneers. With Armageddon so close they felt there was no time to lose. Back then it meant the world to the Lett family, devoutly united in their Watchtower-inspired faith – until the non-event of 1975 when, like so many other disillusioned and bitterly disappointed Jehovah's Witnesses, they eventually woke up to reality over a painful three-year period of realisation and withdrawal – except eldest son Stephen who chose to remain faithful to the Watchtower Society.

Prodigal son Steve's eventual return to his spiritually divided family may well have been motivated by his undivided loyalty to Jehovah's organisation and it could be the case that he has indeed been 'turning over all income' from his private real-estate 'work or personal efforts' in the Lett family business to the Watchtower Society all along. However, so keen was he to secretly retain his economic entitlement and legal connection to Lett Builders and Development that when he was elevated to Governing Body status in 1999 and busier than ever before, he issued a power of attorney (POA) document from Watchtower Headquarters, in the form of a hand-written note authorising brother Tim to take care of his business interests on his behalf *'in regard to any estate and/or real estate including Moonraker Apartments, Gulf Shores, Baldwin County, Alabama'.*

In recent years, for example, the Lett brothers made a down-payment on a Gulf Shore waterfront investment property for $595,000 in October 2013 – 'fifty-percent ownership to Timothy R Lett, with the other undivided fifty-percent interest to Mark Stephen Lett and [his wife] Susan Lynn Lett.' The Vendors Lien Deed further states: 'The property will not be the homestead of Grantee Timothy R Lett nor a second home of his or his spouse and the property will not be the Homestead of Grantees Mark Stephen Lett nor [his wife] Susan Lynn Lett.' The purchase was completed and fully paid off in September 2019. Tim and Steve's most recent, and similarly worded financial deal, in a smaller $60,000 Gulf Shores waterfront property, was completed in January 2020 just a couple of months before the Coronavirus pandemic made its world-wide presence felt in earnest.

Having privately concluded his latest cash investment in a Gulf Shore waterfront property as a real-estate property consultant in the family business, Steven Lett publicly assumed his Governing Body member status in the Spring of 2020 when he sounded Watchtower's latest doomsday alarm in a broadcast on JW.org: 'So, the [Covid-19] events unfolding around us make clear that we are living in the final part of the Last Days. Undoubtedly, the final part of the Last Days – shortly before the last day of the Last Days. Having food and clothing we will be content with these things.' He then quoted Jehovah, warning Jerimiah's secretary Baruch: 'You have what you need, stop storing up great things, be content with what you have for I am about to bring a calamity over all flesh. So, if you get the mastery over all this, I will grant you your life as a spoil.'[229]

Eventually, as worldwide lock-down, social distancing and a ban on public meetings became the lawful order of the day the Governing Body of Jehovah's Witnesses reluctantly announced the cancellation of all local and national conventions planned for 2020 along with a temporary closure of Kingdom Halls and all other meeting places. There would be no more door-to-door preaching or manning of literature carts in town and city centres and Kingdom Halls everywhere would remain closed until the global lock-down 'state of emergency' was lifted. For the first time in its 140-year history the Watchtower Society, Jehovah's corporate voice of doom, was publicly silenced as Covid-19 brought the world to a standstill.

Today's organisation is structured as a series of interconnected business corporations under the overall control and command of the Governing Body of Jehovah's Witnesses. Each administration within the complex is a hive of activity swarming with play-acting, virtue-signalling busybody workers (think North Korea), trapped in a pernicious vortex of negative thinking, low self-esteem, and mental inertia as they thoughtlessly engage in an elaborately contrived divorce from reality in futile pursuit of an impossible dream as life passes them by.

Many commentators and critics of the movement consider the spate of property sell-offs and acquisitions of recent years could be the organisation's last hurrah; a valedictory show of defiance of an outdated morally bankrupt enterprise on its last legs as it limps, posturing and preaching into the darkness of incomprehensibility. Having reached a stonewall 'Ultima Thule' of its own making – (a date-ridden psychological cul-de-sac) – on its inglorious road to paradise, the movement is now on the backfoot craftily tailoring a new set of clothes for the Emperor of the Watchtower Society as it seeks to relaunch itself with a more user-

[229] Jerimiah 45: 4,5. NWT

friendly identity. Perhaps a new fund-raising announcement introduced at conventions back in 2019 – 'Please make your cheques payable to the *Christian Congregation* of Jehovah's Witnesses.' – was a tentative first step in the direction of a new clean-sweeping brand name. Time will tell.

Nonetheless, given its pious canvassing history of bogus fortune-telling 'prophecies' in tandem with its present-day futuristic agenda of international property dealing, investment banking and stock market trading, the tax-free machinations of the Watchtower Society – by any other name – suggests itself as nothing more than a celestial Ponzi scheme; a spiritually tempting, shamelessly fraudulent scam that generates promising returns by attracting a continuous stream of guileless investors, thereby bolstering the forlorn hopes and fanciful expectations of millions of innocently gullible established and prospective stakeholders alike, while prolonging the fictional pay-out timeline indefinitely.

***

Toward the end of the 19th century Pastor Russell claimed to have identified the star Alcyone, in the centre of the Pleiades constellation as the exact spot in the visible sky 'from which the Almighty governs his universe'.[230] This eccentric belief was later endorsed by Judge Rutherford when he declared, 'One of the stars of that group is the dwelling place to which the inspired [prophet] referred when he said: "Hear thou from thy dwelling place, even from heaven" that it is the place to which Job referred when, under inspiration, he wrote: "Canst thou bind the sweet influences of Pleiades, or loose the binds of Orion?"'[231]

This tone-deaf attempt at harmonising theological fiction with astrophysical fact and biological reality was eventually abandoned in 1953 when the Watchtower Society cautioned: 'it would be unwise for us to try to fix God's throne as being at a particular spot in the universe.'[232] However, in 1981 the same organisation decided to restrict Jehovah's movements through time and space when it boldly declared: 'God being an individual, a Person with a spirit body, has a place where he resides, so he could not be at any other place at the same time.'[233]

For a moment, we might well ask ourselves, just where does this 'heavenly father', along with his son and *his* mother really live? Having

---

[230] Studies in the Scriptures, Vol III – Thy Kingdom Come, 1890

[231] Reconciliation, J F Rutherford – WTBTS 1928. (Chron 6:21; Job 38:10).

[232] Watchtower – Nov 15, 1953.

[233] Watchtower – Feb 15, 1981.

specific gender relationships with other spirit creatures that seem to mirror those of a typical human family, makes it so easy for us to identify with and believe in him as the creator of all things and the giver of life. He can do anything. Indeed, it is difficult, if not impossible, for us to imagine something he cannot do. He listens to us when we talk to him, and he can even read our minds – because that is where he lives.

Yes, Jehovah, like all other gods, lives in the imagination, and once he takes up residence, he often proves to be a stubbornly tenacious lodger – difficult to evict – especially if he had moved in during the householder's childhood. However, once his non-existence is understood sufficiently enough to invalidate his tenancy, the best way of getting rid of him altogether is to ignore him completely. Turn the notion of religion on its head, and *imagine* he is *not* there.

Sooner or later, he will return to his rightful place in history, alongside Zeus, Mythras, Osiris, Romulus, Zalmoxis, Adonis, Inanna, plus numerous gods of the Sun, and of the Moon, and countless other 'gods', most of which were there long before Jehovah was collectively dreamed up by succeeding generations of primitive sheep and goat herders in an obscure corner of ancient Syria some 4/5000 years ago – a comparative blink of an eye in the exponential time line of the universe.

Every form of life which has evolved on planet Earth, from the most basic unicellular organisms, which formed some 4 billion years ago, to the relatively recent fossilised evidence of the primitive beginnings of humanity 66 million years previously tells us more about our origins and life expectancy than any so-called 'Holy' book of ancient wisdom. Religious belief itself developed in tandem with the physical and mental evolution of mankind.

Today's enlightening telescopes and revealing microscopes tell us that life in all its forms – animal, vegetable, and mineral – is finite. In short, a death is the natural end-product of a life or existence. It was an embryonic concept of an omniscient, invisible God that gave birth to the apprehensive notion of human immortality, a rudimentary understanding that was borne of ignorance – indeed, it thrives on it. The words of German philosopher Artur Schopenhaur (1788-1860) come to mind: 'Religions are like glow-worms; they need darkness to shine. A certain degree of ignorance is the condition for the existence of any religion, the element in which it alone lives.'

Organised religious belief is a dishonest social stratagem which continues to be nurtured and solemnly addressed by the self-serving God-blessing manipulative weasel words of power-hungry politicians, deluded religious leaders, and ruthless depots the world over. For too long religion has been reverentially formalised and universally foisted on mankind as 'Faith' – aptly described by Richard Dawkins as 'the biggest cop-out of all'. We might add to that the much-bandied nebulous attribute – 'spiritual'.

For example: In July 2016, Russian President Vladimir Putin approved legislation which outlawed the Watchtower Society as an 'extremist organisation preaching the exclusivity and supremacy' of their beliefs in much the same way as the Islamic State militant group (ISIS) and Neo-Nazi movements. Having blocked Russian internet access to Watchtower's JW.org channel in 2015, the president let it be known that he did not want 'foreign religions' in his country. Many of Russia's 175,000 Jehovah's Witnesses were charged with organising prayer meetings. All Kingdom Halls throughout Russia were shut down and the New World Translation of the Bible was banned because of the prominence of the name Jehovah in place of God or Lord. Meanwhile, over in America, President Trump announced that he would 'protect religious freedom'.

On May 3, 2017, the Russian president decided to play 'good cop – bad cop' when he awarded 'Parental Glory' to Valeriy and Tatiana Novak, Jehovah's Witnesses from Karelia, who had raised eight children with 'extraordinary care for their family's health, education as well as their physical, mental and moral development, thereby strengthening the family institution'. However, the ceremony, which was reported in the Russian press and shown on television to showcase Vladimir Putin's supposedly softer 'non-sectarian' family-friendly values, proved to be nothing more than a heartless PR stunt.

The following year Watchtower property, to the value of some $57 million was violently seized by the state. In a concerted police action code-named 'Judgement Day', doors were kicked down in dawn raids on the homes of Jehovah's Witnesses as terror-stricken families fled and sought refuge in neighbouring countries. Many arrests were made at gunpoint, with some JW men facing ten-year prison sentences as dictator Putin announced he has the power to reduce America to 'volcanic ash'.

Religious persecution in Russia was at its height during the official Atheist State of the Soviet era in which some 200,000 members of the Russian Orthodox Church were executed while millions of none-Orthodox Christians risked imprisonment. Today president Putin's some two-decades long rulership of Russia is described by Patriarch Kiril of the

Russian Orthodox Church as 'a miracle of God' while the Watchtower Society publicly hails the resolute martyrdom of its followers in that country with its customary claims of 'power beyond what is normal'. The only losers in this ongoing triumvirate game of east-west political bluster and the religious bluff of the Watchtower Society are the Russian Jehovah's Witnesses themselves – hapless victims of their own innocent ignorance.

From its birth in the 19th century and throughout its phenomenal growth throughout the 20th century there was at least a semblance of scholarship and research – of a kind – behind the doomsday philosophy of the early Bible Students and their Jehovah's Witnesses progeny. Those were the days when charismatic leadership and slick presentations of 'honest to God' biblical truths of the day seemed to echo the sentimental yearnings of millions. However, mankind has grown up since then and the world has moved on. Meanwhile, today's stubbornly mutating Watchtower Society – in plain sight of indifferent taxpayers and religiously compromised tax-collectors on both sides of the Atlantic – continues its financially-focused demographic nose-dive into the exploitable depths of institutionalised ignorance.

***

I form the light, and create darkness:
I make peace, and create evil:
I the LORD do all these *things*.

(Isaiah 45: 7, KJV)

An Accidental Autobiography
Barbara Grizzuti Harrison, Haughton Miffin 1996.
Answering Jehovah's Witnesses
David Reed, Baker Books, 1996.
Apocalypse Delayed
James Penton, University of Toronto Press, 1985
Babylon the Great Has Fallen
WTBTS 1963.
Bible Students in Britain
Albert O Hudson, Bible Fellowship Union, 1989.
Bible Students Souvenir Convention Report
Dr L W Jones, Chicago. USA, 1910.
Inside the Brotherhood
Martin Short, Grafton books, 1989.
The Brotherhood
Stephen Night, Granada publishing, 1984.
Crisis of Conscience
Raymond Franz, Commentary Press, 1983.
In Search of Christian Freedom
Raymond Franz, Commentary Press, 1991.
CULTS IN FRANCE
Expression of Moral Freedom or Factors of Manipulation
(No 2468: NATIONAL ASSEMBLY – December 1995).
Cults of Unreason
Dr Christopher Evans, Harrap & Co. Ltd, 1973.
The Emphatic Diaglott
B Wilson's translation of Vatican Mss 1209, WTBTS.
English Economic History
Georg W Southgate, Dent & Sons, London WC2, 1934.
Faith on the March
A. H. Macmillan, Prentice-Hall, 1957.
Famine 1975
William & Paul Paddock, Little-Brown, 1967.
The Gentile Times Reconsidered
Carl Olof Jonsson, Commentary Press, 1986.
God Has A Plan
Albert O Hudson, Bible Fellowship Union (5th edition), 2014.

Giza – The Truth
Ian Lawton & Chris Ogilvie-Herald, Virgin, 1999.
The Great Pyramid
Morton Edgar, Bone & Hulley, 1924.
The Hiram Key
Christopher Knight & Robert Lomas, Century, 1996.
Index of Watchtower Errors
David A. Reed, Baker Books, 1990.
The Jesus Mysteries
Timothy Freke & Peter Gandy, Thorsons, 1999.
Jehovah's Witnesses – Proclaimers of God's Kingdom
WTBTS, 1993.
Jehovah's Witness Literature
David A. Reed, Baker Books, 1993.
Jehovah Talk
David A Reed, Baker Books, 1997.
Jehovah's Witnesses in the Divine Purpose
WTBTS, 1959.
Paradise Restored to Mankind
WTBTS, 1972.
Pastor Russell's Sermons
Peoples Pulpit Association, Brooklyn, NY, 1917.
Pyramidology
Adam & James Rutherford, (ISBN0-903402-10-6) 4 volumes 1986.
The Pyramids of Egypt
I E S Edwards, Penguin Books, 1947.
Thirty Years a Watchtower Slave
William J. Schnell, Baker Books, 1971.
Revelation – Its Grand Climax at Hand!
WTBTS, 1988.
Reasoning from the Scriptures
WTBTS, 1985.
The Sign of the Last Days
Carl Olof Jonsson - W Herbst, Commentary Press 1986.
The Secrets of the Freemasons
Pat Morgan, Arcturus Publishing, 2007.
The Secret Societies Handbook
Michael Bradley, Cassell Illustrated, 2005.
The Riddle of the Pyramids
Kurt Mendelssohn FRS, Thames & Hudson, 1974.

The Seven Wonders of the World
J & E Romer, Michael O'Mara Books, 1995.
Religion and Unbelief
Edward Royle, Longman Group, 1971.
What Pastor Russell Said
L.W. Jones, 1917.
Watchtower & White House
Saturday Evening Post, May 3, 1952.
Six Roads from Abilene
John McCallum, Wood & Reber, 1960.
The Eisenhower diaries
Robert H Fervell, 1981.
The Great American Heritage
Bela Kornitzer, Farrar Straus, Cudahy, 1955.
Documentary Historical Series, Box 4
J Earl Endacot, Eisenhower Library.
Pastor Russell's Sermons
People's Pulpit Association (IBSA), 1917.
Reasoning from the Scriptures
WTBTS, 1985.
Revelation – Its Grand Climax at Hand
WTBTS, 1988.
Jehovah's Witnesses in the Divine Purpose
WTBTS, 1959.
Visions of Glory
Barbara Grizzuti Harrison, Touchstone, 1978.
NWT – New World Translation of the Holy Scriptures.
KJV – King James Version.
NEB – New English Bible.
ASV – American Standard Version.

Printed in Great Britain
by Amazon

66990989R00165